D0297851

A House Divided?

Errata

p. 25, line 4 from top ... 'it becomes' read 'becomes'.
p. 73, line 16 from bottom ... for 'Exclusive' and 'segmentary' read ''Exclusive'' and ''segmentary''.
p. 91, line 17 from top ... for 'that followers' read 'that follower's'.
p. 100, line 12 from bottom ... for 'about almost any kind of' read 'about by almost any kind of'.
p. 121, line 17 from top ... for 'and who to be discriminated' read 'and who was to bc discriminated'.
p. 129, line 4 from bottom ... for 'an acute rural and urban gap' read 'an acute rural/urban gap'.
p. 151, line 15 from bottom ... for 'compete for labour' read 'compete for the labour'.
p. 162, line 2 from top ... for '(Leach,' read '(in Leach,'.
p. 175, line 15 from bottom ... for 'medium-scale was' read 'medium-scale farmers was'.

A House Divided?

Anthropological Studies of Factionalism

Edited by M. Silverman and R. F. Salisbury

Social and Economic Papers No. 9

Institute of Social and Economic Research,
Memorial University of Newfoundland

ISBN 0-919666-13-2

Canadian Cataloguing in Publication Data

Main entry under title:

A House Divided?
(Social and economic papers; no. 9)

Bibliography: p.
ISBN 0-919666-13-2

1. Social conflict – Case studies. 2. Ethnology – Case studies. I. Silverman, Marilyn, 1945– II. Salisbury, Richard F., 1926– III. Memorial University of Newfoundland. Institute of Social and Economic Research. IV. Title: Factionalism. V. Series.

HM136.H69 301.6′3 C78-001024-8

Printed in Canada by University of Toronto Press

Contents

Acknowledgements

This book is based on discussions among the participants of two conferences. The first conference was generously supported by the Canada Council; Office of the Dean, Faculty of Arts, York University; the Programme in the Anthropology of Development, McGill University; and the President's *ad hoc* committee, Senate Committee on Research, York University. The second conference was financed by the Programme in the Anthropology of Development, McGill University; Office of the Dean, Faculty of Arts, York University. Their contributions are gratefully acknowledged.

Thanks are due to Irene Wensley, Administrative Assistant, and Leo Smits, graduate student, both of the Department of Anthropology, York University for the considerable time they spent on administrative matters. We would also like to thank Alice Johannsen, Director of the Gault Estate, McGill University who hosted our second conference.

This book has been published with the help of a grant from the Social Science Federation of Canada, using funds provided by the Canada Council.

The excerpts from *The Masters* and *The Affair* are quoted with the permission of the author and Penguin Books.

Marilyn Silverman
Toronto, Canada
February, 1978

Richard F. Salisbury
Montreal, Canada
February, 1978

An Introduction: Factions and the Dialectic

1

Richard F. Salisbury and Marilyn Silverman

"A house divided against itself cannot stand." This is the conventional wisdom of St. Mark on the subject of factions. But is it true? The question mark in our title indicates our doubt. It is also intended to draw attention to our skepticism of other conventional wisdoms found in the literature on factions. Are factions the first indications of falling 'houses,' or conversely, the mark of stable but stagnant societies? Are they simply a 'game' played by elites to divert attention from the solution of important social issues? This book, in presenting the view that factions are best seen as evanescent structural forms which occur in predictable patterns within a dynamic political process of factionalism, shows that these wisdoms are at best only partial truths; at worst they are simply wrong.

The key element is the emphasis on *factionalism rather than on factions*. An approach which considers only individual factions or particular aggregates of people tends either to become static and classificatory or to look for the equilibrium states, as groups within which there is conflict, resolve disputes, maintain a balanced opposition, or split into new units. In contra-distinction, analysing factionalism as a total ongoing political process involves looking at the conditions in which it occurs, at the way in which multiple aggregates emerge within a collectivity, at how they oppose one another in particular situations, and at how the interactions of opposition produce decisions, social restructuring, or social rigidification. It is, in short, a particularly fluid process that may produce a variety of outcomes, some of which have been delineated by conventional wisdom: fission in the wider group, or increased power and formalization for a conservative winning faction. Alternatively, however, factionalism can result in the formulation of a new ideology, the emergence and differentiation of new political interest groups, or the crystallization into consciousness of a new social structure. This book tries to relate 'outcomes' to the *sequences* that precede them in the process of factionalism.

More succinctly, divided houses do not fall. Rather, every house, or moral community, has informal subdivisions based on differential interests. There is perpetual change in those interests and, as long as the subdivisions remain informal, perpetual reorganization of space in the house. Each reorganization, whether it is of invisible personal space, or involves the building or destruction of walls, conditions what happens in the next reorganization. Change of the house exterior may or may not be apparent. Anthropological orthodoxy has ignored this dialectical process of successional remodelling. This book shows, in a series of case studies from seven different societies, how patterns of *network manipulation*, of *transactional strategies* of factional leaders, and of *class and ideological concerns* of participants recur in regular enough combinations to be characterized as 'sequences' within a wider dialectical process of factionalism.

Factions and the Authors

The book did not emerge as a single person's revelation, but from a long period of comparison and discussion. In the period 1967–74, four of the present authors independently wrote historical studies of local politics in societies in South Asia, Latin America and the Caribbean. Each focussed primarily on a different aspect that was topically in vogue – the composition of factions, leader-follower relationships, the game of politicking, or the changing class structure. Each hesitated to generalize about factions on the basis of a single study; yet there were many convergences in their thinking, arrived at independently since individual fieldwork and writing-up schedules had prevented discussion. Salisbury, who had read all the studies as they developed, suggested at the Canadian Sociology and Anthropology Association meetings in Toronto in 1974, that a conference be organized to explore the commonalities and divergences in the several studies. Silverman organized such a meeting at Lake Couchiching, Ontario in April 1975, inviting as well, five other scholars who had also studied factional politics. In her description of the aims of the conference, she pointed out that critical issues had been raised in the literature on factions which had not been fully explored, while other issues seemed to have been lost in indifference over time and left without discussion or resolution. She suggested that all papers discuss one or all of the foci delineated by Bujra (1973:133–134): the structure of factions, the process of political conflict and the relations between factions and the wider socio-political context. Nine papers resulted, and all were concerned with long-term histories, though this was not a topic that was solicited in the letter of invitation.

We shut ourselves away for three days in the April snows of Ontario. At the first session the issue was raised, particularly by Bailey, as to whether the study of *factions* was not a 'dead horse' and whether the conference was not a post-mortem. Those whose research had indicated new aspects of factional politics beyond those delineated in the literature argued the contrary, sometimes going to the extreme of saying that because factions had been an integral part of cumulative social change in the societies they studied, this was a universal phenomenon. One common ground, presaged by Bailey's explicitly definitional paper, was a concern not with the factions, but with the wider phenomenon of factionalism as a process. A second common ground was the concern for longer-term history, in which the specific factions appeared as transient epiphenomena of more basic underlying processes. As we sought to clarify this process of factionalism, placing it in contexts of local resource use, or wider political frameworks, we found we could argue on common ground about the similarities and differences of our case studies. By concentrating on a limited range of aspects, each participant gained new insights into his/her own material, even if the idiosyncratic aspects of each study indicated how immense were the potential avenues for future comparisons.

After the conference we revised our papers in the light of the discussions and Salisbury and Silverman wrote drafts of this introduction. In December of 1975 at Mont St. Hilaire, Quebec, we again locked ourselves away, with the exception of Bailey and Boissevain. This time, we discussed mainly how well the draft introductions reflected the common ground shared by the contributors. Absolute consensus, it was felt, was neither possible nor desirable. No contributor felt that harm had been done to his/her position, though each felt that his/her emphasis went beyond the introduction in particular directions. Contributors felt an introduction should not be a bland statement of common elements but should present also some synthesis of its authors; this we attempt in the following pages. Each paper in the book illustrates some of the commonalities, but each also has its idiosyncratic viewpoint and indicates a new direction for future research, beyond the present synthesis. We hope that this introduction will summarize firm findings for readers and that the case studies will be read for both documentation of findings and for their own creative ideas.

The Dialectic of Ideas

What we, as individuals, experienced in gestating this book in many ways reflects the pattern of the emergence of new scientific concepts that Kuhn (1962) has talked about as "scientific revolutions". As he formulates the dialectic of ideas, an orthodox paradigm or explanatory framework is adhered to long after individuals have described data for which the paradigm provides an inadequate explanation. Only when a dramatically different paradigm is proposed, which accounts for the observed deviations from orthodox theory, is notice taken of the deviations. New theory emerges in jumps, each seemingly a revolution of new displacing old, though in the longer view there is progress and cumulation. In the same way we felt our individual dissatisfactions with the theory of factions were crystallized by our discussions of the new concept *factionalism*.

A review of the dialectical process out of which the theory of factions emerged will reveal the intellectual roots of this book. It will also conveniently lead us into the central topic of the book: the role of factionalism in the historical transformation of societies and institutions, or what we call, the dialectical process of factionalism.

For the generation of anthropologists reared on *African Political Systems* (Fortes and Evans-Pritchard, 1940), politics was defined as the process of maintaining social order, balance and the *status quo*. The mechanisms discussed were those of the organized use of force (or the threat of its use) by centralized state structures, or by egalitarian and acephalous corporate groupings, which alternately opposed and supported each other. The term "faction" did not appear in the vocabulary of the time except as a pejorative term for sub-groupings which threatened group unity.

The succeeding generation, in a typical dialectical process, focussed on polar opposites in its definition of politics. It stressed conflict over stability; it was concerned with non-corporate groupings rather than with corporate groups; it rejected the emphasis on structures, and looked for processes or for the use of structures through organization. Factions, the epitome of conflict, of the lack of corporateness and of the pragmatic use of relationships to attain goals, became the archetype of political units studied.

If one wished to date this shift of paradigm it can be seen as starting in the early 1950's. Gluckman's (1953) *Rituals of Rebellion* and Coser's (1956) *Functions of Social Conflict* did treat conflict, but as something to be explained within a structural-functional paradigm – a mechanism to restress basic values and to return the system to equilibrium – rather than as a new paradigm in its own right. So too, Firth's (1957) symposium on factions treated them as informal counterparts of formal political groupings – how people really organized themselves for political action, utilizing the formal political structure.

The shift of paradigm became clearer as Frankenberg (1957) and Barnes (1959) emphasized a focal concern with politicking as a process, rather than politics as structure, and as Siegel and Beals (1960a and b) discussed factions as products of endemic conflict. With the appearance of Banton's (1965) *Political Systems and the Distribution of Power*, Swartz, Tuden and Turner's (1966) *Political Anthropology* and Swartz' (1968) *Local-level Politics*, the shift of paradigm was completed, and a new orthodoxy focusing on conflict established. As far as factions were concerned, the orthodoxy was best expressed in Nicholas' (1965) definition of them as non-corporate groupings, involved in conflicts and recruited by leaders on the basis of diverse principles.

But as with all dialectic processes, what appears on the surface to be a substitution of antithesis for thesis was, in fact, not so. There was an oblique movement of theory since the two paradigms were not really mutual opposites. On one level what occurred was a broadening of interest from a focus on pre-colonial, pre-industrial politics in Africa to a concern with village societies on every continent, particularly colonial or post-colonial villages or small towns having relations with surrounding nation states. The analysis of traditional states or of lineage politics was not discarded as invalid but treated as being relatively unproblematic, and not at the cutting edge of theoretical concern. The critical object for study was the endemic conflict observed in local-level politics, and how factions articulated with traditional groupings and with state super-structures.

On another level we would argue that the conflict paradigm, in fact, contained many elements of the earlier paradigm, and was really a dynamic-equilibrium paradigm. It often treated conflict as having emerged from colonial change, with factions as a major symptom of the disorganization following change. It looked forward to smooth dispute resolution without factions when a new moral community had been established. It considered that factions could become endemic, as in the case studies of Siegel and Beals (1966), if a community remained disorganized and anomic and could in extreme cases lead to community fission. Factions were viewed as undesirable social forms, in much the way that Madison viewed them (see Bailey, this volume), in contrast with the desirable forms of structured political parties, and (can we breathe the words?) dynamic equilibrium.

Yet the definitions that emerged (for example, that of Nicholas) did contrast factions radically with the political units discussed by the previous generation on the dimensions of corporateness/non-corporateness, permanence/*ad-hoc*ness, role structure/leader-focus. A dialectic had occurred.

Since 1968 a dialectical process has been less easy to perceive. No one has been ready to argue that the definition of factions is inappropriate, needing radical change. Some further work was done within the conflict paradigm (Bujra, 1973; and Alavi, 1973) and is extensively noted by the authors of the present volume. Both Alavi and Bujra do express some disquiet at the tendency for factions to be seen in relation to equilibrium states, but otherwise accept the paradigm and propose no opposing one. Interest in factions and political anthropology – under those rubrics – so declined, that by 1973 there were no sessions devoted to these topics at the meetings of the American Anthropological Association. It was as if the definitions of 1968 were too good; they created a synthesis and so halted the dialectical process. Factions, as such, seemed a dead and unproblematic topic, as researchers in the period 1968–1975 adopted unrelated approaches in their work, ignoring the faction approach instead of attempting to change it by substituting an opposing concept. Data which did not fit the concept of "faction" were not systematically reviewed in the light of a more productive paradigm.

The contributors to this volume all worked in empirical situations in which factions and factionalism were identifiable, but they chose instead to relate their work to other currents of anthropological thought – approaches that we label "networks," "transactions," and "class structure" (although others could be added) – even if they had been stimulated by the literature on factions in their field work. None felt called upon to be explicit about why they felt that the faction paradigm was an inadequate one. We suggest that there are various reasons, but the central one is that a new model of social change has become current in anthropological thinking, one that makes the concept of "faction" appear static and lifeless.

Briefly the model is one of societies continually adapting themselves to an environment of other societies and of changing resources and technology; the adaptations cumulate historically, each one being a product of the previous adaptation and the new reality; the mechanisms of adaptation involve individual choices and decisions, but also are constrained by major social forces, such as relations of production, to follow long-term evolutionary directions. A concept of *factionalism*, we argue, is an appropriate one for use in such a model of social change. By dialectically opposing the seeming orthodoxy of *factions* with a new approach – that of *factionalism* – we attempt to see how far an advance in understanding can occur.

The Definition of Factionalism

A minimal definition of factionalism states that it is that part of the political process within a community which is characterized by the interaction and confrontation of multiple non-corporate sub-groupings – groupings that generally satisfy the criteria for being defined as factions (Nicholas 1965). The definition focuses attention, not on the individual faction, its structure, goals, or tactics, but on the process by which a *number* of groupings *compete* to *mobilize resources*, of which human resources are one major element. Intra-factional behaviour, the relation of a leader to his followers, for example, is important but is seen in a context of what is occurring at the same time in other factions, between the factions, and in society at large. The definition also recognizes the limits of an analysis of factionalism; when either the community ceases to be a community, or the sub-groupings become clearly conscious of their common unity and organize a corporate structure, a different analytical concept may be needed.

The emphasis on political process, on the other hand, stems from the recognition, which evolved as case studies were presented at our conference, that factionalism has an inherent dynamism. Factional confrontations are rarely balanced; one side gains and the other loses ground on every occasion. Each confrontation changes the terms on which the next confrontation will take place. In any confrontation the strategy of one side, or a particular combination of individuals in one faction, does not produce an exact or mirror-image strategy or collection of individuals on the other side. Reactions are, in fact, systematically oblique and groupings are systematically unlike. Factionalism, in short, produces actions and reactions that do not simply balance out, but by opposing groups obliquely, it gives a net movement to the whole society, even if this is in a direction no faction intended it to go.

Within this global political process the disparate aspects of networks, transactions and class structure, which have been the starting points for individual contributors, constitute analytical elements. The papers in this book are grouped as much as possible according to discussions of the same elements, though every paper discusses all of them and other elements besides. The remainder of this introduction spells out the interrelations between the three approaches, and shows how they combine in a series of factional sequences.

A. *Network Theory*

The use of the concept "network" to analyse the organization of non-corporate groupings antedated the emergence of the study of factions and may conveniently be seen as started by Barnes' (1954) seminal study of interpersonal relationships in a Norwegian parish. Corporate group, class, and network principles were each seen as being used for organizing different domains of activity.

But it was notably in the subsequent studies of political conflict that a non-mathematical vocabulary of network concepts emerged. The recruitment of particular individuals for a particular conflict from an individual's network to form an *action-set*, and the potential transformation of that action-set into a *cluster*, or even a *quasi-group* (if they come together often enough), has been noted by many workers (for example, Mayer, 1966; Boissevain, 1971; Gulliver, 1971). Such a quasi-group may be surrounded by a varying number of individuals, each linked to one or more members of the quasi-group, which then appears as the *core-group* of a wider politically-active unit, including a wide *periphery* of members (Nicholas, 1965; Bailey, 1971).

The persistent grouping together of roughly similar assemblages whenever conflicts emerge is characteristic of factionalism, and the network concepts listed above thus crudely suggest a temporal growth cycle for factions. Starting with an assumed total field in which all interpersonal links are of equal strength, the emergence of conflict first groups individuals around two or more focal "big men" (we use the term advisedly, utilizing its connotations in the Melanesian literature; cf. Oliver, 1955; Salisbury, 1962; and others). Recurrence of conflict crystallizes these action-sets and may eventually polarize the entire community into two or more factions, each following a different leader. If a faction develops a coherent ideology, and from this a formal corporate identity, it may become a *party* (Boissevain, 1966; Bujra, 1973), a term which can be generalized beyond its customary usage in political science.

This non-dialectic growth cycle is amplified in this volume by many writers, notably by Gulliver. Gulliver describes how Ndendeuli settlements characteristically come into existence as the small kin-related following of a single big man who starts farming in a new area. While the settlement is in a stage of rapid growth, factions are unlikely to occur (a fact Silverman has also reported). But the accretion of new individuals who are loyal to sponsors other than to the original leader provides the potential for such sponsors to become foci for factions. Death of the leader may well precipitate conflicts among sponsors and so also a dual polarization.

What happens once conflicts emerge, however, and once there are enough individuals present who are not so equally allied to both disputants that they must intervene to mute the conflict, is not merely a question of natural growth, but of a dialectic also. The role of the undistributed middle becomes important and is a prerequisite for the dialectic process in which change results from the interaction of structurally different groupings.

Boissevain and Silverman both suggest that it is usual for one faction to emerge as the strongest (at least in any one arena) and to take over the distribution of the rewards which a dominant faction has at its disposal. This faction becomes an in-group or *establishment*, and against it other factions coalesce as an out-group or *opposition*. The two factions are not symmetrical. The establishment faction characteristically has a core group that is connected by multiple links, with a periphery of supporters all allied to an individual member of the core by more specific and single-stranded ties. Gulliver uses the term "dense cluster" for this type of network. The opposition, by contrast, has a much looser structure with little distinction between core and periphery. It may, indeed, have a single focal individual with single-stranded ties to a number of opposition members, but the other members have few interconnecting links with each other. They connect through the leader or through specific interconnecting individuals in what Gulliver terms a "star pattern". These links may be of different kinds. The loose web is held together either by the focal big man, or almost as commonly by the hostility of each opposition member to specific individuals who are members of the establishment. Opposition is the theme of faction unity, although the issues about which opposition is felt may be different for each opposition member. It is as though the establishment were held together by the wide distribution of tangible benefits within it; the opposition is held together by the conviction that only unity will enable them ever to be in a position to distribute benefits; in other words, the opposition is held together by the promise of eventual benefits.

The opposition deliberately tries to organize itself, using more formal patterns than are found in an establishment. These extend to the deliberate attempt to recruit new supporters from the establishment faction by raising new issues and by co-ordinating action around those issues. By contrast the establishment tends to focus on increasing the density of links within its core group, assuming that each member of the core group will retain the allegiance of his own peripheral followers. By this very strategy the establishment lays itself open to two weaknesses: the defection of a member of the core group with his following and the apathetic non-involvement of the periphery. The opposition is open to the draining away of individuals who are attracted by members of the establishment. Silverman clearly describes these two strategies of factional competition – the subversion or collusion of leaders and the seduction of supporters on particular issues – although she does not analyse the differential use of the strategies by different factions.

What happens when such an opposition, linked loosely by simplex ties, becomes a majority faction on a specific issue is a critical step in such a dialectical process. The present volume contains no clear illustrations of this step, although hints of what may occur are provided in Silverman's (1973) description of events in Rajgahr in the 1930's, and in Paine's analysis of C. P. Snow's *The Masters* (this volume). The latter study, admittedly based on fiction and perhaps more stimulating for that reason, suggests that the new master of a Cambridge College, whose election by an *ad hoc* coalition of opposition forms the body of the book, may provide, by the exercise of legitimized power, a focal core group for the former opposition and so relegate some previous members to the periphery. Rapidly the opposition begins to look like an establishment, and in the book's sequel (and Paine's epilogue) twenty years later, the full cycle has been turned.

Even more dramatically, the build-up of an opposition and the new strategies used for acquiring support and for achieving factional unity alter the entire nature of the factional game. Silverman, Nagata, Schryer and Attwood all describe these dramatic alterations, ascribing them, in part, to changes in the surrounding social environment. Both Salisbury and Gulliver, however, point out what may occur when a relatively large number of individuals with some access to resources are not directly involved in every conflict. The presence of neutrals means that an establishment cannot behave as absolutely as it can when it is a majority; oppositions do not need to recruit individuals if small dense clusters occur in the society outside the establishment. Any of the smaller dense clusters may, with the right leadership, recruit majority support on a particular issue and gain its case, without at the same time becoming an establishment. *Multiple clusters*, with weak links between the clusters, would characterize such a total social network.

By contrast, a situation is hypothetically conceivable in which no dense

chance matter. In the long run, it does not matter which side wins or loses, for no change occurs. However, this would be another erroneous conclusion based on false premises.

Transactional analysis immediately suggests why this is necessarily the case: it is that a relationship exists between the availability of resources and the nature of the transactions. In this volume the most dramatic empirical demonstration of changes occurring in factional transactions, when resources abruptly decline into almost complete non-availability, is provided by Islam. He returned to the area of Bangladesh, where he had previously studied factions, shortly after the 1971 war with Pakistan. In a climate of extreme poverty, suspicion, and the likelihood that armed men, who claimed to be Freedom Fighters (Bengalis who had fought independently of the Indian army for Bangla independence), would use force to get their wishes, all alliances seemed at an end. Public recognition of pre-existing ties within the village was minimal, since any such linkage might be a starting point for accusations and violence; political ties of individual Freedom Fighters to politicians in the capital of Dacca provided them with resources, principally access to foreign relief shipments. The well-organized factional structure within the village of elite/patron establishment and loose opposition, which Islam describes elsewhere (1974), had disappeared; the leader of the old establishment was in exile, accused of collaboration with Pakistan, whereas the leaders of the opposition cautiously remained in the city as successful private individuals.

The situation described by Islam, of an apparent war of all against all, may even be taken as a close approach to an idealized *opportunistic* transactional condition – one where each individual is seeking short-term personal advantage and negotiating dyadically to obtain it through alliances.

Ironically Nagata, in his analysis of a stable and even affluent Hopi group at Moenkopi in Arizona, shows that the same pattern of shifting and impermanent coalitions, with much individual calculation of pragmatically advantageous strategies, occurs under other conditions of resources. Another common denominator between the Bangladesh and Hopi situation is, however, the lack of an agreed unit of political community at the local level (Easton, 1959), or what Salisbury terms a "circumscribing corporate grouping". In Bailey's terms such an absence means that there is no moral consensus. In a transactionalist analysis, the absence of a wider political unit means that no added rewards appear to accrue to transactors in achieving a wider group agreement: there is no positive-sum game present, no reward for winning a conflict and no incentive for weaker parties to settle. In fact, as Nagata phrases it, there is a positive gain for all parties in having conflicts continue unresolved. Many earlier analysts of factions (notably, Firth, 1957) have pointed to this phenomenon in a negative way, saying that factions exist where institutional means do not exist to resolve conflicts. In the present context this should be re-phrased: endemic opportunistic strategies occur in the absence of a political community fostering combined action and so producing additional rewards for the winner to distribute.

Attwood in an earlier paper (1974), Silverman in the present volume, together with Paine, Boissevain, and Islam in indirect descriptions point to the importance of the resource of group support, which can be utilized by group mobilizers. They point out that treating factions or interest groups as though they were recruited only by elite leaders offering their resources in exchange for the individual support of followers is sometimes inaccurate. A non-elite mobilizer may often find himself in possession of committed supporters for various reasons – the Freedom Fighters in Bangladesh suggest themselves as an example – and may then use his control of that support to bargain with elite leaders for the resources they control in order to obtain them for distribution among his followers. This strategy produces a factional structure different from the establishment-opposition structure previously described by such terms as "elite-council" (Bailey, 1965) and considered as typically involving strategies of patronage.

From the transactional approach, then, we identify at least three patterns of factional strategies: the prevailing *patronage* pattern, linked with establishments and oppositions; the *group mobilization* pattern, and the *opportunistic*, unstructured pattern. Each pattern can be related in a synchronic transactional analysis to a different pattern of resource availability in the society concerned.

Any transactionalist would readily agree that should resource availability change over time, the pattern of factional strategies would likely change also. What the dialectic analyst asks is whether there is a necessary temporal connection between these three patterns and the accompanying patterns of resource availability that would constitute a dialectic. Attwood, in the present volume, answers with a resounding yes. Although exogenous changes in resource availability are those most commonly talked about, the factional strategies used at one moment in time do, in and of themselves, affect the volume and type of resources available for the future and the distribution of those resources within the society. Each pattern contains within itself the seeds for the patterns that potentially succeed it, so that cycles may occur dialectically. To take only one example, group mobilizers can, by organizing their supporters, both obtain major resources from the wealthy and create new productive forces. Their role as intermediaries with the wealthy may then lose its importance, and a new strategy may become appropriate for those concerned with the exchange of resources for political support in the new environment. But since Attwood's argument also bears on the class-structure approach we shall not present his whole argument here.

c. *Class Structure Analysis*

The classic position of class structure analysts is that factions are groupings, recruited across class lines, which are separated from one another by vertical cleavages; the class lines themselves represent horizontal cleavages (cf. Brass, 1965; Nicholas and Bailey, 1968). Followers from less privileged groups attach themselves to leaders who are members of elites. But the conflicts giving rise to factions really concern only the interests of the elite leaders. The involvement of the supporters in these conflicts merely diverts their attention away from the significant conflict in society – the conflict between social classes. Only when the populace ignores factions will it acquire class-consciousness and an awareness of the issues of class conflict. Factions are a device of the elite to prevent the masses from acquiring class-consciousness. This is indicated by their lack of ideology and exclusive reliance on self-interest and personalism (Alavi, 1973; Bujra, 1973).

The analysis of variations in factional structures and factional strategies that has already been presented indicates that this may sometimes be the case, expecially when establishment factions use patronage stragegies; but even there opposition factions typically extend their recruitment of followers outside the elite. In other factional structures the cross-cutting recruitment of factions presents opportunities for the interests of lower social classes to assert themselves, in particular in the form of group-mobilization strategies.

In this volume Schryer analyses the structure of establishments and oppositions in a backward area of Mexico. Elsewhere (Schryer, 1975), he has related the existence of this elite pattern to the relatively small size of haciendas and the multiplicity of small-holders or tenant farmers in such an area. This has the dual effect of providing a class of middle peasants with vested interests and of making patronage from the state the most significant resource for local elites. In the 1920's only large landowners competed for benefits deriving from the national government. In the 1930's merchants in the small towns entered the competition, and sought local support (and official PRI approval) by espousing agrarian reform, though not putting it into effect. By the mid-1940's a new group of middle peasants joined the opposition, which again sought peasant support by espousing land reform. In 1957 a large landowner finally achieved the break-up of one opponent's estate by encouraging peasant occupation of the property.

Schryer argues that a continuing pattern of elite factionalism has persisted throughout this era, involving few landless labourers: the call for agrarian reform was a hollow one in practice. The detail of his study permits an equally feasible analysis in terms of (1) a steadily increasing involvement of new class groupings in the politicking, as opposition factions sought to involve new supporters outside the elite; (2) ideologies being used both to recruit followers and to persuade national politicians to grant benefits (a group mobilization strategy, in fact); and (3) slow percolation of benefits to disadvantaged groups who become politically conscious during periods of factional competition.

That the early 1960's subsequently proved to be a period of group-mobilization politics fits this analysis. Issues emerged such as clericalism/anti-clericalism, middle-peasants/day-labourers, cooperatives/merchants, as well as land reform (though allegiances differed on different issues). Factionalism brought the issues out into the open, increasing public awareness. A little more land was distributed as a result. The process of change may have been a slow one, but factionalism contributed to it.

This argument builds on the network and transactional analyses of this paper, which show that even within elite factionalism, the opposition faction is not the mirror-image of the establishment. The opposition faction seeks to circumvent the establishment's resources and network ties by attracting outside supporters, by appealing to ideology, and by formalizing its organization. Boissevain's paper (this volume) presents this argument at length.

Attwood's and Islam's papers indicate the possibilities for other patterns of class participation in factional activities. Attwood (and to some extent Schryer) shows how the opposition between factions is over issues of class conflict in a situation where the formal structure of monolithic political parties provides no avenues for the conflict to be overtly expressed. The group mobilizers who articulate this conflict may well be of the same class as the interest they represent, and in such a case each individual faction may be of a single class group. The evidence is, however, insufficient, and on other grounds it may be suggested that it is group mobilizers who can identify with the class of their faction, while having the ability, training or background to communicate with the classes of other factions who are the most successful. If such people exist, the conflict may find expression in factionalism; if they do not, then the conflict may either remain unexpressed, or be expressed more violently. If the usually reported pattern is one of *elite participation* in factional conflict, with minimal participation by members of other classes, then what Attwood indicates is an alternative to *class participation* in factions, with minimal membership in each faction of members of other classes.

Islam suggests a third type of participation, for which we propose the label "bourgeois participation". Involvement in factional activities is widespread in all classes, but the issues are not ones of continuing class interest. The composition of factions fluctuates rapidly, and the leaders are not clearly defined elite figures or populist orators, but rather shadowy influence brokers. Participation seems principally to be on the basis of momentary, situational self-interest as individuals perceive it. Bourgeois participation would appear to demand an environment where individuals are potentially able to achieve social mobility by dissociating themselves from the interests of a class group – elite or popular – and to do so through opportunistic factional alliances.

D. *Factionalism and Factional Sequences*

The argument to date has identified inductively three polar types of network structures, of transactional strategies and of class participation in factionalism. It would be simple to combine the three distinct analyses into a single typology in which each 'pure' type combined one form of network with one transactional strategy and one basis of class participation. To do so would do harm both to the complexity of the case studies and to our theoretical argument that every factional situation contains within itself elements of all 'pure' types and is thus dynamic. Yet it may help the reader to remember the separate typologies by linking them together. Thus, we could classify factionalism as *conservative* if it is marked by establishment-opposition networks, by patronage transactions and by élite participation; as *revolutionary* if it combines group mobilization transactions, participation by class and multiple clustering of networks; and as *progressive* where strategies are opportunistic, participation bourgeois and networks open.

But the over-generalization of such a typology is evident the moment one tries to apply it to any particular situation. Only conservative factionalism has been described by earlier writers, as though it were a stable state, and then, as the case studies of the present volume suggest, this has been possible only because the ethnographers have omitted to analyse non-conservative elements in the factionalism. Class participation in persistent opposition is such an element, and is probably common. If one accepts the fact that conservative factionalism is a steady state, then one would argue, along the lines suggested by Paine's fictional case study, that even class-based opposition factions lose their revolutionary potential when they gain power. After twenty years the establishment and the opposition may change places and labels, but the factionalism remains conservative. The analyst can ignore class-based oppositions as being momentary deviations from a stable condition to which a system returns in repetitive cycles.

Yet we do not know whether such cycles are repetitive. It may be that in real life the dialectic of change is more common. If an opposition gains power, the informal understandings that govern decisions in a densely linked establishment no longer hold. The more explicit and specific bases for common action by an opposition will differ. They may crystallize into an ideology as Boissevain's paper suggests; they may gradually modify themselves into the informal understandings of a new establishment – but the new understandings will be different from those of the old establishment. Even if the cycle were repetitive, the dialectic would produce some change, at some level of analysis. More research is clearly needed to test empirically the satisfying intellectual model of cyclical recurrence provided by the fictional case.

By contrast, Attwood's paper suggests that no factionalist state is a stable or even cyclical one, but that all contain a dynamic for long-term change. Within a condition of elite conservative factionalism the incentive for the opposition to recruit outside the elite class is great. If it does so, the potential exists of a move towards group mobilization by elite individuals and of an expansion of political awareness or even class-consciousness among non-elite classes. Emergence of non-elite group mobilizers, of multiple dense clusters as nuclei for non-establishment factions, and of the wide distribution of resources within a community appear as further steps in a sequence that moves from conservative factionalism to revolutionary factionalism.

But revolutionary factionalism itself is no steady state. Even if it starts as merely associations of individuals, it is likely to lead further. The associations may formalize themselves into parties or into political movements, and so cease to be factional. Or if they remain factional within a wider community and effectively carry out a redistribution of resources through group mobilization, they can radically alter the pattern of resource availability on which revolutionary factionalism is based. Attwood's case suggests that when multiple sources of benefits are available, and multiple interest groups have already been mobilized in an earlier phase of revolutionary factionalism, then the networks activated become more open, and the strategies used more opportunistic. In short, bourgeois factionalism can succeed revolutionary factionalism.

Yet Islam's case study describes bourgeois factionalism immediately succeeding conservative factionalism after the war had altered the state of resource availability. And Schryer describes how revolutionary factionalism can change to conservative factionalism if leaders become coopted into an elite. Clearly, bourgeois factionalism itself can potentially change into either conservative or revolutionary factionalism, if it produces innovative politicians who can competitively gain mass support for elite or for socialist productive activities.

Do particular types of factionalism tend to follow other types more frequently than randomly? Does the internal dialectic of factionalism that we have described for establishment-opposition, patronage and elite factionalism predispose a system to move through particular sequences? What are the necessary conditions for a particular sequential change to occur, rather than another? These, and a host of other questions for future long-term historical studies are suggested by this book.

To be more provocative, even if the patterns of factionalism change, how much are whole societies changed thereby? Are the patterns of factionalism repetitive? Have we succeeded in merely amplifying Pareto's analysis of the circulation of elites as 'lions' of patronage politics temporarily are replaced by 'foxes' of opportunistic politics? At what point in a situation of factional politics do different classes achieve self-consciousness, do different cultural rules governing politics become established, different interest groups become incorporated as parties, or different productive processes become instituted, so that politics cease to follow a factionalist logic? Does the locus of a factionalist analysis then merely switch to studying political behaviour, within the newly formalized moral communities, which is acted out according to pragmatic strategies not normatively accepted, as Bailey suggests?

E. *Other Analyses*

We have gone far enough to suggest that the pardigm of factionalism, dialectically opposed to a paradigm of factions as groupings, is clearly compatible with alternative anthropological approaches such as those of networks, transactions and social class. More importantly, the use of the paradigm enables us to combine these approaches and to gain a fuller understanding of the relationship between local conflicts and long-term political change. The paradigm forces us to look more closely at the way variations in factionalism can correlate with variations in resources, class structures, institutions and cultural rules.

But the three approaches listed do not exhaust the approaches which the contributors to this volume use in their work. Bailey's insistence, following Madison, on the illegitimacy of factionalism suggests that a study of 'illegitimate politics' might provide a wider paradigm. Many contributors suggest that a relationship may exist between the type of factionalism surrounding an issue and the nature of the issue itself; generalizations on this question remain to be made. Nagata's study of Hopi factionalism – a factionalism in which each faction denies that the other faction exists and thereby makes a confrontation or resolution impossible – recalls Nicholas' earlier analysis (1965) of Iroquois factionalism of the 1920's. Is there a distinctive pattern of American Indian factionalism? Or, as Paine would phrase it, should there not be a cultural analysis of factionalism? Are the cultural rules, within which the factional process takes place, not worthy of study? Do the rules change with the factional process? Is academic (or novelistic) factionalism different from other kinds of factionalism? How would C. P. Snow's novel have ended if it had been set in North American academe?

We hope that this study provides a dialectical step along the path of research into factionalism. We hope our advance may provoke the next step in dialectic with us.

REFERENCES

ALAVI, H.
1973 "Peasant Classes and Primordial Loyalties." *Journal of Peasant Studies*, 1:23–62.
ATTWOOD, D. W.
1974 "Patrons and Mobilizers: Political Entrepreneurs in an Agrarian State." *Journal of Anthropological Research*, 30(4):225–41.
BAILEY, F. G.
1965 "Decisions by Concensus in Councils and Committees: With Special Reference to Village and Local Government in India." In M. Banton (ed.), *Political Systems and the Distribution of Power*. New York, Praeger (ASA Monograph 2, London, Tavistock).
BAILEY, F. G.
1968 "Parapolitical Systems." In M. J. Swartz (ed.), *Local Level Politics*. Chicago, Aldine.
BAILEY, F. G.
1969 *Strategems and Spoils*. Oxford, Basil Blackwell.
BAILEY, F. G.
1971 "The Peasant View of the Bad Life." In T. Shanin (ed.), *Peasant and Peasant Societies: Selected Readings*. Harmondsworth, Penguin Books.
BANTON, M. (ed.)
1965 *Political Systems and the Distribution of Power*. ASA Monograph 2, London, Tavistock Publications.
BARNES, J. A.
1954 "Class and Committees in a Norwegian Island Parish." *Human Relations*, 7:39–58.
BARNES, J. A.
1959 "Politics without Parties." *Man*, 59:13–15.
BARTH, F.
1959 "Segmentary Opposition and the Theory of Games." *Journal of the Royal Anthropological Institute*, 89:5–21.
BOISSEVAIN, J.
1966 "Patronage in Sicily." *Man* (N.S.), 1(1):18–33.
BOISSEVAIN, J.
1971 "Second Thoughts on Quasi-Groups, Categories and Coalitions." *Man*, 6(3):468–72.
BRASS, P. R.
1965 *Factional Politics in an Indian State*. Berkeley, University of California Press.
BUJRA, JANET
1973 "The Dynamics of Political Action: A New Look at Factionalism." *American Anthropologist*, 75(1):132–52.
COSER, LEWIS
1956 *The Functions of Social Conflict*. New York, Free Press.
EASTON, DAVID
1959 "Political Anthropology." In B. J. Siegel (ed.), *Biennial Review of Anthropology*. Stanford University Press.
FIRTH, R. W.
1957 "Introduction: Factions in Indian and Overseas Societies." *British Journal of Sociology*, 8:291–95.

FORTES, M. and E. E. EVANS-PRITCHARD (eds.)
1940 *African Political Systems*. London, Oxford University Press.
FRANKENBERG, R.
1957 *Village on the Border*. London, Cohen and West.
GLUCKMAN, M.
1953 *Rituals of Rebellion in South-East Africa*. Manchester, University Press.
GULLIVER, P. H.
1971 *Neighbours and Networks*. Berkeley, University of California Press.
ISLAM, A. K. M. A.
1974 *A Bangladesh Village: Conflict and Cohesion – An Anthropological Study of Politics*. Cambridge, Mass., Schenkman.
KUHN, T.
1962 *The Structure of Scientific Revolutions*. Chicago, University of Chicago Press.
MAYER, A. C.
1966 "The Significance of Quasi-Groups in the Study of Complex Societies." In M. Banton (ed.), *The Social Anthropology of Complex Societies*, ASA Monograph 4. London, Tavistock.
NICHOLAS, RALPH W.
1965 "Factions: A Comparative Analysis." In M. Banton (ed.), *Political Systems and the Distribution of Power*. ASA Monograph 2. London, Tavistock.
NICHOLAS, RALPH W.
1968 "Structures of Politics in the Village of Southern Asia." In M. Singer and B. S. Cohn (eds.), *Structure and Change in Indian Society*. Chicago, Aldine.
OLIVER, D. L.
1955 *Solomon Islands Society*. Cambridge, Harvard University Press.
SAHLINS, M.
1967 "On the Sociology of Primitive Exchange." In M. Banton (ed.), *The Relevance of Models for Social Anthropology*. London, Tavistock.
SALISBURY, R. F.
1962 *From Stone to Steel*. Cambridge, Cambridge University Press.
SALISBURY, R. F.
1968 "Formal Analysis in Anthropological Economics: The Rassel Island Case." In I. Buchler and H. G. Nutini (eds.), *Game Theory and the Behavioural Sciences*. Pittsburgh, Pittsburgh University Press.
SCHRYER, FRANS J.
1975 "Village Factionalism and Class Conflict in Peasant Communities." *Canadian Review of Sociology and Anthropology*, 12(3):290–302.
SIEGEL, BERNARD J. and ALAN R. BEALS
1960a "Conflict and Factional Dispute." *Journal of the Royal Anthropological Institute*, 90:107–17.
SIEGEL, BERNARD J. and ALAN R. BEALS
1960b "Pervasive Factionalism." *American Anthropologist*, 62:394–417.
SIEGEL, BERNARD J. and ALAN R. BEALS
1966 *Divisiveness and Social Conflict: An Anthropological Approach*. Stanford, Stanford University Press.
SILVERMAN, M.
1973 "Resource Change and Village Factionalism in an East Indian Community, Guyana." Unpublished Ph.D. Dissertation. Montreal, McGill University.
SWARTZ, M. J. (ed.)
1968 *Local Level Politics*. Chicago, Aldine.
SWARTZ, M. J., V. W. TURNER and A. TUDEN (eds.)
1966 *Political Anthropology*. Chicago, Aldine.

The Definition of Factionalism[1]

2

F. G. Bailey

Introduction

One reason why the study of factions and factionalism by anthropologists over the past ten years has been slight may be that, like surgeons, we have cut out the cancerous parts which happen also to be the interesting parts. We make our definitions out of features such as impermanence, lack of ideology, or diverse recruitment; we notice, almost in passing, that factions lack legitimacy. But we do not build *centrally* into our analysis the fact that everywhere people deplore factions, think they are a sign of decay, and brand them as immoral.

Secondly, beyond noting that factions engage in contest and are therefore of political significance, we have tended to regard them as, *sui generis*, odd forms of behaviour somehow peripheral to the central field of understanding how institutions and organizations work,[2] and we have not completed the job of definition by noting those features which link factions with other kinds of political groups.[3]

My aim, then, is to define factionalism in a way which takes account of the shady connotations of that word at the same time showing that factional behaviour, certainly frequent, is also 'normal,' in the sense that its features are shared by other political styles, and that it is not a uniquely aberrant thing.

Near Horizons, Personalizing, Covertness, and Normality

A famous description of factionalism is that of Thucydides in the third book of The Peloponnesian War between sections 82 and 85. In the fifth year of the war between Athens and Sparta a civil war broke out in Corcyra. The people of this island were subordinate allies of the Athenians. Several hundred of their sailors had been made prisoners by the Corinthians, allies of Sparta, and Thucydides traces the beginning of the disturbances in Corcyra from the release of the sailors, their return home, and the attempt of the Spartans and Corinthians to persuade the people of Corcyra to change sides. At that stage the people of Corcyra were very sensible: when a ship from Athens and a ship from Corinth arrived with representatives, they listened to both, and voted to remain allies of the Athenians and at the same time maintain friendship with the other side, the Peloponnesian League.

Then the freed prisoners-of-war, who constituted the party in favour of

Corinth and Sparta, brought to trial a man called Peithias who, as Thucydides puts it, "had voluntarily offered to look after Athenian interests in Corcyra and who was the leader of the democratic party." He was charged with betraying his country. He was acquitted and promptly brought five of the other party to court, on the charge of cutting vine props out of a sacred grove. Found guilty, they were fined a large sum, but instead of paying they took refuge in temples and begged that the fine should be made less. Peithias, however, was a member of the council, and his arguments persuaded his colleagues to insist on the "full rigour of the law." At this point the five accused men gathered together a raiding group, broke into the council, killed Peithias and murdered sixty other council members.

They then took over the government, announced a policy of friendly neutrality, and sent a delegation off to Athens to give a plausible account of what had been done and to take whatever steps they could to prevent the Athenians from stirring up a counter-revolution. The Athenians promptly arrested them.

In Corcyra civil war broke out. For the first few days the fighting was among the people of Corcyra who were divided into the democratic party and their opponents. Later Athenian and Spartan fleets appeared, each coming to help that faction of the Corcyrans which supported them. Some indecisive battles were fought. Then the Spartans, hearing that a strong Athenian fleet was approaching, sailed quietly away during the night, leaving to their fate that faction of the Corcyrans which had supported the Spartan cause.

Then, Thucydides says, "There was death in every shape and form ... people went to every extreme and beyond it." There follows the well-known passage in which the author describes factionalism (which in Greek is *stasis*), the circumstances which produce it, the style of politics which characterizes it, and its consequences for the individual and the state.

How, then, is factionalism to be defined? The first and obvious point is that it can exist only in contrast with a set of 'normal' conditions. An alternative translation for *stasis* is civil war: the splitting apart of a whole which *all concerned claim should be united*; without this idea of a whole there can be no factionalism, just as without health, there can be no sickness. Secondly factionalism is a form of contest. But contest is an attribute of all political systems; to be of use in analysis, it has to be capable of variation. Our next task is to identify alternative states of the political arena (that is, of contest), and find out what features distinguish factionalism from normal styles of political contest. Out of the description given by Thucydides emerge the following characteristics:

(1) There is a set of features which can be summarized by the words "near horizons." A "*thoughtless* act of aggression" becomes courage; "to think of the future" becomes cowardice; if alliances are made, they are

temporary and made for a particular purpose, to be broken the first time it is advantageous to do so: "Their one standard was the pleasure of their own party *at that particular moment*"; and so on (emphasis added).

Connected with short-term planning and plotting is a liking for precipitate action.[4] To try to understand a question from all sides and to think it through is to proclaim oneself unfit for action. It is good to anticipate the opponent by striking first. To think too much about the long-term consequences of action is the mark of a coward. The result is the elimination of those who have "superior intelligence" because their opponents, mistrusting their own capacity for intrigue or debate, go straight into action (as in the murder of Peithias and his fellow councillors in Corcyra).

Moreover, this action is violent, outside the existing rules of competition, urged on by a fanatical enthusiasm, and unhindered by considerations of justice or fairness. In the historical account it is the violence which catches one's eye and which is immediately destructive; but from a comparative point of view what matters is that violence usually also means "outside the existing system of rules for political competition."

All these characteristics, the lack of concern for the future, the preference for action and the limiting of what might be called the "moral horizon" to members of one's own faction or party, the fanaticism and the refusal to think rationally about the interests of the whole or to remember "that there may come a time when they, too, will be in danger and will need (the protection) of the laws" – all these characteristics hang together.

(2) The second cluster of attributes can be described as the 'personalizing' of politics. This is not the familiar modern proposition that factions are leader-centered, for in the passage on civil war Thucydides has nothing to say about that. Rather it is the frontier notion that in the last resort every man must look after himself, because it is the man rather than the system which is effective: "... instead of being able to feel confident in others, they devoted their energies to providing against being injured themselves." Elsewhere Thucydides writes, "... men take it upon themselves to begin the process of repealing those general laws of humanity ... ." The sense that politics is about persons and their doings rather than about ideas and policies and programs comes out most strongly in the several remarks about revenge. To inflict vengeance men commit "unheard of atrocities." Revenge becomes more important than even self-preservation. In all this we can see an implicit despair of order and systematic action. When things go wrong, there is no point in asking how the system was at fault, but every point in putting the blame on someone and punishing him or eliminating him. Rehabilitation of those who offend is nowhere considered, only retribution; hence, the violence and the atrocities. Such an attitude fits well with swiftness of action and impatience with planning and foresight, for the death of a man is more easily achieved than the reform of a system.

Out of this emerges a feature of political systems which seems a theodicy, a theory explaining why evil exists and what should be done: whether people are to blame or systems are to blame.

(3) The third characteristic is covertness. To be successful in factional politics one had to plot to work behind the scenes, to go behind the backs not only of one's enemies but also of those who appeared to be one's friends, and to set a high value on secrecy and conspiracy. There is a simple explanation of why people engaged in factional politics would want to keep their plans secret: in a contest it pays to do the surprising thing, to throw one's opponent off balance, and to hinder him from anticipating and therefore parrying the blow that is coming.

But the element of surprise is not the only consideration. There is also in factionalism an element of shame, anticipated in being caught in the act of employing such tactics. Although there may be cases in which the actors do not care what the world thinks of their behaviour (indiscriminate terrorism is a contemporary example), but certainly in the cases described by Thucydides, the conspirators looked for ways of justifying publicly the goals at which they were aiming and of concealing the means which they employed to attain these goals. Thus, in the case of Corcyra, all these atrocities were committed either in the name of "political equality for the masses" or "safe and sound government of the aristocracy." This is not so much a code of conduct specific to the factional arena (analogous to those myths of the fair fight in the romances of the frontier), but rather the survival of dominant values which existed before *stasis* began. The factional fighters, for all the disgraceful things they delight in doing, nevertheless have their eye on an orderly past and still more on a future in which order will reign; they will be the rulers, and they will have need of a code which discourages their opponents from hitting below the belt. Factionalism may be the negation of orderly government, but in the desire to conceal actions of a kind that deny fundamental moral rules on which orderly government rests, lies a dialectical intention to return one day to orderly government (or at least a wish to keep that option open). Whatever the negative results of their actions, faction fighters have – or like to appear to have – positive intentions.

This again seems to me to be a feature of any political style: the varying degrees to which the actors are willing to be held openly accountable for the tactics which they employ. The unwillingness to put things in writing, the use of the telephone, the reliance on personal contracts in bureaucratic organizations (where all this is not, of course, legitimate) are all instances of the "backstage" or shady side of politics (that area where goals are achieved by ignoring or bending rules, but in secret) where faction fighters like to operate.

There is a final characteristic at which Thucydides hints: "Everyone had come to the conclusion that it was hopeless to expect a permanent settlement ... ." Factionalism seems like the millennium, but in reverse: it is a positive feedback system, self-liquidating because the discords amplify one another until in the end life, if it continues to exist at all, it becomes "solitary, poor, nasty, brutish, and short." The positive expectations of those anthropological observers who regard factionalism as a period of experimentation do not seem to be shared by the actors themselves; as they see it, constructive action is impossible because their opponents are not working towards a solution, but away from it; factionalism, unless countered by other modes of politics, can only lead to extinction. In the eyes of many, that is the situation in Northern Ireland today, as it must also have been in fifth century Corcyra.

Let me summarize. Out of the description of factionalism given by Thucydides the following attributes have been extracted: the near horizons, the personalizing of politics, the covertness, and paradoxically, a concern for and pessimism about a larger order. Those engaged in factional politics prefer action to planning, the objective being immediate rather than for the distant future; and they concentrate, *almost* in a single-minded fashion, on the interests of their own group to the detriment of the wider community to which they formerly belonged. Secondly, those who are active in the political arena of factions are careless about, if not contemptuous of, ideas about systems and organizations. They prefer rather to think of persons, who serve either as the object of unswerving and unthinking loyalty or, in the same mindless way, as scapegoats for disaster, since disaster does not so much call for better planning and more sophisticated organization as for revenge upon those whose criminal activities have created the disaster. Thirdly, factional politics are covert: whatever stories are told in public, the effective action is kept behind the scenes. Finally, the commentary upon factionalism is suffused with a concern for order and with pessimism: factionalism is the descent into ruin, an addiction which compounds itself at every indulgence and must end in self-destruction.

Through this list runs a feature which is a central concern in the study of factionalism: an apparent contradiction, an uncertainty about where to draw the boundaries of the moral community. Factional activity is kept covert partly out of a sense of shame (that is, a concern with one's own reputation), indicating that those concerned have an eye on the future and on a wider public than the members of their own faction. Evidently they look back and forward to a 'normal' state of affairs from which factionalism was and will be absent. For all the pessimism and Gresham's law which states that factional politics must drive out 'good' politics (indeed, Thucydides argues that the good men are the first to go the wall), there is, nevertheless, at least an idea of a non-factional state of affairs and of a responsibility to a community which is larger than one's own faction. If this were not true, there would be no way of explaining why nowhere do we find a political group proclaiming itself to be a faction. On the contrary, the term is used for one's opponents. Even those groups which, from the point of view of the historian, seem to have followed a path of total irresponsibility and destruction, nevertheless had – and may well have believed in – their 'cover story': they were out to save the world or the nation or the city of the people, a body larger than just themselves.

Scale and Open Politics

In *The Federalist* IX and X, there is a well known discussion of "domestic faction and insurrection." Max Beloff, in his Introduction (1948:XLVI), notes that the authors of these papers were sharply aware of the conditions under which they lived: "... to their contemporaries had been given the chance of constructing from the ground upwards a new political society, approving by experiment what had been hitherto only food for abstract speculation." This was an age of experiment and of uncertainty. Whereas Thucydides watched and wrote about the descent into disorder, these men wrote about ways to control it. They offer us a design for society, together with a definition of what factions are, an explanation of why they arise, and a recommendation on how factionalism can be controlled.

It is impossible to read the history of the petty republics of Greece and Italy, without feeling sensations of horror and disgust at the distractions with which they were continually agitated, and at the rapid succession of revolutions, by which they were kept perpetually vibrating between the extremes of tyranny and anarchy ... From the disorders that disfigure the annals of those republics, the advocates of despotism have drawn arguments, not only against the forms of republican government, but against the very principles of civil liberty.

These passages occur near the beginning of *The Federalist* IX and the point is made again in X, in the famous essay by Madison. "The instability, injustice, and confusion, introduced into the public councils have, in truth, been the mortal diseases under which popular governments have everywhere perished; as they continue to be the favorite and fruitful topics from which the adversaries to liberty derive their most specious declamations." Despotism will end factions, but the cure is no better than the disease. "Liberty is to faction what air is to fire, an aliment, without which it instantly expires." But to prevent factionalism by taking away liberty would be like protecting people from fire by removing the air which they breathe.

There will always be faction: the question is how to keep it under control. If one asks why there will always be faction, the answer turns out to be that such activity is in the nature of man: as Thucydides put it "... human nature, always ready to offend even where laws exist ... incapable of controlling passion, insubordinate to the idea of justice, the enemy to anything superior to itself ... ." But what appears to be a terminus in

Madison's reasoning, the appeal to human nature as an axiom, in fact leads him on to a description of what factions are and how they arise.

A zeal for different opinions, concerning religion, concerning government, and many other points, as well of speculation as of practice; an attachment to different leaders, ambitiously contending for preeminence and power ... have rendered (mankind) much more disposed to vex and oppress each other, than to cooperate for their mutual good. So strong is this propensity of mankind, to fall into mutual animosity, that where no substantial occasion presents itself, the most frivolous and fanciful distinctions have been sufficient to kindle their unfriendly passions, and excite their more violent conflicts. But the most common and durable source of factions have been the various and unequal distributions of property. Those who hold, and those who are without property, have ever formed distinct interests in societies. Those who are creditors, and those who are debtors, fall under a like discrimination. A landed interest, a manufacturing interest, a mercantile interest, a money interest, with many lesser interests, grow up of necessity in civilized nations, and divide them into different classes, actuated by different sentiments and views. The regulation of these various and interfering interests forms the principal task of modern legislation, and involves the spirit of party and faction in the necessary and ordinary operations of government.

Evidently, factions are to be recognized not by what they are, but by what they do. They can be "a manufacturing interest," or a "landed interest" or "those who are without property"; ... a religious sect may degenerate into a political faction ..."; "a rage for paper money, for abolition of debts, for an equal division of property, or for any other improper or wicked project ..." can bring about the factional style of politics. Madison does not offer a list of attributes with which to identify factional styles (analogous to those suggested by Thucydides), but relies on the single dominating criterion: that the action is taken in the interests of a sectional group and damages the interests of the whole. "By a faction, I understand a number of citizens, whether amounting to a majority or a minority of the whole, who are united and actuated by some common impulse of passion, or of interest, adverse to the rights of other citizens, or to the permanent and aggregate interests of the community." It should be noted that in all this the interest to be safeguarded against the destructive activities of factions is not that of the majority (which itself can constitute a faction), but rather that of the whole community.

So far there is no substantial point of contradiction between the criteria which Thucydides and the writers of *The Federalist* papers use to identify factionalism against a context of normal political activity. Thucydides distinguishes more of the attributes of factional activity; Madison provides a richer list of the kinds of groups which may turn towards factionalism. But the richness of this list (creditors, debtors, those without property, those who advocate such "wicked projects" as "an equal division of property" and so on, rather than just the simple opposition of "political equality for the masses" against "safe and sound government of the aristocracy") turns out to be of considerable importance when Madison goes on to talk about ways of controlling factionalism. Further, he suggests that a discussion of factionalism will be incomplete without a consideration of *scale*.

There will always be factions. "The diversity in the faculties of men, from which the rights of property originate, is ... an insuperable obstacle to an uniformity of interests." Yet factionalism is beyond control only when a single faction dominates, and is able to govern in its own interests to the detriment of the whole community. (No doubt a polar situation in which only two factions were present in the arena, as in the case of Corcyra, would also be regarded as deplorable.)

The weakness of "pure democracy" lies in its small size: "... a society consisting of a small number of citizens, who assemble and administer the government in person, can admit of no cure from the mischiefs of faction. ... Theoretic politicians, who have patronized this species of government, have erroneously supposed, that by reducing mankind to a perfect equality in their political rights, they would, at the same time, be perfectly equalized and assimilated in their possessions, their opinions, and their passions." Madison, in short, stands behind Professor Srivinas in asserting that face-to-face communities are better described as inevitably "back-to-back."

On the other hand, large-scale political operations (a characteristic of the republican form of government, but not of "pure democracy") provide their own protection against factionalism. They do so in three ways, Madison claims. Firstly, he says (forgetting an earlier statement that "neither morals nor religious motives can be relied on as an adequate control") the larger the pool of candidates from which rulers are elected, the more likely it is that men of good will, capable of just action in the interest of the whole community, will find their way to office. Secondly (and not entirely consistently with the first statement), it is harder to rig large elections than small ones. (At the present time, it is not easy to be persuaded by either of these arguments.) The third argument turns out to be that of the political free marketplace: if there are many divergent interests, then the competition between them will ensure that no single faction, or even a pair of factions, will ever be in a position to dominate the political arena. Although there might be some danger that factionalism could reassert itself among the governing elite, this tendency is controlled by the many and divergent interests which they represent.

Before this is written off as, at best, Dr. Pangloss and Pollyanna, and at worst, as a sophist's defense of the propertied classes, the argument about scale deserves closer examination, for it suggests another attribute of factionalism.

After the description of what went on in Corcyra and the other city states of classical Greece, there is no need to ask why both, those concerned in the event and the historians who recorded them, regarded factionalism as disastrous. When people in Bisipara (Bailey, 1968) said that there was too much "party" in a village, they meant both that an undue proportion of resources was being expended in political activity, and that this activity was destructive. It was destructive because in a well-ordered political system, the quantity of resources consumed in political competition is limited by the rules of the system. When the controlling rules fall into disuse, there is no *numen*, a word which I have used elsewhere (Bailey, 1972) to refer to the entity which, so to speak, "holds the ring" – a useful metaphor since it indicates the need to prevent fighting from spreading outside the ring, and to make sure that the contest within the ring remains relatively orderly. *Numen* means a "nod," then a "command," and comes to stand for the divinity which both symbolizes and maintains the common values of the contestants.

The point of factionalism is that *numen* is weak in two senses. Firstly, factionalism is politics without order, an arena in which nothing is likely to be lost by breaking the rules by which an unwary opponent thinks he is protected, because there is no one around to enforce the rules. From this comes the covertness, the precipitate action, making the person rather than the rule the object of attack, and the alleged lack of foresight in that the contestant is himself destroying the rules which he might one day need for his own protection. Secondly, in a more literal sense, in the case of total polar factionalism, everyone is commited to one side or the other and no one is left to play the role of *numen*.

Madison seems to suppose two kinds of *numen*. One kind, which is less emphasized, is internalized and moral, and appears in the patrician view that a properly elected governing elite will be more likely than the masses to possess sensitive political consciences. But more important than this is the other version of *numen*, whose amoral incarnation is the self-regulatory mechanism of the political free marketplace. Given *many* divergent interests, any *one* must (assuming that the distribution is appropriate) be in a minority. If it asserts its interests too strongly, then the rest will gang up against it and so bring it under control. Since no one can have all of what he wants, everyone has the better chance of getting something and so the general interest of the whole is preserved.

The step missing in this argument is the explanation as to why size alone should produce divergent interests. One wonders why those relatively sophisticated Greek city states did not also have "a landed interest, a manufacturing interest, a mercantile interest, a monied interest, with many lesser interests ... ." They surely did. The question then is why this divergence should be more easily sunk into a pair of dominant factions than the larger divergence of 18th century America ("larger" in the sense that a greater number of people were involved). Clearly, something is missing in the argument: there is no way as yet of explaining why Corcyra too could not have had its *numen* in the form of the self-regulating mechanism of a free political marketplace, nor why American politics should not eventually be polarized into two fanatical factions.

The argument about scale can be salvaged only if it is the case that when contesting political groups grow beyond a certain size, they must divest, of necessity, some or all of the attributes of a faction, and somehow make room for the re-emergence of *numen*.

If one looks again at the list of attributes derived from Thucydides, the argument that this in fact must happen seems plausible. A large-scale political organization requires a bureaucracy. A bureaucracy is impersonal, based on rules rather than on persons, and men are required to act in the open much more than are members of a faction. Moreover, a large organization which attempts to run its affairs on the principle of the "near horizon" must soon dissolve into chaos (one sign of which is the emergence of factions within it). Organizations are ill-adapted to precipitate action, they set a low value on fanaticism and a high value on reason, and finally, organizations make people specialize in their political activity; a faction, on the other hand, preserves the frontier ideal that most of the tasks of life are simple enough for every man to carry out for himself.

Madison's argument, I think, rests mainly on the divergence of interests: that the pack would always pull down a would-be leader. Against this, I am urging his other argument, one which in the end takes a less pessimistic view of the human condition; the assertion that "neither moral nor religious motives can be relied on as an adequate control" grows less effective as the size of political organization increases, providing one interprets "moral and religious motives" to mean shame rather than guilt. I hasten to add that this is not a claim that people who work for General Motors have better developed consciences than the man who runs the corner repair shop. Rather it is that the techniques required to run a large organization make necessary a form of relatively public accountability. Of course covert backstage operations still go on. But at least there is a front office, where respectability (*numen*) must appear to reign. Whether the existence of this office sets some limit on the transactions which can take place through the back door, or whether it is the other way around – the dirtier the deals, the bigger the façade – is an interesting question.

But the conclusion is firm enough: large-scale politics require forms of behaviour which are not factional; but these may not be pervasive enough to eliminate factionalism and certainly will not eliminate the milder forms of shady politics. In just the same way, factionalism does not entirely dispense with open politics: factional politicians seem not to be able to do without a cover story designed to eliminate the charge of factionalism.

This brings us back to the familiar statement that factions tend to be small face-to-face groups. The large "faction" could not be a faction. Just where the line is drawn between "large" and "small" poses many problems, of the same nature as those involved in setting a size to a "little community." At this stage it is enough to say that the distinctively factional style of operating becomes more difficult as the size of the contesting political groups increases. The larger the group the less likely is it to be concerned exclusively with the skilful application of political devices, and the more likely is it to insist upon open discussion about the public approval of political ends. At the same time, within such bodies will emerge specialized groups still small enough to have the characteristics of factions and to use their political devices.

Politics in the Open and in the Shade

Covert modes of political activity, attention to persons rather than to policies or principles, and an overwhelming interest in today and tomorrow at the expense of long-term planning separate the shady side of politics from the relatively open world of parties or movements or nations pursuing their interests through open competition or open diplomacy. These three modes of activity identify not only factionalism, but also what is done by pressure groups and by lobbyists, in patron-client relationships and courtly or palace politics – and even in the activities of the Mafia. One other feature which all these share is that *particular operations* engage only small numbers of people, even when quite large numbers of people are engaged in the *same kind* of exercise: as soon as there is an attempt to mount a large-scale operation, some of the features which are characteristic of open politics must appear.

In order to separate factionalism from other modes of shady politics, the distinction between shady and open politics requires elaboration. Any normal political system develops shady institutions in order to supplement the channels of open interchange. A normal system will covertly recognize procedures through which personal influence can be exercised, favours can be granted and prizes gained without having to go through the scrutiny of open processes of justification or through the trials of open competition. At least it is hard to find a system in which there are no complaints about this being done. People deplore it when they are on the losing end, but when benefited, they will defend it (either discreetly or with an overcompensating aggression) as being a fact of life, or the oil without which the machine would come grinding to a halt, or a liberating device from the thraldom of bureaucracy, or something of that kind – the favoured justifications varying from one culture to another. But of those who deplore it, few would be found (even within the ranks of a bureaucracy) who felt that because the odd favour was done or a little graft was detected from time to time, the whole fabric of their society was about to be torn apart. Probably this is true even with such institutions as the Mafia; certainly Plunkitt's concept of "honest graft" was not his alone, nor *mutatis mutandis* confined to Tammany Hall.

We can think of shady politics as a continuum, from clique at one end (barely political, if political at all) to factionalism at the other. Movement towards factionalism marks an increasing seriousness of the threat against the continued existence of the entire system of orderly political life.

Cliques exist because organizations never seem to be able to use up man's capacity and need for affection. To be human is to belong to a small face-to-face group, where one is accepted in the round as a moral person, rather than a mere instrument serving an organization. Especially on the frontier where there are no organizations, or in conditions of uncertainty where normal organizational arrangements have broken down, men have, so to speak, a lot of unused loyalty, and under such conditions the tendency, to which Eric Wolf has drawn attention (1966), will be to assert a common humanity by discovering mutual affection and respect and associating in small face-to-face groups.

These groups, even when not intentionally political, contain the seeds of such activity. They are created by a sense that the rest of the world is different and is dangerous, and there is certainly an idea that the goals and purposes of the larger organization will be sacrificed, if the need arises, to protect a fellow member. The standard of morality and mutual forebearance is infinitely high within the group, and very low across its boundaries. In short, they have near horizons, are personalized, and covert.

Although the members of such groups, which Boissevain (1973) calls *cliques*, may have no political intentions beyond the minimal ones of wanting to be left alone to enjoy one another's company, and although they are not in combat with other groups such as factions, they are readily suspected by others of conspiracy. In fact, they are well adapted to enter the political arena as factions. Cliques are, in a way, proto-factions.

Insofar as a clique acts politically, this action is primarily defensive, taken to maintain a boundary and to exclude a larger world. The clique represents withdrawal from an unpleasant situation, rather than an attempt to change that situation. Once the group attempts to gain resources and actively to manipulate the world, it becomes a pressure group or a gang or, in the extreme case, a faction.

Lobbyists, pressure groups, and criminal organizations such as the Mafia intervene more directly than cliques in the political process. Undoubtedly they belong on the shady side of politics; but, as we noticed earlier, legitimacy – or at least a pragmatic necessity – is claimed in varying degrees for such activities. Arguments are advanced that they make the system work and adjust it to reality, and in so doing, far from being a threat to open and respectable action, they make such action possible. Their existence is both a sign of and a condition for political stability.

Those involved in faction fighting will also claim altruistic intentions. But their goal is not that of adjusting the system, but rather that of cleansing and reforming it by eliminating destructive persons and destructive practices. In other words, along the line of shady politics which stretches from cliques through lobbyists, pressure groups, and criminal organization to factions, the break between factionalists and the others is marked by *their recognition of crisis and breakdown*.[5] In a paradoxical way, factionalism turns back towards open politics because its practitioners hold up as an ideal the possibility of a political process that is clean and respectable.

The recognition of a particular point along this line is a complex thing because recognition, itself, is often a political act. From outside, and in the mode of common sense, one can suggest that the movement towards the factional end of the continuum means that fewer resources for living are being distributed through open and fair competition, or through a rational debate about the best interests for all concerned. Certainly, by the time one reaches cases such as Corcyra, it seems that no route to personal survival exists except through that of the dark side of politics; as usual, extremes pose fewer difficulties than the intermediate cases.

Since we do not, in fact, have any way of arriving at an indisputable statement of the amount of resources which go in one direction or the other, in practice we fall back on the culture-given rank order which determines: (1) that lobbyists and pressure groups pose so small a threat that they can be considered normal; (2) that more open graft – especially when it results in successful prosecutions – is more serious; and (3) that Mafia-like activities, because they are against the law and involve violence, are yet more serious. But all of these are – depending on where you stand – activities which are useful ancillaries to the clumsy open system or, at worst, parasitic upon it. They are not a direct threat, either in the *de facto* form of factional disorder or in the plain and open intentions of revolutionary bodies.

Given such a scaling, the words themselves become political weapons with which to strike an opponent, and every contestant tries to make sure that no one can pin on him the next most serious term in the line. Thus, we meet terms such as "honest graft" and the notable patriotism of American Mafia figures – so the story goes – in adventures against the nation's enemies.

Nevertheless, there are points on the line at which there can be little dispute about the appropriate term. What went on in Corcyra was the extreme of faction-fighting – not lobbying nor graft, whether honest or dishonest. Our definitions, in short, are not entirely subjective and we can identify points which are clear enough to resist the obfuscation of political claims.

In brief, politics are like the Indian months in having a light half and a dark half. Unlike the two halves of the month, these two modes of politics exist at the same time and influence one another: an increase in one mode may intensify or may diminish the other. Within the dark half, the 'gloom' intensifies as one moves from the parasitic modes towards, at the extreme, the obvious destructiveness of factionalism. Beyond this is the total darkness of chaos: no system at all.

NOTES

1 For their comments on an earlier essay of which this is a drastically shortened version I wish to thank the following: participants in the Geneva Park Conference, Kevin Avruch, Ray Larsen, Mark Mochary, Mike Orbach, Mel Spiro, Marc Swartz, and Don Tuzin. *Patruriunt montes ....*

2 To have an interest in factions was, at one time, itself a factional posture. Those who disdained to use the word "faction" were the leaders of structural-functional anthropology. The word does not occur in the index to any of Evans-Pritchard's three books about the Nuer, in either of Meyer Fortes' books about the Tallensi, in Gluckman's book about the judicial process among the Barotse, nor even in the index to Schapera's *Government and Politics in Tribal Societies*. Lucy Mair, who has never been slow to pick the needed hole, does not index the word in her *Primitive Government*. Whatever the behaviour to be summarized in that term, it evidently did not seem worthy of distinct categorical recognition. Obviously factional behaviour was written off as unstructured behaviour, unpredictable and irregular, and therefore beyond the scope of structural analysis. In carving out the statuesque form of structure, factions (like individuals and choice) fell among the material discarded in order to reveal a form.

Looking back, it is not surprising that the first symposium convened explicitly to discuss the theoretical significance of factions was directed by Raymond Firth (1957). The participants in that conference were all young men recently returned from the field, and it was clearly not an occasion for hanging up the red flag. In effect, the meeting pointed out that there are regularities in factional behaviour and that these regularities might have adaptive functions. If this was a revolution against the concepts of "structure" and "corporate group," it was no more than a small part of Firth's lifelong contest on behalf of "individual" and "choice" and, like the rest of that contest, conducted without excesses.

The same kind of patient exploration and classification was carried on in two other conferences. One product is the article published by Ralph Nicholas eight years later (1965). The other is a collection of articles which appeared as part IV in *Local Level Politics* (Swartz, 1968). Only recently (Boissevain, 1974) has the red flag of the "manipulating individual" been run up: "Unquestionably those who have helped shape this theory [structural functionalism] and carried out their initial research under its influence, hold, or held until recently, the senior university chairs in their profession" (p. 20). "... entrenched power hierarchies in the scientific community thus inhibits the development of scientific theory" (p. 23). In other words, horses with names such as "factionalism" or "the manipulative individual" did not get to win a race because the race track and the stables were, until recently, owned by the structural functionalists.

Whether or not this is true, or the extent to which it is true, I do not know. Maybe the young horses cannot run that fast anyway, or do not have the stamina. But the scene itself is wholly that of incipient factionalism: little gangs of conspirators forced to work behind the scenes and beyond the rules because they fear the disapproval of their rulers, and going beyond the mistaken idea to attack the malevolent person who supports it.

3 Certainly many have seen factions in the context of other "informal" or "unstructured" political groups. Firth, Siegel and Beals, Nicholas, Boissevain and Bujra have all insisted that factions are to be analysed from a dynamic point of view, and this can hardly be done without at least one other form of political group out of which or into which a faction may develop. I have drawn upon these authors' writings, but my intention is not the same as theirs. Firstly, I have made no attempt in this essay to identify the environmental or contextual variables which might account for the appearance of one or another of the unstructured groups. Secondly, I have tried to make explicit those features which can be used to discriminate between the various unstructured groups and to distinguish between that domain and the domain of open politics.

4 One feels uneasy in reading that Spiro's factional politicians in his Burmese village (Swartz, 1968:418) were all talk and no action (although he adds, appropriately, that words are themselves a form of action). In the same way, when later in this essay I use "recognition of crisis and breakdown" as a criterion for distinguishing between factionalism and other 'shady' modes of political action, I am uncomfortably aware not only of Bujra's (1973) discussion of "institutionalized" factions, but also of my own descriptions (in Swartz, 1968) of the game-like way in which 'factions' in Bisipara (referred to by the people themselves in their use of the English word "party") were conducted. Something which is institutionalized or game-like can hardly indicate an incipient breakdown.

But to think in this fashion is to fall into the trap of believing that a definition must somehow average out or include every way in which the word has been used up to now. Yet definitions are for use in solving problems (ultimately my problem is the dynamic between 'open' and 'shady' politics), and if I violate the way in which the term has been used in the past, that does not matter. The short way out is to say that the Burmese 'factions' or "parties" in Bisipara's *doladoli* are not factions, but some other kind of contest group. One is then free to go on to a more constructive level by asking, for example, what, in the context of the Burmese village or Bisipara, is it that eliminates the "liking for action" component which I have built into my definition of factionalism.

5 See note 4.

REFERENCES

BAILEY, F. G.
1968 "Parapolitical Systems." In M. Swartz (ed.), *Local Level Politics*. Chicago, Aldine.
BAILEY, F. G.
1972 "Tertius Gaudens aut Tertius Numen." Burg Wartenstein Symposium, No. 55.
BELOFF, MAX (ed.)
1948 *The Federalist*. Oxford, Basil Blackwell.
BOISSEVAIN, J.
1974 *Friends of Friends: Networks, Manipulators and Coalitions*. Oxford, Basil Blackwell.
BOISSEVAIN, J. and J. C. MITCHELL (eds.)
1973 *Network Analysis: Studies in Human Interaction*. The Hague, Mouton.
BUJRA, JANET
1973 "The Dynamics of Political Action: A New Look at Factionalism." *American Anthropologist*, 75(1):132–52.

FIRTH, R.
1957 "Factions in Indian and Overseas Indian Societies." *British Journal of Sociology*, 8:291–95.
NICHOLAS, RALPH W.
1965 "Factions: A Comparative Analysis." In M. Banton (ed.), *Political Systems and the Distribution of Power*. Association of Social Anthropologists, Monograph No. 2. London, Tavistock.
RIORDAN, WILLIAM L.
1963 *Plunkitt of Tammany Hall*. New York, Dutton.
SIEGEL, BERNARD J. and ALAN R. BEALS
1960 "Conflict and Factional Dispute." *Journal of the Royal Anthropological Institute*, 90:107–17.
SWARTZ, M. J. (ed.)
1968 *Local Level Politics*. Chicago, Aldine.
THUCYDIDES
1954 *The Peloponnesian War*. (Trans. Rex Warner). Harmondsworth, Penguin Books.
WOLF, ERIC
1966 "Kinship, Friendship and Patron-Client Relationship in Complex Societies." In M. Banton (ed.), *The Social Anthropology of Complex Societies*. London, Tavistock.

Networks and Factions: Two Ndendeuli Communities

3

P. H. Gulliver

Introduction

There are four general purposes in this essay. First, there is ethnographic analysis of the Ndendeuli people of southern Tanzania. I present a summary reiteration and re-analysis of some materials in my book, *Neighbours and Networks* (1971), together with additional supporting data. The intent is to examine these materials specifically in the context of cooperation and conflict over the access to, or allocation of, scarce resources and the concomitant association of people in alliances as a result. Second, the focus is on factional development in two separate communities where the courses of events were quite different. An attempt to explain these different developments may contribute to understanding some of the variables in factional processes. Third, this study of factionalism is made within the specific framework of network analysis. It is hypothesized that this is an essential framework, though here I seek no more than to demonstrate its validity and usefulness in the particular context. I do not use 'network' as a kind of generalized, fuzzy metaphor but as a theoretical concept concerned with the particular kinds of interdependence and feedback in the relationships between people. Of special concern is the use of subsidiary concepts of action-set and cluster in their reference to factionalism. Fourth, this particular ethnographic context is one of the 'simplest' milieux in which factionalism has been reported. Among the Ndendeuli there were no corporate groups, no social stratification, virtually no economic differentiation in what was a near-subsistence economy. There were no institutionalized and distinct roles and relationships of an economic, political, religious, friendship, or other kind. Relationships, especially those which involved rights and obligations, were framed within the powerful idiom of kinship. Any important, on-going relationship was marked and morally endorsed by kinship reference: acknowledged kinship connection implied a commitment to active, reciprocal support and assistance. Another feature of this 'simple' milieu comes from the fact that the two communities which are compared comprised 32 and 42 households respectively. That is, factionalism occurred among 32 and 42 men, the household heads. These small numbers in the context of the 'simple' kinship network bring out some of the variables in factional analysis in starker form than is the case in larger, internally more differentiated, and more complex social situations.

Kinship Network
In the Ndendeuli case the network comprised a ramifying and convoluted chain of primarily dyadic linkages expressed in the idiom of non-lineal, multi-lateral kinship, cognatic and affinal. These kinship linkages were, effectively, though not solely, representations of exchange relationships. A request for support and assistance of some kind from another person, and acceded to by that person, presupposed in both practical and moral terms, a commitment to reciprocate in kind at a later time. This was a mutually recognized expectation. But a straight, once-and-for-all reciprocation seemed to Ndendeuli to be inadequate, indicating at best a tentative relationship, an absence of commitment. True reciprocity and a true relationship for them entailed a series of transactions over time in which there was a flow of assistance both ways and a reasonably reliable expectation of its continuation.[1] In essence such a relationship – and primarily that – was confirmed by the designation and acknowledgement of kinship. The reverse was also true, but with reservations. Acknowledged kinship meant a more or less active exchange relationship and reciprocity; yet almost every man knew of persons genealogically linked to him who were "not really kin" – that is, *not* acknowledged as kin – because there was no practical and moral relationship. On the other hand, almost every man did acknowledge kinship with some others whose genealogical connections were most tenuous, or not even known, but with whom a persisting exchange relationship existed (Gulliver, 1971:216ff.).

For present purposes I emphasize two features of the network of kinship linkages and its patterning. First, because a man had linkages with many kinsmen, he sought – as he had to and perceived he had to – as much as possible to make his exchange commitments congruent with each other in order to avoid troublesome or intolerable conflicts of interest and purpose, and to ensure reliability of expectations. Empirically this was often problematic. To take a simplistic example: X could scarcely expect Y to give him support in his competition with Z when Y was strongly committed to or dependent on Z. Were X seeking support from Y in a situation where Z was not involved, then it might be possible and advantageous for Y to accede. Yet it might not; for Y could consider the implied commitment to X as likely to jeopardize his relationship with Z in the future; or Z might actively attempt to interfere and to hinder such support of his erstwhile and potential rival. X could seek to offer more to Y than the latter could expect from Z, but this might not be possible. This kind of consideration, and the action-choices coming out of it, were of course multiplied geometrically as the number of involved persons increased.

These dyadic relationships were not, then, free-floating. They were interconnected and therefore interdependent. This was expressed by the Ndendeuli in the kinship idiom, for it was evident that an individual's links with two kinsmen were affected by their several kinship links with others and, perhaps, by their link with each other. Among other things, this meant that an individual could not freely manipulate relationships for his own purposes. He had to take account both of his own range of commitments and those of his kinsmen. These ranges overlapped in varying degrees but they did not usually coincide. Therefore the network, in one sense, represented a range of possibilities and of constraints for choice and action. This remained true even though the people concerned neither carried a complete picture of the network in their heads nor fully appreciated all of the possibilities and constraints it entailed. The kinship idiom provided a useful, if only approximate guide. In practice, Ndendeuli quite often 'experimented' to see what might or might not work under the circumstances.

Second, the network of kinship linkages as it existed at any one time was the product – in large part the epiphenomenon – of action-choices to make claims, to accede to claims, and to engage in coalitions beyond the dyadic level through a past period by the people involved – and by some persons who were no longer directly involved. The network was the result, intended and unintended, of past interaction in both cooperation and competition, and subject to the possibilities and constraints already referred to. Thus, how the network of linkages had come to be as it *was*, and how it could be used and manipulated *now* involved the same kind of interactional processes.

To examine these characteristics further and to use them in the analysis of competition, cooperation, and factionalism, it is necessary first to give a preliminary account of the Ndendeuli context.

Local Community and Bounded Network

The Ndendeuli, some 20,000 people in 1957, live in the Songea region of southern Tanzania, about 100 miles east of Lake Nyasa. They were shifting cultivators in the prevailing conditions of poor soils and slash-and-burn, hoe agriculture. Their principal crop was maize, supplemented by some cassava, beans, and sweet potatoes, which provided a living not much above subsistence level. Cash crop cultivation of tobacco, sales of food crops, and young men's labour migration to far distant plantations injected some cash (about one hundred shillings a year per household in 1953) into the local economy, sufficient barely to meet minimal needs for cotton cloth, taxes, and tools (Gulliver, 1955:18ff.).

In the second half of the nineteenth century, the Ndendeuli had been a subject people of a Ngoni military-predatory chiefdom in that region. Towards the end of the century they had begun, in the course of the shifting cultivation regime, gradually to drift away from Ngoni centres (Gulliver, 1973:94 and *passim*). During half a century of colonial administration this effective separation was continued and confirmed so that the Ndendeuli were largely free of the government-recognized Ngoni sub-chief, the nominal ruler of their area. Official headmen, subordinates of that sub-chief, in practice did little beyond assisting in tax collection. Each headman was responsible for a set of people, and not a prescribed area and its population. These people were dispersed as a result of shifting cultivation and free residential movement among several or many local communities where they became the immediate neighbours of people of other headmen. There was no resident headman in most communities. In brief, the Ndendeuli were lightly administered and had no tradition of chiefship nor institutionalized roles of authority. In a remote part of a remote province of a poor colonial territory, impingement of the outside world had been rather slight and tardy.

The Ndendeuli lived in discrete local communities of thirty to fifty households (man, wife, unmarried children, dependents) scattered in small hamlets (together with their fields, past and present) over two to four square miles. Each community was separated from others by stretches of unoccupied woodland. Because of limited cultivable land and soil fertility, communities persisted for about fifteen to twenty-five years, until locally available land became exhausted and before natural regeneration of soils was sufficient to allow recultivation of old fields. Residential movement between communities or the establishment of a new community in unoccupied woodland was virtually uncontrolled and quite common, although membership of a community tended to be fairly stable at least in the short term.

Individual rights to land were gained by clearing a piece of woodland; but in practice rights were gained only for the two to four years during which it was worthwhile to cultivate a cleared area before yield fell below acceptable limits. In general, land was freely available with an overall density of about five persons per square mile. Locally, where a community had been established for a long time, accessible land became more distant as available woodland was used up.

A local community was begun by a group of about a dozen pioneers and their households by clearing house sites and fields in unoccupied woodland. The pioneers focused on the leader of the enterprise. They were all related to him, cognatically or affinally; that is, they were recruited by the leader on the basis of kinship. Thus, although not all kin to each other, they were all indirectly linked via the leader and perhaps via others also. The leader was the man of initiative in the pioneering phase, but he gained no authority nor preferential rights over his collaborators. Once a community was established, after two or three years, he might emerge as a 'big man,' one of the *de facto* leaders, although this was not invariable.

Newcomers joined the group, seeking new land to cultivate and/or wishing to leave their former communities. A newcomer was always sponsored by an existing resident who was his kinsman: the newcomer's credentials were thus assured whilst he himself could expect invaluable assistance in house-building and field-clearing in the arduous first year of residence and thereafter. In this way all newcomers were linked by kinship directly with one or two existing residents and therefore indirectly with all others. As newcomers increased in number, so did the range and complexity of direct and indirect kinship linkages. This complexity was augmented by intra-community marriage and by the development of new reciprocal relations between neighbours which became confirmed by the mutual acknowledgement of kinship. However large the community and however long its existence, all its members fitted into a single, continuous and convoluted network of kinship linkages. This network could, in fact, be represented by a single extended genealogy, although members of a community were unaware of this and made no claim to kinship with all or even most of their current neighbours. An example of such a kinship network is given in Figure 1.

A number of features are to be noted. First, each man had many kinsmen scattered among a number of communities. The kinship network of a single community was, therefore, a partial network whose boundaries were defined in terms of residence and not of kinship *per se*. Second, acknowledged kinship links followed no particular pattern, emically or etically, and had no lineal structuring and little distinction in concrete practice between cognates and afines. Third, within this bounded network, each man had his egocentric range of kin-neighbours: that is, those with whom there was mutual acknowledgement of kinship and exchange of regular support. This range was different from that of most or all other men, including his closest kin. It overlapped in varying degrees with the ranges of a man's neighbours, both kin and non-kin. Lastly, although specific kinship terminology existed, it was common for the Ndendeuli to use the simplest set of terms. Thus all kin-neighbours were referred to, described, and addressed as "father" (*tati*), "brother" (*nkuru*), or "son" (*mwana*), with the additional use of "grandfather" and "grandson" when relevant. For example, MBS, FBS and WF were "father": more importantly, attributed to them were the characteristics and expectations of "own father." All four were normally "big father," whilst other kin-neighbours of senior generation were normally "small father," although that usage was ever subject to situational and strategic requirements (Gulliver, 1971:292ff.). These usages were congruent with actual practice – expectations and fulfilment. Therefore a closer approximation to the Ndendeuli model of network linkages is exemplified in Figure 2.

Action-sets and Clusters

Within his community a man wanted support from his kin-neighbours for a variety of needs. Although he gave and sought support in purely dyadic situations, most commonly and more importantly it was given in collective

This is a model constructed from genealogical data collected piecemeal from the 32 men concerned. It is not necessarily true objectively but is based on the contemporary memory of those men. For example, the mothers of B3 and B10 may not have been sisters, in the sense of being daughters of one mother (and/or one father): they might in fact have been cousins or even affines. Similarly, there was reason to suspect that C11 and C12 were not first cousins (that their parents were not sister and brother of the same mother). Genealogical memory had most probably been affected by recent and contemporary relationships between the men concerned.

In any case, Ligomba men had no such model as this in their minds.

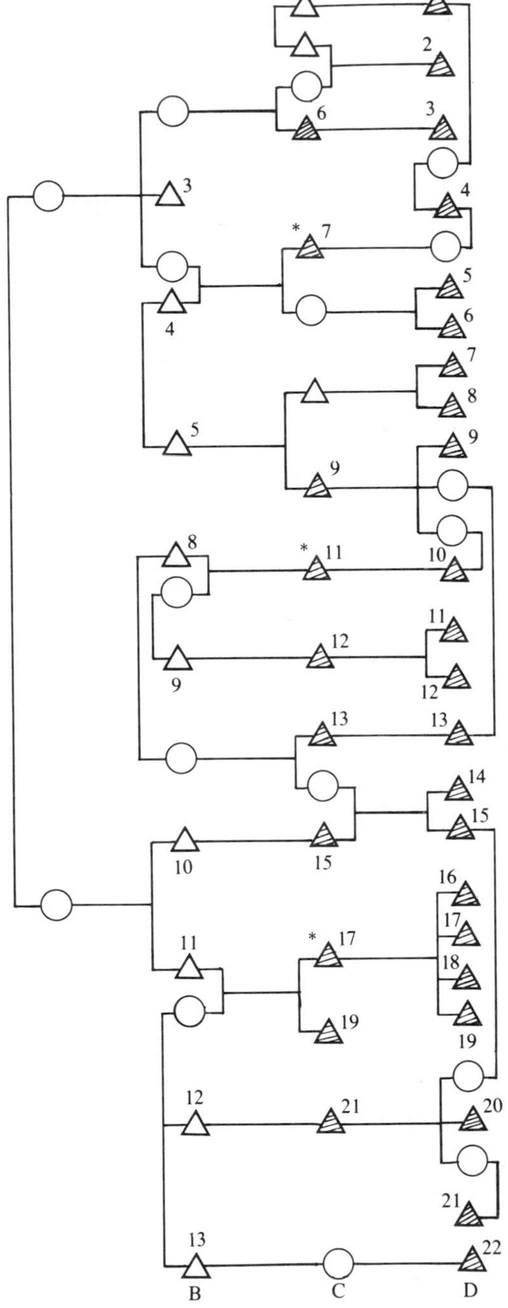

▲ resident in Ligomba
* notable

Figure 1 *The Ligomba Kinship Network in Genealogical Form*

Figure 2 *The Ligomba Kinship Network in Terms of Emic Kinship Categories*

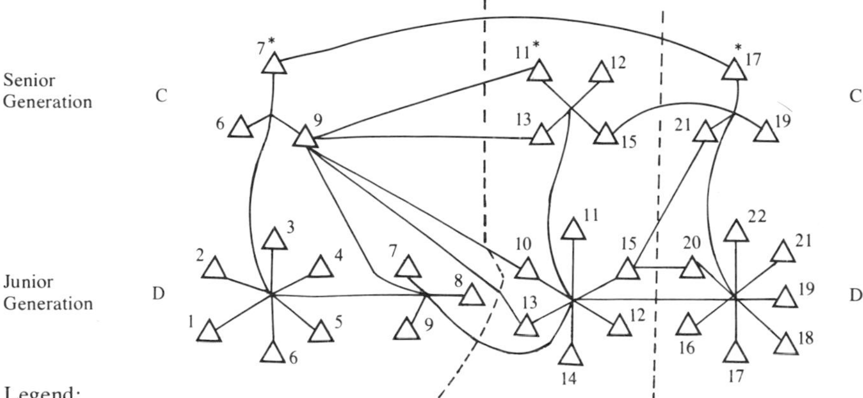

Legend:
Lines from one generation to the other represent "father-son" links
Lines within a generation represent "brother" links
Dashed lines indicate the approximate boundaries of clusters
* indicates a notable

N.B. This is not wholly an emic model, partly because none of these men had a concept of the total bounded network in his mind. Not all the emic relationships are included in this diagram: e.g. D7, D8, and D9 usually referred to C6 or C7 as "small father" and did not always perceive that relationship as mediated through either C9 or the set of "small brothers", C1–6. Similarly, C9 sometimes referred to C12 as "small brother" but at other times recognized him only as the kinsman of a kinsman ("big brother" of a "big brother"). To give a more complete emic model, it would be necessary to provide a series of egocentric models superimposed on each other.

action in which several kin-neighbours joined together. Such collective action pursued or defended a man's interests in a number of ways: work-parties for agricultural tasks (clearing woodland, hoeing and planting, weeding, fencing) and for house-building and repairs, teams for ritual performances in life crises and in dealing with sickness and misfortune; teams to negotiate disputes with other neighbours; parties to engage in beer drinks, and feasts for honouring visitors or for purely convivial reasons. Each year the agricultural requirements of a household called for three or four work-parties, and at least one or two occasions for other collective action would arise. For these purposes a household head recruited an action-set from among his neighbours.[2] He sought his kin-neighbours and, as far as he could and wished, the kin-neighbours of those kin; for example, cousin's cousin, affine of MB, or in Ndendeuli terms, a "brother's brother," a "father's brother." The extent of recruitment depended, broadly speaking, on a number of situational factors: (i) the importance of the interests concerned; (ii) the simultaneous recruitment of an action-set by another neighbour: a man might be in direct conflict with that other neighbour, as in a dispute, or both might be engaged in the same activity (such as hoeing their fields) and perhaps, therefore, in competition for some of the same neighbours, whether or not the principals themselves were fairly closely linked; (iii) the strength of the claims a man could exert on his kin-neighbours and, through them, on their kin-neighbours; (iv) the assessed advantages to those neighbours such as obligating the recruiter for reciprocal support, allying with some or all other members of the action-set, expressing hostility to members of a competing set, being able to demonstrate influence, to gain prestige, and to exercise leadership.[3]

Ndendeuli were convinced that the various forms of collective action were essential to their social lives and livelihood. In developing and maintaining their kinship links, they were consciously seeking to ensure adequate supporters who could be recruited for these requirements and in so doing, ensure security. *It was these supporters who were the primary scarce resources in this society.*

The only people available for all these purposes were the members of neighbouring households whose assistance was obtained on a reciprocal basis. This often involved competition as claims were organized through acknowledged kinship links. Within a local community, considerable and conscientious efforts were made to arrange the recruitment of action-sets so as to prevent or at least minimize competition for the same people. Again, the guiding principle was kinship. Two household heads, whether kin-neighbours or not, should not attempt simultaneously to recruit an action-set if they can legitimately make claim against some of the same people. For instance, A should not seek to recruit his cousin, B, and perhaps B's affine, C, at the same time as D could legitimately seek to recruit his ZS, C, and perhaps C's affine, B. Either A or D should assemble his action-set at a different time. This was the ideal, and it worked with some efficiency.

But there were recurrent organizational problems, partly of a logistic kind, partly because of individuals' unwillingness to accommodate their needs to those of others. The interconnectedness of kin links within the network made the recurrent task highly difficult and never wholly successful. There were obdurate men who, through selfishness, ignorance, fear, or the desire for self-assertion, were unwilling to give way – particularly during the hectic few weeks of the early wet season when the security of harvest depended on getting the soil turned and the seed planted. Not everyone's fields could be dealt with in the first week; someone had to be last. Sometimes the time of ritual performance could not be easily changed nor, in matters of illness and danger, were men altogether disposed to do so. When disputes arose, two action-sets were automatically required, one by each disputant; and then it often happened that disputants, already in conflict, competed for some of the same neighbours. Finally, there were the 'big men,' the *de facto* leaders, who actively sought to share or take over the leadership of the action-set. In their competition with each other, these sometimes encouraged intransigence.

Much of this competition for people could perhaps have been avoided had a local community specifically divided itself into a number of discrete units such that each contained enough people to accomplish the tasks required and each was small enough to make logistical problems unimportant. Such a solution was difficult for the Ndendeuli if only because there were no logical, cultural, or organizational points where the network of kinship linkages could be interrupted by segmental boundaries. Wherever a boundary might have been put, there were kinship linkages on which individuals depended, linkages which each man saw no good reason to relinquish and thus to threaten his own personal (ego-oriented) security. Nevertheless, something approaching this kind of a solution did occur, as sets of neighbours came to develop persisting coalitions, within each of which there was a relatively high degree of cooperation and interdependence based on practice rather than kinship definition.

These coalitions were clusters within the total bounded network. In the formal terms of network analysis, a cluster refers to a set of actual linkages which exhibits a relatively high density and regularity of interaction and which has "a relatively low ratio of external relations as compared to internal relations" (Boissevain, 1974:43).

Clusters cut across the kinship network in a somewhat arbitrary fashion, not operating entirely consistently with kinship linkages. Many men maintained active links with kin-neighbours outside the cluster, and not all men within it were close kin; some were on the limits of kinship recognition where genealogical knowledge was slight or even absent. Yet clusters were perceived emically as sets of kinsmen. They emerged empirically as a result of neighbours seeking to concentrate and make congruent their reciprocal commitments in order to obtain security in their claims for support in on-going social life. They emerged out of men's experiences in the recruitment of successive action-sets over a period.

Each cluster had a single *mundu mukurungwa* (literally "big man") or notable.[4] The cluster focused on him in the perceptions both of members and non-members. He became its reference point within the ambiguities of the network. In a most important sense, he was so recognized and accepted because he was useful in dealing with recurrent problems of action-set recruitment and in providing leadership. He offered his time, efforts, skills, and experience beyond the normal level of support given by other neighbours. One might say that a notable was precipitated as the relatively high density cluster began to emerge, in order to serve the interests of the men involved. This would be but a half-truth, however, for a notable was not simply a creature of his fellows nor the embodiment of functional requirements. He actively sought leadership, influence, and prestige and in so doing was, in part, the creator of the cluster, giving his usefulness in return for those values.

Examination of action-set composition over a period shows the repeated appearance of the same men in certain sets: those sets recruited by one of their number.[5] However, a cluster was by no means unambiguously clear. It was sometimes referred to as "the people" or "the kinsmen" or "the neighbours" of its notable, but such terms also applied to action-sets and even the whole community. More importantly, few action-sets comprised only members of a single cluster. Any member could and commonly did recruit other neighbours to his action-sets as he sought to obtain whom he could in particular circumstances. But although action-sets seldom comprised only men of one cluster, seldom were such men absent from each other's sets.

Figure 3 gives empirical data on action-set recruitment by members of the cluster focusing on the notable, C11, in Ligomba local community. In one ten-month period all but one member participated in at least two thirds of all sets. Another thirteen neighbours, not members of that cluster, were on one or more occasions members of these sets, but none of these were regular participants. On the other hand, it is significant that, as far as information goes, only on two occasions were some other neighbours not involved at all. Moreover, twenty-three of the thirty-two household heads in Ligomba did participate at least once, whilst members of the cluster were severally recruited to the action-sets of other neighbours at the same time. This cluster of highly interdependent men did not usually engage in social action as an exclusive unit.

To sum up the argument so far, many activities in a local community were undertaken collectively as each individual recruited his kin-neighbours, and perhaps the kin of kin, into an action-set. Because of the complexity of the kinship network, men had discrepant loyalties which produced recurrent problems and conflicts of recruitment. In seeking to gain reliability of support in action-sets and some congruence of commitments, men came to concentrate their primary recruitment within a cluster of neighbours among whom there could be a high degree of coordination and interdependence. Such clusters were, in effect, a systematization of action-set recruitment, although they were not the exclusive pool from which sets were composed. Each cluster focused on a notable as its leader and coordinator.

These clusters were not, as such, necessarily factions in political conflict and competition. They did, however, furnish the basis of factionalism as co-members supported each other in conflict situations and as notables sought their own individual prestige and influence. Factionalism enhanced

Figure 3 *Participants in Action-Sets Recruited by Members of a Cluster in Ligomba*

Members of the Cluster		Non-members of the Cluster	
Household head	No. of sets participated in	Household head	No. of sets participated in
C11	33 (notable)	C7	1 (notable)
C12	30	C9	11
C13	32	C17	14 (notable)
C15	31	C19	12
D10	29	D7	4
D11	31	D9	15
D12	25	D16	14
D13	16	D17	9
D14	27	D19	12
D15	24	D20	9
		D21	2
		D23	2
All but D13 participated in at least two thirds of all action-sets		None participated in half of all action-sets	

Recorded action-sets recruited by the ten members of the cluster, April 1962 to January 1953.

5 in dispute cases
11 in agriculture (dry season clearing, wet season hoeing)
7 in house-building or repair
5 for ritual performance (initiation, birth, sickness)
8 for parties (honour guests, conviviality)

Total 36

Notes: a. References to household heads are those used in Figures 1 & 2
b. Some other action-sets were convened for agricultural work and possibly for other purposes during the period.
c. In many instances other members of a household (wife, children over 8 or 9 years old, dependant) also participated in these action-sets.

unity and coordination within a cluster, further strengthening cooperation in action-set recruitment and operation. This, in turn, tended to encourage factionalism.

Ligomba Local Community: Cluster and Factionalism

The history of Ligomba shows how, over the years, each of the three notables (C7, C11, C17 in Figure 3) was assiduous in building up and sustaining his own cluster. Each had done this, sometimes in competition with other aspirants to the role, by sponsoring newcomers who would be directly linked with, obligated to, and particularly associated with him, by encouraging and helping associates to sponsor similar individuals, and by energetically assisting associates on any relevant occasion. A notable became confidant, adviser, and strategist.

Briefly, clusters and their notables in Ligomba developed as follows.[6] The pioneer-leader, B11, was initially recognized as the notable of the new community. He died some six years after its foundation, and both his son, C17, and his FZS competed for the succession. C17 gained the approval and support of their mutual kin-neighbours and the other man moved away from the community. Meanwhile B4 had been sponsoring newcomers and was building up a set of neighbours increasingly distinct from those more closely associated with B11 and, later with C17. Two clusters were emerging in the still young community. On B4's death, his son, C7, and his WB, B3, competed for his role. In two successive intra-cluster disputes, C7 gained the principal adherence of their co-neighbours and recognition as leader and notable. B3 moved away. Further newcomers were sponsored by C7 and his kin-neighbours. At this point, some nine years after its foundation, the kinship network within Ligomba had become differentiated into two clusters.

These clusters did not operate as factions, at least not if a critical criterion is the existence, even fostering, of conflict between the two sets of people. A few still-acknowledged kinship ties linked some men of different clusters, including those between the two notables themselves. That is, some men of each cluster continued to participate in some of the action-sets of members of the other cluster. These cross-linkages were not numerous enough to cause serious problems of competitive recruitment to action-sets; to the contrary, they provided useful bridges for cooperative friendliness between clusters. The community at this time remained small enough – probably seventeen or eighteen households – to resolve fairly easily most logistical problems of action-set recruitment. It is significant that the two notables retained the kinship link (second cousins) between them.[7] Both apparently went to considerable effort to play down inter-cluster conflict when it occurred and to prevent confrontations. Once or twice each notable was able acceptably to act as mediator in intra-cluster disputes relating to the other. Neither notable attempted to subvert supporters of the other; rather, each sponsored newcomers and occupied himself in consolidating his own cluster and his leadership within it.

It is impossible to say if this tolerant, collaborative condition could have persisted as the size of the community continued to grow, bringing increasing difficulties of organization. In any case a new development began as a direct result of persisting animosity between the notable, C17, and his FBS, C15. This was an intra-cluster matter in which the common kin-neighbours of the two men largely supported their notable. The other notable, C7, acted as mediator in a major dispute between the two cousins, though with rather obvious bias towards C17. This meant, as C15 saw it, that he was left somewhat isolated in terms of expectations of reliable support from his kin-neighbours. His response, quite typical of Ndendeuli in such a situation, was to sponsor a newcomer – his WB, C13 – and so to gain a reliable associate not directly connected with C17's cluster. Soon after, the two men sponsored C11 and C12, and other linked newcomers followed. This new cluster of kin-neighbours found a leader in C11 who began to gain recognition as a notable. Some members of this cluster were, or became, through marriage, kinsmen of members of the two older clusters. Practical distinctions between this cluster and the other two were rather less clear than the established distinctions between the latter. The notables, C7 and C17, perceived attempts by C11 to subvert some of their own supporters – a new phenomenon and a new dimension in Ligomba. For this and other reasons they resented C11's claim to be a notable and his emergence as leader of the new cluster. This resentment grew as C11 continued to intensify the practical cooperation and interdependence among his associates. It was, of course, to his advantage to emphasize distinctions between clusters for his own role depended on doing this successfully.

Factionalism therefore emerged. Sometimes it took the form of more or less clear confrontations between C11's cluster and one or other of the older clusters. On a number of occasions, however, C7 and C17 allied themselves and their supporters against C11 and his supporters: either overtly as when C7, C17, and their supporters participated in a common action-set against the others, or more indirectly as when one of these notables led an action-set whilst the other intervened as a mediator favouring his ally.

In any case, organizational difficulties increased in frequency as the size of the community grew and the complexity of the network increased. But any conflict was now exacerbated by rivalry between notables. Almost any dispute between men of different clusters was aggravated and intensified and taken as a pretext, although significantly, notables C7 and C17 still sought conciliation and cooperation between members of their clusters. In their view, as expressed to their associates and to me, they shared a common competitor and antagonist. They shared also a somewhat idealized past, "when there was no conflict," and when the connections between their clusters were not such as to raise fears and allegations of subversion.

The emergence of a third cluster brought factional conflict. Distinctions between clusters were less clear than hitherto, problems of action-set recruitment were more frequent and more difficult to resolve, and men saw their security of expectations threatened in meeting the needs for collective support. The first two notables perceived a threat to their leadership, influence, and prestige from C11, whilst he believed (by his own statement) that he had to fight for his own influence and prestige. Although the factions comprised the clusters of C7 and C17 as against the cluster of C11, it was not quite that simple. The factions were not precisely delineated, although most men were clearly in one or the other.

These factions focused on leaders; they competed for scarce resources and took the form of coalitions of men to obtain advantage and security in that matter; they were not corporate units. It is less obvious that they were recruited by a leader and only partly true in fact.

This development in Ligomba and the factional situation at the time of field research appear to have been more or less typical of well-established Ndendeuli communities. In newly founded communities, factions were usually not present. As mentioned, factionalism evolved as the size of the community increased and the kinship network was extended.

The appearance of factions did not produce a major cleavage in a community. Certainly they did not align neighbours in every situation. Participation in action-sets and a good deal of friendliness and visiting occurred across factional lines. On some ritual occasions and at some parties a large proportion of all Ligomba men were present. It was in conflict situations that factions came to the surface. Disputes between members of the same faction were usually worked out internally, whereas those between men of different factions were usually dealt with on factional lines. A larger proportion of all disputes were inter-factional, however. In all cases the notables took a leading part. Ligomba men were somewhat apprehensive about the possibility of factions disrupting otherwise valuable kinship relations which cut across these alignments, and of the community's becoming divided into two clear parts or even breaking up altogether as a residential unit. Their seed of mistrust of the notables was that their activities and ambitions might produce such undesirable consequences.

Sometimes, therefore, men were at pains to minimize clusters and factional distinctions. This could occur in a general way on celebratory occasions which attracted large numbers of neighbours. But it could be more deliberate than that when the threat of divisiveness seemed more obvious. For example, in Ligomba a dispute arose between the two cousins, C15 and C17 – the latest in a long series of conflicts between them.[8] A rather minor issue became loaded with emotional and intransigent antagonism between the two men. The action-sets in the public moot were effectively led by notables C11 and C17 respectively. Both disputants refused reconciliation and talked of the end of their kinship link. Yet kinship and the linkages between their sons and (as kin of kin) between the kinsmen of each man were valuable to the several neighbours concerned: in a practical sense as they sometimes exchanged support, but also because they represented cooperation across cluster boundaries. Some of these men feared that a decisive rupture might occur, especially as the notables on either side took a hostile stance against each other. Eventually the dispute was mediated by men from each side who moved out of their action-sets to the open space in between. It was they, rather than the notables, who suggested negotiating concessions and argued their acceptance, leading to a settlement.

A week later a dispute began when a man complained about his son-in-law's persistent dereliction to fulfill affinal obligations. The man's action-set was unusually large, comprising men of both factions who had, virtually uninvited, joined in order to show friendly cooperation with one another, rather than to support a son-in-law who, it was agreed, was errant and irresponsible. This action-set was led by C17, who was not the notable of the man's cluster, and the opposing action-set was led by his ally, C7. Their common opponent, notable C11, deliberately absented himself, whilst these two notables acted more as mediators in the dispute rather than as antagonists. Factional alignment, then, was deliberately ignored and cooperative unity was expressed instead. This was made clear both in the moot and afterwards in the small feast shared by all the participants.

Notables as Faction Leaders

Notables had nothing that could be called authority, in the sense of Weber's "imperative control," nor sanctions of power over their supporters. They could only seek to demonstrate their usefulness to their supporters. They exercised influence in the sense of persuasion: a man could be induced to act in a certain way "because it is felt to be a 'good' thing for *him*" (Parsons, 1963:44). The successful notable took care not to seem to exceed persuasive influence by, for example, demanding accedence to his wishes or strategy. Although he usually took the initiative, as he was more or less expected to, in discussions leading to decision-making, he was but *primus inter pares*. He had to recognize the rights of his associates to speak, to question, and to differ. His approach was typically oblique, tactful, and regardful of a trend of opinion among his followers.

The principal conflict between the notables in Ligomba was in terms of relative success in competitive action against each other, overtly on behalf of their respective supporters. This was most obviously shown when, in a case of dispute, confronting action-sets were each led by a notable. Each sought the negotiated settlement which, by and large, was most favourable to his own supporters: a prime aim that was neglected (as it occasionally was) only at risk to his accepted leadership. A notable had to appear to gain advantage for his followers. This called for a judicious combination of open sympathy and firmness on behalf of the supporters, together with sufficient flexibility that could lead to acceptable compromise without too damaging concessions. But notables endeavoured to accumulate reputation and to score points against each other in the presentation and negotiation of a case. There was credit to be won, too, in the felicity and humour of an argument, in the ability to remain unruffled under attack or when making concessions, in using appropriate aphorisms and Koranic references, and the like. Much the same behaviour occurred in the frequent discussions over work-party arrangements. Notables also sought to display and compete in their knowledge of such matters as proper ritual performance, agricultural and house-building techniques, the kinship networks of nearby communities and so on.

Although the major scarce resources for all Ndendeuli were reliable supporters, for the notables there was the additional scarce resource of prestige. By this I mean deference and respect as well as willingness by others to seek and accept advice and follow a lead.[9] Prestige was acquired by successful leadership, diplomatically exerted, from which followers saw their interests defended and promoted. But it was acquired also in confrontations with other notables, although not necessarily in zero-sum competition. The promotion of factional confrontation was advantageous to a notable, both as a means of gaining or consolidating prestige and as a means to strengthen the identity of a faction and his leadership of it. But it was largely the notable who sought and gained the prestige, rather than his supporters. He had an interest over and above theirs to which, however, he had to appear to conform.

Ligomba men, like other Ndendeuli, were ambivalent in their attitudes to their own notable. They admitted and welcomed his usefulness, and yet disapproved of his desire to gain prestige and to influence and lead other men – particularly when it was thought that this led a notable to put greater importance on that desire than on resolving supporters' problems. Ndendeuli valued egalitarianism among heads of households who were married men with family responsibilities and therefore fully adult. A man should not claim superiority over another. Reciprocal commitments between kinsmen were essentially equal, tempered slightly by some deference to one of senior generation. Thus a notable transgressed a cultural ideal practised by most other men. He sought and achieved something of a different quality. There was admiration for his ability and for the time and energy he gave beyond what an ordinary man gave. He displayed virtues of hospitality and generosity. Yet this generosity itself was troublesome because it was seen as obligating a supporter to give, in recognized return, the acknowledgement of superior influence and prestige that was disapproved of. "It is hard," said one Ligomba man, "to live with a big man. But it is harder to live without him."

It seems quite possible, but without sufficient evidence in the field data, that Ndendeuli were off-loading their discomfort, maybe even guilt, about the obvious contradictions between egalitarian ideals of concord and amity between neighbours and the fact that tensions, competition, and conflict occurred in the local community as a direct result of structural and cultural arrangements. Organization was often inadequate; interests or even basic livelihood were, or were felt to be, under threat. When conflict emerged in open dispute, negotiations in public moots and elsewhere were sometimes bitterly conducted; nor did they always resolve basic issues of contention. Notables, were, I believe, held responsible (not altogether unfairly) for this unhappy state of affairs and the contentiousness which it involved. Factionalism was not an approved mode of social behaviour, although virtually all men engaged in it. But the notables were the factionalists *par excellence* and they were the outstanding persons who benefitted from it.

Factionalism in Namabeya Local Community

There is good reason to think that Ligomba will not segment because of factionalism in the future. Not only were efforts made to counteract tendencies that way, but such developments did not occur in other Ndendeuli local communities which had persisted as long as Ligomba. Political conflict was contained, largely because of inter-factional, cross-cutting links of persisting importance among neighbours.

A remarkable exception to this general condition was demonstrated in one local community a few miles from Ligomba. There, in Namabeya, factionalism led to a decisive cleavage within the community which culminated in fission as the members of one faction moved away to found a new community elsewhere. Ndendeuli informants agreed on the exceptional results in this particular instance, which was one of only two or three such cases that were remembered over the previous twenty-five years. This case is now described as a direct contrast with that of Ligomba.

In about a dozen years this community had grown from thirteen to forty-two households, containing just over two hundred people dispersed in hamlets over some three square miles. By that time, in 1952, there were four clusters of kin-neighbours each focusing on a notable. The kinship network is shown in Figure 4.

Two of those notables – Lihamba, Q8, and Amiri, Q16 – had been among the pioneers. They had begun to compete for prestige and influence in the new community when the original leader fell chronically ill and lost his vigour and initiative. Amiri was more acceptable to a majority of their neighbours; but an energetic sponsoring of newcomers gained Lihamba a growing body of kin-linked supporters. Fairly soon, in a matter of six years, two distinct though interconnected clusters emerged. Factionalism seems not to have begun at this period, although informants said that the two notables often failed to cooperate sufficiently in order to coordinate routine action-set arrangements satisfactorily. One point that informants stressed was the personal antipathy which existed more or less from the beginning between the two men. Whether this was cause or effect is hard to say.

As newcomers joined the community, two more clusters developed by the time Namabeya was ten years old. Each new cluster with its notable (Q4 and R29, respectively) was closely linked with one of the older clusters and its notable. These four clusters provided the essential basis for the arrangement of action-set recruitment. At this time, just prior to my field research, alliances of pairs of clusters had begun to emerge as opposed factions. No particular critical occasion was cited by my informants as marking this new phase. Possibly it was at the time of the first of the following events when the factions were overtly and generally recognized by Namabeya people. Thereafter and for a little over two years, factionalism dominated the social life of the community. A summary account of the more important events in that period shows the development which resulted. (Reference should be made to the Namabeya kinship network diagram in Figure 4.)

(i) *Adultery and witchcraft.* R16 had formerly associated closely with his cousin, R14, and the latter's "brothers" within Lihamba's cluster. In a series of quarrels he found himself increasingly isolated from them and as a result, he began to associate himself more with his WB, R22, and the latter's kin-neighbours in Amiri's cluster. This was encouraged by Amiri and his supporters. On the sudden death of R14's wife, R14 accused R16 of committing adultery with her and thus of being partly responsible for her death. In the subsequent moot, the action-sets of the disputants were led by the respective notables. For the first time R16 showed himself to be a follower of Amiri: his action-set contained men only from Amiri's cluster under that notable's leadership. Earlier such a dispute had been treated as an intra-cluster affair under Lihamba's leadership. The dispute was bitterly contested in the moot, eventually leading to mutual recriminations by the two notables. Imputations of witchcraft were made on each side, effectively announcing the probable severance of relations between R14 and R16 with the disavowal of kinship. Neither notable attempted to repudiate these accusations (as was usual), in effect declaring the impossibility of settling the dispute by negotiated agreement. As Namabeya informants noted, this expressed a state of considerable antagonism, not only between the disputants but also between the two clusters and their notables. The moot ended without settlement.

Soon after this, R16 shifted his house near his wife's brothers. The work-party for the purpose contained most of the men of Amiri's cluster, including the notable himself. At the end-of-work party these men were joined by Amiri's ally, Mohammedi (notable R29) and several men of his cluster who, in this way, showed their friendliness to those involved.

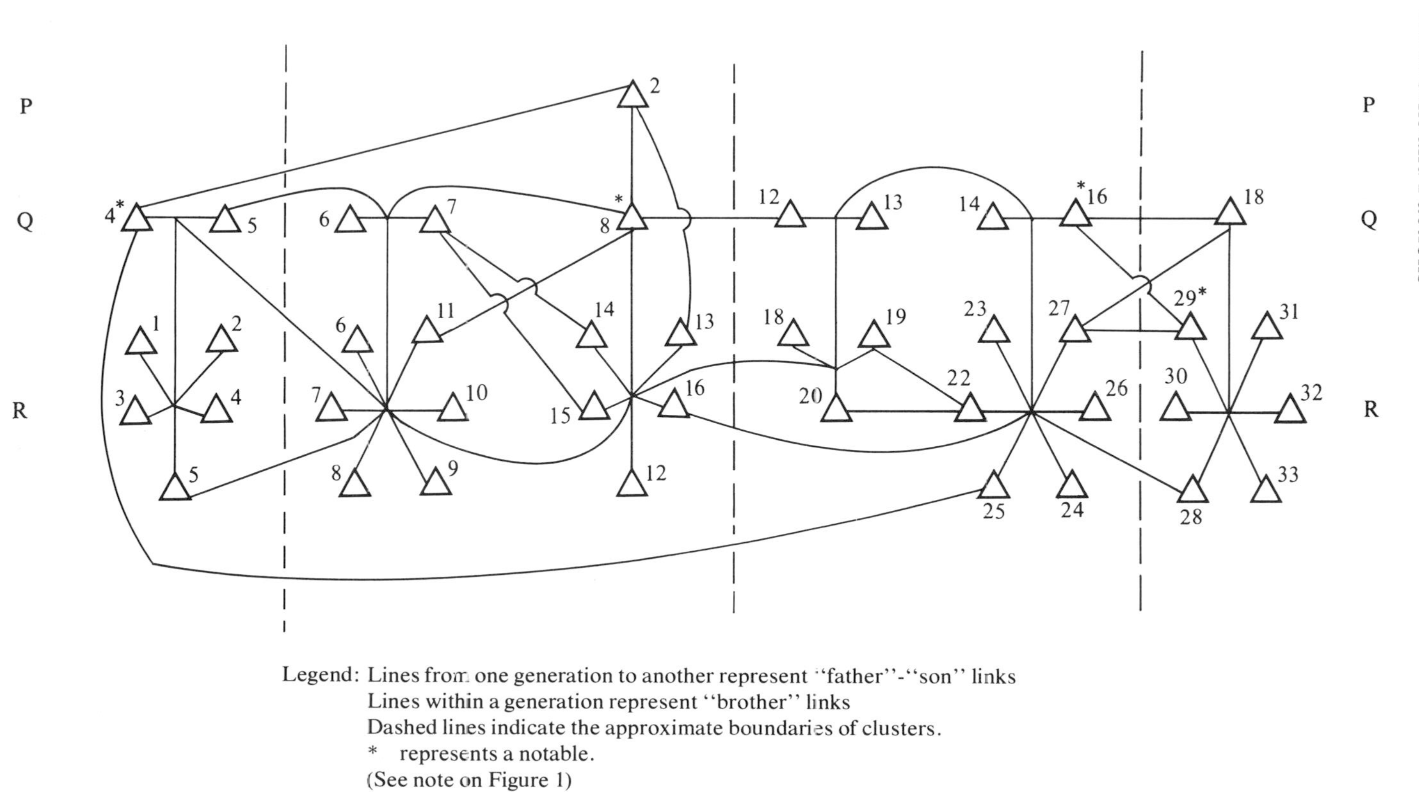

Legend: Lines from one generation to another represent "father"-"son" links
Lines within a generation represent "brother" links
Dashed lines indicate the approximate boundaries of clusters.
* represents a notable.
(See note on Figure 1)

Figure 4 *The Namabeya Kinship Network, 1951*

(ii) *Road construction.* At about this time the possibility of cultivating tobacco as a cash crop was introduced into Namabeya. This was already well established in some Ndendeuli areas, but had not begun here partly because of the problem of transporting the bulky crop some eight miles to the nearest storage and buying centre. Amiri advocated the self-help construction of a lorry track with the technical and financial assistance that was available from the local cooperative society. Lihamba made it known that he was opposed to this innovation, chiefly (he said) because such a motorable track would bring increased governmental intervention into the community. Amiri went ahead, secured the outside assistance and himself took charge of the volunteer labourers in building the track. These workers were almost entirely members of the clusters of Amiri and Mohammedi – a fact which Amiri publicly noted.

(iii) *Mosque repairs.* A few months later there arose the matter of communal repairs to the small hut used as the community's Friday mosque. Previously this work had been done by casual volunteers, but now Amiri and Mohammedi called a general meeting (itself a rare phenomenon) to discuss arrangements. Lihamba (a non-Moslem), the notable Kambi, and most of their supporters (including some who were Moslems) did not attend. Lihamba announced that he was against community action and compulsion in this matter. Subsequently repairs were carried out by a work-party consisting of men from Amiri's and Mohammedi's clusters, although a few Moslem supporters of Lihamba also participated. It appeared that Amiri was seeking to create an issue and to join Islam to his side; in any case the two leading notables acted in open opposition.

(iv) *Tobacco cultivation.* In the following wet season most supporters of Amiri and Mohammedi planted tobacco. They had the advantage of advice in this enterprise, which required novel techniques, from Amiri who had attended a short course the previous dry season at Cooperative Union headquarters. They obtained fair crops and managed to cure the leaf moderately well. Some supporters of Lihamba and Kambi also tried the new cultivation, but without Amiri's assistance and with relatively poor results. When disparaging comparisons of the results and cash yields were made at a later party, fighting broke out between men of either side.

(v) *Arson.* As a direct result, so it was held, R16's new house caught fire the next day. He and his associates, supported by Amiri, accused R14 of arson and repeated the earlier accusation of witchcraft against him. No moot was held, as would normally have been the case, and so the matter went unsettled as had the previous one between them.

(vi) *Local government.* During this period a movement was afoot among the Ndendeuli to persuade the colonial administration to allow them a local government independent of the Ngoni chiefdom.[10] Amiri was enthusiastic about this. He convened a meeting in Namabeya to be addressed by one of the Ndendeuli spokesmen currently touring the country. Most men attended, including Lihamba. He opposed support of this political movement on the grounds that the Ndendeuli were effectively already independent of the Ngoni chief. Formal autonomy and a new local government would, he said, only bring increased interference by officials and probably increased taxation. He accused Amiri of seeking personal advantage, deriding his alleged ambition to become an official headman under the new regime. He openly denounced Amiri for seeking authority over everyone in Namabeya and (the ultimate epithet) for wanting to be "like an Ngoni or a European." The notable, Kambi, fully supported Lihamba, saying that Amiri "wants to be the big man over all of us. But he is not my big man nor am I his kinsman." Amiri replied in comparable invective terms. The dichotomous alignment within the community was marked at this meeting as the two sets of men sat in separate groups, giving vocal support to their leaders.

(vii) *Bridewealth debt.* Kambi (the notable, Q4) claimed bridewealth payment from his son-in-law, R25, newly returned from labour migration. R25 wished to use his accumulated savings to start a small store in Namabeya now that the new motor track was open. This would have been the first store there and he could have expected customers from other communities beyond. Amiri favoured this kind of innovation, and in any case, R25 was a member of his cluster and was, therefore, to be supported in his dispute. Had not factionalism existed, Lihamba might well have acted as mediator in such a case. However, he joined Kambi's action-set, bringing with him most members of his cluster, and assumed leadership of it. Kambi acceded to this. In the moot, therefore, the opposed action-sets, containing almost all Namabeya men, were led by the two principal notables, the faction leaders. This was a direct confrontation, a demonstration of supporters, and a show of strength. Discussion in the moot concentrated on the projected store and its possible effects, rather than on the bridewealth debt, and developed into a general and rancorous debate on the advantages and disadvantages of potential innovations. In the end it was agreed that R25 should make a small installment of bridewealth, and so the moot was not a complete failure in its overt purpose. Yet to the people themselves, the crucial significance lay in the public confrontation of the two factions.

This event occurred about fourteen months after the adultery case. The community now was, and was seen to be, sharply divided into opposed segments. It was the early dry season and schedules were being arranged and work-parties assembled for agricultural and house-repair work. All of these comprised only men from a single faction. The same happened in the following wet season. All of the cross-linking ties between kinsmen and the kin of kin that had previously been activated at such times were now ignored.[11] These formerly acknowledged kinship ties were not specifically repudiated: for the Ndendeuli it was sufficient and significant that they were ignored in practical, reciprocal assistance. Active relations had lapsed. In contrast, the affected men began to rely on other associates in order to make up action-sets who were co-members of the same faction. On either side the notables encouraged these innovations and helped to work out novel recruitment patterns and logistics.

Whether or not these lapsed cross-linkages would have been reactivated, thus repairing the bisected network, is a matter for speculation. In the event, a crisis occurred which precipated final segmental separation. During heavy rains, part of the new motor track was washed away. Considerable realignment and reconstruction was required to make it usable again. This the local cooperative society was not prepared to support. Namabeya tobacco farmers had much difficulty in getting their crop to the buying centre that year. The consensus of opinion among them was that further tobacco cultivation was not a viable enterprise. After much discussion, Amiri persuaded almost all his men to pioneer a new local community some seven miles away on the existing main road where tobacco could be grown and readily marketed. Lihamba and his faction remained in Namabeya, except for two men who shifted to a spot where they too could cultivate tobacco in the future. The old pioneer leader and his three associates also shifted away.

Figure 5 summarizes the dispositions of household heads in 1951, before open factionalism, and in 1954, after residential separation.

During a period of little over two years, though covertly beginning somewhat earlier, factionalism in Namabeya had developed to the point of decisive cleavage within the local community, culminating in fission. Why did this quite rare development occur? Why, in contrast with Ligomba and other Ndendeuli local communities, did all social activities, including action-set recruitment and leadership, become oriented around this factional cleavage? The simple, immediate answer is, of course, that the kinship network was cut; cross-linking kinship ties were severed and cooperation in practical matters became restricted to a single faction-segment. But that is too simple and insufficient an explanation for what happened.

Some negative points can be made in order to clarify discussion. First, this factional segmentation cannot be directly attributed to the size and age of the community. There were numerous other communities at that time as large or larger than Namabeya, some of which had existed for a longer time without segmentation. Second, segmentation and fission were rare. Ndendeuli local communities persisted for about two decades before each gradually dwindled when cultivable woodland became locally scarce. Residents shifted away in small groups of one to four or five households. At the time of field research Ligomba was forseeably approaching that point.

Figure 5 *Namabeya: Dispositions of Men Before and After Fission*

1951: Clusters*	
Kambi (Q4) with Q5, R1–4, R5*	7 households
Lihamba (Q8) with P2*, Q6, Q7, R6–15	14 households
Amiri (Q16) with Q12*, Q13*, Q14, R16*, R18–20*, R22–26, R27*	14 households
Mohammedi (R29) with Q18, R28, R30–33	7 households
1954: Residence	
In Namabeya:	
Lihamba (Q8), Kambi (Q4), Q5–7, P2, R3–15	19 households
In the newly founded community:	
Amiri (Q16), Mohammedi (R29), Q14, Q18, R16, R20, R22–28, R30, R32, R33	16 households
In an already established community, 'X':	
Q12, Q13, R18, R19	4 households
In an already established community, 'Y':	
R1, R2	2 households
In an already established community, 'Z':	
R31	1 household

* Membership of clusters was not as clear and unequivocal as this listing suggests. Starred men were notably uncertain or ambiguous in their alignments.

(Letter-numbers refer to men in Figure 4)

But Namabeya, in its rarity, did not represent any regular stage in a developmental cycle. At that time land was still conveniently available by Ndendeuli standards.

Third, it is tempting but inaccurate to explain the Namabeya problem as resulting from the beginnings of social change. Several of the issues of conflict arose over innovations; people at that time were uncertain of the future and of themselves. Certainly there was no consensus in the perception of changes and their implications. Hitherto Namabeya had been relatively remote, difficult of access, and seldom visited by officials; it was peripheral to political, economic, and religious trends. Yet issues of innovations did not necessarily have to engender specific, aligned conflict. They did not do so in Ligomba nor in other Ndendeuli communities which had already been affected by them.[12] It is reasonable to assume, therefore, that new issues were used, and even partly contrived for factional advantage. It is possible, of course, that factionalism might have been contained had those novel conditions not obtained: at least the conditions exacerbated conflict. Had the new motor track not been destroyed, creating a valid reason for residential movement, there would have been opportunity for bridging links between factional segments by, for example, reforming clusters and coalitions with the arrival of newcomers and departure of some residents in the normal turnover of neighbours.

Structurally the kinship network in Namabeya early began, and thereafter continued, to be segmented. There was not the convolution and interconnection of linkages between clusters that was characteristic of other Ndendeuli local communities. Two factors were crucial in its initial years: the relative weakness, both practical and symbolic, of linkages between Lihamba (with his son-in-law, R11) and the other pioneers, and the early chronic illness of the pioneer leader, Q12. Because of the first factor Lihamba, in quite typical Ndendeuli fashion, was energetic in sponsoring newcomers who became closely associated with him rather than with other neighbours. In any case, given Lihamba's apparent ambition for influence and prestige, this would probably have brought him into competition with any other aspirant notable. As it was, he came into immediate contest with Amiri to take up the focal leadership role left vacant by Q12's illness.

As the size of the community grew quite rapidly, the two clusters, focused on Lihamba and Amiri, became increasingly discrete with few bridging links of acknowledged kinship and of cooperation. The later emergence of the two smaller clusters further localized network densities. It is possible that the expansion of Namabeya had been more rapid than was usual in Ndendeuli communities: my data impressionistically support this. If this were the case, then the consequent rapid extension of the kinship network contributed to persistent, effective segregation within it. There were no bridge-links at all between the two newer clusters. This must have been partly fortuitous: that is, none of the newcomers had acknowledged kinship before coming to Namabeya, which they could have continued to use. Why this was so is not known.

Whatever the reasons, the kinship network continued to be fairly clearly bisected, each segment containing two inter-linked clusters in political alliance. The principal bridges between these segments were the kinship links of the original pioneer leader, Q12, and his close associates. He himself was withdrawn from public life and had little influence, whilst his brother-in-law, Q13, was an ineffective simpleton, and their sons were often absent in labour migration. After event (vi), when Q12 attempted to mediate, he was simply disregarded by the leaders of each segment. He had no political resources to use.

This structural segmentation was fundamental to the peculiar factional development in Namabeya within which other factors operated. Some of the latter had a feedback effect which strengthened segmentation.

In practical terms, all this meant that action-set recruitment was largely restricted (beyond each cluster) to a single segment. Men perceived their security to be within the alliance of clusters. Potential competition there appears to have been resolved by the successful cooperation of the two notables concerned.[13] The explanation seems to be that, in each case, the dominant notable (Lihamba and Amiri) wished to gain and retain the support of the other notable in his segment. This being so, then it was advantageous not only to promote internal cooperation but to emphasize external conflict in inter-segmental rivalry and factionalism.

This is suggested, without unequivocal evidence, as a reasonable explanation of the persisting competitive rivalry between the leading notables. That rivalry had its seeds in the early conditions in Namabeya, but there were also differences of experience, attitude, and aims between the two ambitious men with incompatible personalities. Structural distinction, therefore, permitted and encouraged active hostility.

Lihamba was an elderly man who had had little contact with the outside, non-Ndendeuli world. He was a conservative, a 'traditionalist,' who took (as I understood it) a genuine stand against innovations. He was not even a nominal Moslem, and so belonged to a minority of Ndendeuli at that time. His conservatism was not simply against each innovation itself, but also against the more general implications of outside interference and the perceived threat to existing culture which novelty promised. His leadership was, by Ndendeuli standards, exemplary: he was seldom accused of claiming authority (rather than influence) or unacceptable superiority. Yet his prestige and influence were considerable and seldom were his advice and strategy not followed by his supporters.

Amiri, in contrast, was in his middle forties. He had made several labour migration trips to distant estates, eventually becoming a field foreman. He genuinely wanted the innovations which he advocated, although he was ready to take advantage of Lihamba's opposition to them. For example, Amiri and his supporters could not have been prevented from cultivating tobacco, and as events showed, they were able to build the new road with little help from Lihamba's supporters. Nor could Lihamba prevent Amiri and other Moslems from repairing and using the mosque.

These personal differences and the mutual dislike and mistrust between the two leaders were also important in determining some of the issues over which factionalism developed. It is significant that the two factions were occasionally referred to as "conservatives" (literally, "those who stay") and "progressives" ("those who go on"). I think that neither man really disapproved of these labels, perceiving some usefulness in them as symbols. Each notable was able to obtain the consistent adherence of his supporters in the particular matters that became *causi belli.* Yet this was more the result than the cause of factionalism. Not all the tobacco cultivators were on Amiri's side, nor did they all favour Ndendeuli local government autonomy. Conversely, not all of Amiri's supporters agreed with his expressed views on these issues. There was no real reason why they should, for the basis of recruitment to, and continued participation in a faction were established by quite other criteria: acknowledged kinship and the opportunity and value of continued practical cooperation in action-set operations. It is, therefore, significant that few if any members of either faction spoke out in opposition to his leader. Ideology and issues were not unimportant, of course, even though they could become matters of competitive convenience rather than fundamental difference.

There were also real cases of dispute between members of different factions. These kinds of dispute were not uncommon in a local community, and were handled by negotiations in a public moot. There, despite typical posturing of antagonism and the desire of a disputant to secure his rights, concession and compromise towards an agreed settlement were the practical norms. This was patently not so in Namabeya. Those cases were treated as inter-faction affairs. Two of the principal cases were not resolved in the moots, leaving open antagonism and resentment. In the bridewealth case, although an agreed settlement was reached, the disputants did not resolve the problem of their relationship, and the entire moot was conducted in a hostile manner. The notables scarcely attempted to engage in negotiations to achieve a genuine settlement. Instead they exacerbated the disputes, using them as opportunities to rally supporters, express antagonism, and compete with each other. This was especially so concerning the witchcraft accusations which were understood to have serious implications. A Ndendeuli notable would generally dissociate himself and his supporters from such accusations since they expressed failure not only to reach a settlement but also to engage in normal neighbourly relations. Neither Lihamba nor Amiri attempted to deny his supporter's allegations, and so tacitly endorsed them. This was a declaration of implacable hostility and of irreconcilable differences.

Lihamba reportedly saw the adultery case and its consequences as direct subversion of a supporter. He may have been correct. Certainly R16 had previously been his supporter; afterwards R16 shifted his residence near Amiri's associates and thereafter supported Amiri.

Conclusion

The contrast between factional processes and development in Ligomba and Namabeya, fortuitously presented to me in the field, is worth emphasizing since it focuses attention on differences in variables. It is not unimportant to enquire why in the one case, factionalism was contained and in the other, why it led to segmentation and fission.

Firstly, in Ndendeuli local communities the scarce resource was people – co-neighbours – who gave assistance and support in vital collective action of various kinds. The emergence of effective clusters within a community was the result of men's efforts to promote congruence of commitments and expectations and to obtain some reliability in them. A cluster was not, as such, a faction: it did not necessarily engage in competition and conflict with another cluster. In fact, as in earlier Ligomba and Namabeya, where individual cross-linkages were not too numerous, not too productive of competition over neighbours, they served as useful bridges for cooperation. An increase in numbers of neighbours and in cluster overlapping brought increased competition and conflict in action-set recruitment, with fears and allegations of subversion. More importantly, cluster leaders took advantage of and stimulated conflict in their particular competition for a different resource: prestige and influence.

Secondly, there was a fundamental contradiction in Ndendeuli social organization. On the one hand, men sought to concentrate clusters of interdependent relationships and commitments of reciprocal support. On the other hand, individual men wished to continue their several relationships and commitments with other men not of their own cluster. An individual was not prepared, and could not be constrained, to commit himself altogether to his cluster. As I have previously noted, clusters were inevitably an arbitrary disjunction in the kinship network: they were not founded and directed in purely kinship terms, but at least as much in pragmatic terms of practical cooperation. In other words, Ndendeuli were not consistent in their kinship idiom. Egocentric ties conflicted with cluster coordination.

In Ligomba – and in most other local communities, to the best of my knowledge – this contradiction was at once a source of the growth of factionalism and of its limitation. Men continued to seek support from, and to give it to, men outside their cluster so that claims were not altogether cluster-coordinated. Competition as well as uncertainty resulted. Yet that competition was muted precisely because men were not prepared wholly to commit themselves to a cluster and would not accept all-out factional alignment.

In Namabeya, however, bridging links were few and became fewer and more fragile as the network became increasingly extended without much convolution. Yet factionalism not only continued, but was intensified when, *prima facie*, it seemed that there was a decrease of practical occurrences of competition and conflict in the critical area of action-set recruitment. That factionalism became unconstrained was the direct result of the absence of inter-cluster links. The persistence and growth of factionalism, and its more or less deliberate aggravation, were advantageous in emphasizing intra-factional cooperation and interdependence. And it was advantageous to each faction leader in enhancing his prestige, influence, and leadership among his supporters. Leaders could do this without much check precisely because there were so few active cross-linkages: almost no one's prime interests were being damaged. In a sense, the two faction leaders were in collusion, though probably not deliberately or overtly. In this situation, ideological differences and personal animosity between faction leaders became important, tending to prevent containment and to encourage polarization.

In general there are four main sources of factionalism: (1) conflicts of interests and competition over scarce resources, together with (2) competition for power (or for influence) between leaders, within (3) a fluid or flexible network of social relationships without well-defined groups or other clear alignments which channel conflict, and where perhaps (4) ideological and personal differences exist or are contrived. Factionalism, by these criteria, would be inevitable in an Ndendeuli local community – a regular development as it grew in size.

In the Ligomba and other similar cases, a more or less stable situation of containment was achieved because of the fundamental contradiction between cluster identity and overlapping ties, loyalties, and interests. There was, therefore, some effort to prevent decisive encounters, potentially damaging to almost everyone's interests, whilst there was a good deal of indecisive confrontation. This containment did not necessarily prevent changes in (1) faction membership altogether, or in (2) some short-term advantages. It did, however, in effect give systemic stability.

A second, distinguishable, developmental process occurred in Namabeya. Because of bisection of the network, factions hardened into discrete segments, leading ultimately to the fission of the community. That need not have happened if, for instance, geographical movement had been less easy and residential stability had persisted. Thus, a third factional process could be the hardening of factions into opposed political groups or 'parties' as the environment encouraged or even forced this. A fourth possible process would be that in which little or no stability is achieved and where, neither, is there a hardening of the factions into something else, something new. In that case, factional alignment and leadership would be short-lived: confrontations occur and are won and lost; there is no containment and new factional formations are created. Here the socio-cultural context would contain both interests and scarce resources that are various and variable such that fairly clear, persisting alignments are never obtained.

The present essay provides examples of only the first two of these developmental processes, indicating the kinds of pertinent variables involved. Further research and consideration are required to substantiate and/or modify the range and interconnection of these variables cross-culturally and to discover also the relevant variables operative in the other two processes which are not exemplified among the Ndendeuli.

NOTES

1 Cf. Gouldner (1960:169): "giving and receiving are mutually contingent" and "there can be stable patterns of reciprocity *qua* exchange only insofar as *each* party has both rights and duties." But whereas Gouldner largely concentrates on giving in return for receiving, the Ndendeuli put at least as much emphasis on giving in order to gain or strengthen the right to receive in the future.

2 Only occasionally were non-neighbours so recruited.
3 A fuller discussion of the concept of action-set is given in Gulliver, 1971:18ff.
4 Because the roles and cultural characteristics of these Ndendeuli, leaders differed in critical respects from those of the well known Melanesian big men; I prefer to use the alternative of "notable."
5 The data for such demonstration are available with reference to Ligomba in Gulliver, 1971:138–79 and 197ff.
6 More detailed accounts are given in Gulliver, 1971:87–119.
7 On the other hand, C7 did not continue to acknowledge as kinsman the brother of C17, nor did C17 so recognize his other second cousin, C6.
8 See page 48 *supra*.
9 Cf. Nadel, 1951:171, Scheffler, 1965:182.
10 See page 39 *supra*.
11 Only Q12 (the original pioneer leader), Q13, and their sons refused to align themselves on one or the other side. They suffered as a result, being unable to get the assistance in work-parties of former kin-neighbours in either faction.
12 For instance most Ligomba men had come to accept Islam, many had taken to tobacco cultivation, and regular labour migration had become increasingly uncommon; nor was there any real opposition to local government changes. Factional conflict did not occur on any of these issues although consensus was never complete.
13 Just as inter-cluster relations were kept fairly free of conflict in the earlier period of Ligomba when there were only two clusters.
14 The Bisipara *doladoli* situation seems to be similar (Bailey, 1969:88–91).

REFERENCES

BAILEY, F. G.
1969 *Strategems and Spoils*. Oxford, Basil Blackwell.
BOISSEVAIN, J
1974 *Friends of Friends: Networks, Manipulators and Coalitions*. Oxford, Basil Blackwell.
GOULDNER, A.
1960 "The Norm of Reciprocity: A Preliminary Statement." *American Sociological Review*, 25(2):161–78.
GULLIVER, P. H.
1955 *Labour Migration in a Rural Economy*. Kampala, East African Institute of Social Research.
GULLIVER, P. H.
1971 *Neighbours and Networks*. Berkeley, University of California Press.
GULLIVER, P. H.
1973 "Negotiations as a Mode of Dispute Settlement: Towards a General Model." *Law and Society Review*, 7:94.
NADEL, S. F.
1951 *The Foundations of Social Anthropology*. London, Cohen & West.
PARSONS, T.
1963 "On the Concept of Influence." *Public Opinion Quarterly*, 27:44.
SCHEFFLER, H.
1965 *Choiseul Island Social Structure*. Berkeley, University of California Press.

Village Council and Factionalism: Definitional and Contextual Issues[1]

4

Marilyn Silverman

This paper examines the relationship between factionalism and council decision-making patterns. First I describe the village context to indicate the intimate relationship between village council organization and local factional politics. The second section presents an operational definition of factionalism, followed by a synthesis of the features thus far identified as relevant to council decision-making patterns, which are then discussed specifically in part four. Section five investigates the precise nature of factionalism in the council context and the implications for the definitional issue. Finally, both the decision-making process and factionalism are located within the wider political-economic context of village and state.

I. THE SETTING: VILLAGE COUNCIL AND LOCAL POLITICS

(a) *The Village*

Rajgahr Village District, located in West Berbice County in Guyana, South America is an Indo-Guyanese community within a "plural society." Located approximately sixty miles from the capital city, Georgetown, a journey of about two hours by hire-car, the population totals approximately 3,100 in slightly under 500 households.

The village was founded in 1902 as a land settlement scheme for former indentured labourers. Today, it is regionally renowned because of population size and extensive acreage, and spoken of as a "prosperous rice farming village with a tractor to every house." This popular characterization is incorrect on two counts: first, most people are not rich, and secondly, rice cultivation is not the sole occupation of the village. Rather, the local economic division of labour is complex and belongs to the "dual occupational pattern" typical of the West Indies (Comitas, 1964). In this case almost all households plant some rice (at least two acres for home consumption) but branch into numerous other occupations including estate labour, wage labour for government and village projects, shopkeeping, huckstering, smithing, white collar jobs (teachers, clerks), cattle herding, and businesses transcending village boundaries such as transport and construction. Such vertical occupational groups are additionally cross-cut by 'class.' As a result of differential access to land[2] and differential success in private enterprise, incomes of villagers range from under $900 per annum to over $15,000.

This economic complexity is a product of cumulative growth over the past seven decades, stemming from external inputs as well as from the decisions of family groups made as early as 1919. At that time, the crown made available, for sale or lease, Abary land located seven miles behind village farm lands.[3] Lessees of the first depth, the most accessible sub-area, were also given prior access to subsequent depths. Despite exceptionally harsh physical conditions, some farmers gave their descendants access to almost unlimited acreage and expansionary possibilities. For example, access to Abary land gradually increased a family's capital savings because of high returns in both rice and cattle. This enabled investment in larger land holdings, the education of children for white collar employment, investment in more cattle, and investment in other businesses. On the other hand, some families chose a more traditional economic strategy: combining small-scale village cultivation with estate labour. By 1969, all village lands were in use and wage labour opportunities were limited largely because of underemployment in the society in general. The only possibilities for expansion lay in Abary land, with access limited by tenure regulations, and in economic enterprises requiring a supra-village capital investment in education or business. Rajgahr Village is thus characterized by scarce resources in which the rich have the competitive advantage.

(b) *The Village Council*

The formal political structure of the village, according to the Local Government Ordinances of 1907 and 1945, consists of a village council of twelve members elected every two years to act as a local authority "entrusted with the management of the administrative and financial business of the district and with its government generally" (The Laws of British Guiana, Chapter 150, Section 28 [1]). In other words the council is invested with legal power, the control of physical and human resources, and as a result of these, with a great deal of informal influence which can be, and is, wielded. For example, the council is responsible for local taxation, public works (maintenance of drainage, dams, and trenches), leasing village and crown lands within its jurisdiction, and similar tasks. In monetary terms, the budget for 1970 involved the collection/expenditure of almost $80,000. The council is thus a major employer of casual labour for its public works projects and is also responsible for hiring a permanent administrative staff consisting of an overseer, an assistant overseer, three village rangers, and several watchmen. With both land and appointments at its disposal, the council is an instrument of a great deal of potential patronage.

As a body, the council is formally accountable to both the government hierarchy and the public it represents, and it provides the communication link between the two. For example, if a villager wishes to complain to a high authority, his communication must pass to, in ascending order, the council, the chairman of the council,[4] the District Commissioner, the Local Government Board, and finally to the Chairman of the Local Government Board located within the Ministry of Local Government. In addition to finance and land, the council thus controls the communication nexus with the formal national hierarchy.

However, public accountability has been delimited since 1959 when the Suspensions of Election Bill, passed during a constitutional crisis, eliminated local elections and substituted Board appointments for vacancies caused by death or resignation. Knowledge that the Bill can be rescinded at any time and elections called does mean, however, that councillors are aware of public support, if only for the future.

(c) *Local-Level Politics: Historical Dimensions*

It is an anthropological truism that government and politics are not coterminous, that the formal structures provide, simply stated, the resources and constraints within which 'politiking' occurs. In Rajgahr Village, the legal structure of the council has provided the major parameters for actual political organization since the 1920's at which time political relations became characterized by factionalism.

A local elite group composed of two extended families, each owning a village rice mill, gained control of the marketing of produce and the allocation of credit to farmers in a situation of crop uncertainty. Since each mill was associated with the respective head of each family, the economic competition for *padi* and mill clients became phrased as factional politics in which the village council became both an arena of competition and a resource for politically enhancing each family head's/factional leader's economic position. This organization continued for two decades ending ultimately in a 'fight' because of changes in external circumstances: economic change released the majority of villagers from debt, and a newly introduced electoral system enabled the masses to support second generation elites aspiring to council seats and political power. These events coincided with massive economic expansion and the emergence of the People's Progressive Party (PPP), representing Guyanese nationalism, which siphoned off certain members of the Rajgahr elite for competition in the national arena. Since every family was busy consolidating its expansionary economy, village council politics were aimed at conciliation of disputes with minimum competition for resources. The political sphere was characterized by a 'factional peace.'

In 1953, economic expansion, minimum competition, and political conciliation came to an abrupt end. The village, as a result of the expansion, was now cross-cut by complex and opposing vertical occupational groups, and additionally, by groups of families who had been differentially successful in the scramble for resources. This coincided with the suspension of the constitution by the British in 1953. Local activists who had been engaged in national politics returned to Rajgahr as members of a nationalist party aiming for grass-roots organization. They ran in local council elections and came into direct confrontation with other elite members who saw nationalist politics as 'a Georgetown story.' Factionalism again became the means of organizing political relations and continued until 1970 with only one major alteration.

In the mid-'50s, the nationalist PPP split into two factions, each associated with a different ethnic group: the PPP became the East Indian party; the new People's National Congress (PNC) became the African party. In 1967, with the PNC in control of the national arena, and with its support mainly among the Afro-Guyanese, a Muslim wing was formed with the purpose of subverting East Indian Muslim support from the PPP. The strategy of this encapsulation policy of 'incorporation'[5] has been noted elsewhere (Silverman, forthcoming). It resulted in a faction leader being designated local PNC activist, and therefore middleman, so as to enable the exploitation of the factional game for PNC subversion goals.

(d) *Local-Level Politics: 1969–1970*

Ebrahim Sultan, designated PNC activist, is priest of the Muslim mosque and has been involved in factional politics since the early '60s through PPP affiliation. A member of the village council, he has often been chairman when his supporters had a majority of seats. His major opponent, P. T. Premsingh, entered factional politics and the village council in the late '30s as a supporter of one of the millers. He too has often been chairman, and received a Member of the British Empire award for his work in local government; in addition, he is a priest in the Christian Catholic Church and a Justice of the Peace.

The council supporters of these two factional leaders (see Table 3) also had a lengthy history of involvement in factional politics. As a group, the councillors represent the elite segment of the village. All are modern, upwardly mobile entrepreneurs with a solid economic base in rice, cattle, and business, except for two long-term factional competitiors whose economic activity, although not extensive, is certainly sufficient to make them financially secure.

Like Sultan and Premsingh, many of the councillors had additional formal roles which were important sources for tapping support. For example, Amin was president of the mosque and until 1970, president of one of the two competing race clubs. He was also a PNC activist within the village and, although not as vociferous as Sultan he was a source of national patronage.

The administrative staff was highly partisan, particularly overseer Singh. Involved in factional politics since the '40s, a member of the elite and highly antipathetic to Sultan, he was also president of both the Sanatan Hindu temple and the local chapter of a national Hindu cultural organization, the Maha Sabha.

The council and councillors thus controlled and had access to political resources from the national arena, from local arenas, from the control of the council, and ultimately from their own positions of personal economic strength. All this was directly related to a factional political game of oscillating encounters in a situation of scarce economic resources.

(e) *Conclusion*

Village council and village factionalism have had and continue to have a close relationship. The council provides the context for factional struggle and a resource that enables the manipulation of other support. Additionally, factional competition appears to have been associated with the village elite since its inception, and in fact, may be viewed as a product of competition among the elite for scarce economic resources, which ultimately provide them with the means for consolidating their position and a means for furthering their competitive advantages. Finally, throughout village history, this pattern is not only predominant, but it is also relevant by virtue of the personnel alignments which have continued since the early years of political competition. Factional politics, the council, and elite personnel have a shared continuity.

II. THE NATURE OF FACTIONALISM

It will be argued that factions comprise the structural aspect of a more inclusive competitive process of political strategizing which can be defined as the initiation of 'ego-centered' political action-sets. Phrased another way, the definition should be concerned with the nature of factionalism as opposed to factions, with the former viewed as a process or means of competitive political strategizing. The emphasis is to be placed on action, and the set seen as a derived structure via an arbitrary stoppage of an ongoing process of strategizing. How is the above logically derived?

Historically, factions have assumed theoretical and empirical importance as a result of studies emphasizing their proliferation in the majority of ethnographic areas and their persistence over lengthy periods of time. The major problem has been to "distinguish them from other kinds of political groupings" (Nicholas, 1965:23) and the literature demonstrates the search for the definition.

Three studies appear to have a degree of acceptability. Nicholas has suggested five attributes as a definitional base: factions are political groups, conflict groups, non-corporate groups, which are recruited by a leader, and which are recruited according to diverse principles (1965:27–9). Boissevain defines factions as "an exclusive coalition of persons recruited personally according to structurally diverse principles by or on behalf of a person in conflict with another person or persons within the same social unit over honour and/or control of resources" (1968:551). Also, Mayer has suggested that factions are "quasi-groups" (1966:116), but agreement is limited as to what, in fact, a quasi-group is (Boissevain, 1971; Yadava, 1968; Lantz, 1971), or how a faction specifically fits into this general notion.

In addition to definitions, it is assumed that factions can be placed on a continuum at a point between public opinion and parties (Boissevain, 1964) or that factions can be opposed to the notion of party (Bujra, 1973) by virtue of the presence or absence of certain specified characteristics.

Factions can of course be fitted into any of the above frameworks or definitions. Doing so, however, avoids the major goal of definitional exercises – that of giving a concept precise and analytic meaning to render it useful both theoretically and empirically (Gulliver, 1971). As the definitions stand now, they make assumptions as to the origins of factions, their persistence, their socio-cultural context and their political significance. The present section attempts to circumvent the problem by offering a precise definition which may gain some acceptance.

There appear to be two contexts out of which the varying definitions have emerged: first, the context of network analysis; secondly, the context of political anthropology. An assumption which both have, however, is a distinction between the intra-factional as opposed to the inter-factional sphere. In fact, analysis has taken two directions: investigation of the internal organization of factions (the network approach) as opposed to the analysis of conflict between factions (the political approach) (Yadava, 1968:898). Underlying this distinction is, of course, the more basic one between structure and process and the view that this is relevant to the analysis of factional behaviour.

For the moment, ignoring definitional problems, let us assume that there is a factional political sphere with the implication that there are factions and factionalism. One of the leaders (there must be at least two) recruits a follower. This action is typically regarded as being a step in building a factional structure, team, and so on; that is, it concerns the intra-factional realm. However, this act of recruitment implies that something was gained – a resource, a supporter. There are at least three possible implications. First, if the game is zero-sum, the other faction leader lost in direct proportion. Secondly, in a non-zero-sum game, the other faction leader must now alter his strategy, at least minimally, if he wishes the support of the recruitee who is now engaged in a relationship with the other leader. Phrased another way, the second leader's strategy is subversion in contradistinction to the first leader whose strategy was recruitment. Thirdly, regardless of whether the game is or is not zero-sum, both leaders' interfactional strategies, that is, their strategies on confrontations and encounters, must now take into account the new fact of leader A's additional support/resource. Simple recruitment to a faction is in fact an act of competition. A distinction between factions and factionalism is, therefore, only a low level of abstraction, and factions, when viewed diachronically, are merely a structural representation of an on-going dynamic.

From this initial position, an advance in definition can be made by meshing the political with the network approach. Let us assume the social network is the basic unit for social analysis. After Barnes (1968) and Gulliver (1971), we accept the view that the basic unit, the network, is what has been labelled the "total network" which is viewed as socio-centric, unbounded, and infinite. Composed of nodes and linkages, the latter of which may be multiplex or uniplex, the total network may be analytically delimited into a "partial network" on two non-mutually exclusive bases: by delimiting "activity fields" or "institutional fields" (Jay, 1964; Mitchell, 1969), or by introducing the element of ego-centricity (Barnes, 1968).

Utilizing the former method, the total network is composed of overlapping statuses and dyadic ties which can be grouped into particular institutional complexes, one of them being the political. At this point, there is a potential *cul-de-sac* in defining 'political.' If we accept as basic, "competition associated with the attaining and exercise of power in the public domain" (Swartz, 1968), a political domain can be defined as those roles and resources (nodes and links; human and physical) which are socially defined as being available for inclusion in political competition. As Bailey notes, many social roles are explicitly excluded from this categorization since politics can be a parasitic activity from which the overall social organization must be protected (1969:11). Every society has definitions of what constitutes 'fair play'; that is, what constitutes political resources, physical and human. Phrased another way, analogous to the "kin-set" which Gulliver (1971) distinguished, every society can be assumed to define a 'political set,' a set of relationships – both physical and human – which can be utilized in political competition.

This notion of partial network or set, is similar to notions of "social categories" (Boissevain, 1971), classificatory "quasi-groups" (Mayer, 1966), and the "class of potential allies" (Boissevain, 1971). Regardless of label, a partial network/set can be abstracted from the total network, and this partial network can be political.

An individual, enmeshed in a total and partial network in general, may initiate interaction. If it is goal-oriented and includes more than one person, namely, more than one dyadic tie (Mayer, 1966; and others), the individual has initiated an action-set. If this action-set is derived from the political set and has been initiated for action in a potentially competitive, or actually competitive, political arena, then that action-set can be labelled a faction.

A faction is thus an ego-centred action-set recruited from within the parameters provided by the political set or partial network. An action-set within a political arena is a faction.

With this definition, there remain several conceptual issues which must still be clarified. First, the definition does not distinguish between the intra- and inter-factional spheres. The activation of a political action-set, simply put, is factional: it is concerned with both building a team (structure) and with competition (process). Further, however, it is suggested that the term action-set, itself, logically implies that action precedes the existence of a set – in this case, a set of political supporters.

Despite this logic, much theorizing has been concerned with trying to delineate the nature of the set. Three approaches seem to be paramount: first, an attempt has been made to deal with the set by defining the arena within which the set is found. Notable here is the concept of "segmentary factional systems" in which the system/arena is factional when membership is totally "exclusive" and "exhaustive" as in lineage systems (Nicholas, 1966). Additionally, there are notions of "bifactional" and "trifactional" systems (Graham, 1968). These ignore the oft-cited character of a faction as being ephemeral and loosely-structured. Except in the case of sociological micro-seconds, a factional sphere can never be exclusive. Not only does such a view not allow for the existence of neutrals and the alienated, it assumes that all actors have a commitment to a faction. In contradistinction, if a 'photograph' of an arena were taken, one would see a lot of people moving in between, in the interstitial areas. Phrased another way, people are constantly negotiating, being subverted, and realigning. This is precisely what accounts for the loose structure and what prevents factions or factionalism from being defined in terms of arenas or systems. 'Exclusive' and 'segmentary' imply a solidarity that must be empirically shown, and an ideological commitment which is seldom found (Bailey, 1969; Bujra, 1973; Spiro, 1968). The crucial point is that the definition put forward here does not zero in on arenas, fields, or on any *a priori* bounded units; instead, by focusing on action-sets, it focuses on actions and interactions of persons composing that arena/field. That is, it emphasizes process and ego-centricity; the set is simply a product of these two facts.

The second approach concerning itself with factionalism as sets is in the literature which deals with distinctions between core membership as opposed to support (Bailey, 1968), notions of direct as opposed to indirect structure (Graham, 1968), and the view that a faction can be recruited on behalf of another person (Boissevain, 1968). Such variations are not incorrect, either empirically or theoretically. If one deals with factions, there *is* variation in structure. However, they are merely variations which are the results of strategic decisions by the leader, the results of strategies of particular supporters, or the product of particular environmental circumstance. Each of these is empirically specific and affect factional competition. They are, however, unnecessary when dealing with a minimal definition of factionalism. It should be noted that this minimal definition of ego-centred, political action-sets does clarify a problem faced by those dealing with structural variation by providing the means for its analysis. Attempts thus far to do this have been characterized by vague dealings with the "degree of solidarity" factions can have (Spiro, 1968) before becoming "parties" (Bujra, 1973). This has resulted in the placing of factions along a continuum of social forms, between "public opinion and *partit*" (Boissevain, 1964), or in the designation of descriptional features such as transience, non-corporateness, and quasi-group.

Basically, these are negative definitional categories and in analysing a factional structure at a given point in time, reference should not be made to other structures or entities. Instead, one should ask which social relationships constitute factional membership at a given point in time and what is the character of the relationships. In network parlance, these questions deal with the morphological and interactional characteristics of an ego-centred network as discussed by Mitchell (1969; 1973). The definition, in short, not only permits the analysis of structural variation, it provides the tools with which this can be done.

Related to the above is the third approach which deals with set/faction. It is characterized by submerging the notion of ego-centricity and by refining instead variations of the quasi-group concept. Beginning with Mayer (1966), Boissevain ultimately concludes that an "interactive quasi-group," one of Mayer's two types, was merely a classification and therefore a social category (1971). This view has been accepted here and incorporated into the definition as being the means of delineating the partial network. However, Boissevain suggests the alternative concept of "coalition" defined as "a temporary alliance of distinct parties for a limited purpose" (1974:171). The aim is to deal with those non-groups, such as cliques and gangs, which are not ego-focused and in which leadership may develop at a later time, spontaneously.

Two points can be made in this connection. First, there are definite problems in dealing with non-leader-centred "non-groups," and Boissevain and others (Van Velzen, 1973a; Blok, 1973) therefore re-define action-set as "a set of persons who have co-ordinated their actions to achieve a particular goal" (Boissevain, 1974:186). The contention here, however, is that it is precisely the characteristic of ego-centricity which enables the analysis of factionalism. Further, methodologically, the action-set as an ego-centred entity is a rather elegant tool with its network implications and its individual focus which allows for the anchorage needed in the analysis of patterns of strategizing. It would be a great loss if this perspective were forgotten. In any case even socio-centred non-groups do not preclude the use of network analysis. On the assumption that all individuals are enmeshed in social relationships, by implication, coalitions, cliques, and gangs are composed of both individuals and networks of relationships. Although a more definitive explanation is beyond the scope of the present paper, social relationships and the networks can still be the basic unit of analysis. The individual must not be submerged into a variation of an institutional framework – the non-group or coalition; rather, the nature of these non-groups could be better elucidated if individuals, with their ability to act, are not forgotten. This is not to argue for the so-called Robinson Crusoe maximizing paradigm (Van Velzen, 1973b); it is merely to accept the fact that people may maximize, and that in any case, they do not simply react.

This investigation has made several interrelated points. First, it is possible to zero in on factional structures or factions, but these should be viewed as a low-level abstraction, a product of action such that the real problem is the nature of this action, and not simply its results. Secondly, the argument is put forward that it is the ego that should be the focus of attention, and not arenas or systems. The latter may be more usefully viewed as the context in which competition takes place and which competition may alter. They are part of the environment, and not the focus.

The diacritical foci of factional politics are thus taken to be ego-centricity and action; that is, the ego-centred political action-set satisfies the minimal definition, with factional 'structures' arising from competition. *The critical issue is not what are factions, but rather, what is factionalism.* It is suggested that factionalism may be defined as a strategy for engaging in political competition.

At this point the issue is, in fact, that of context and the various attempts to deal with the so-called interfactional sphere. How is factionalism related to social change? How does factionalism emerge, develop, and persist? Here we enter the realm of political anthropology and the general problem of how political process is to be perceived. The two major approaches are political process in terms of phase development (Swartz, 1968), and political process as the interaction between political structures and their environment (Bailey, 1968). The former has the tendency to implicitly assume that a system returns to equilibrium; the latter has too narrow a view of process. At this point, the reader is referred to Bujra's analysis of stratification patterns and types of conflict with the attempted specification of the varying directions of factional processes (1973). I suggest that this is the direction which future analyses should take. As such, factionalism is a process which is a rational strategy for engaging in competition for power and resources. It is further suggested that regardless of whether it is associated with social change or transition, or viewed as a system of conflict or of goal attainment, it remains a competitive political strategy which may have variations resulting from differences in the immediate context or environmental structure.

This environment, however, is not the wider sociological context, for this wider context is not to be found within the local arena, village level, and so on. Such a context results only in teleological description, as for example, when the local arena is viewed as conflict-ridden/orderly, so that factionalism becomes viewed as a cause, as an effect, and as a measure of degree, all simultaneously. Our initial description predefines the nature of factionalism; context/factionalism cannot be explained in terms of itself. Rather, the wider social context *is* the nature of social relations and the allocation of power in the wider society, beyond the boundaries of our 'little communities' and 'little contexts.'

III. THEORETICAL ASPECTS OF COUNCIL DECISION-MAKING

The major theoretical work upon which later studies have been based is Bailey's model of two ideal types of decision-making:

A. Councils lean toward *consensus* when they have one of the following characteristics:
   1. An administrative function, especially when they lack sanctions; or
   2. An elite position in opposition to their public; or
   3. Concern with external relationships.
B. Councils proceed readily to *majority voting* when they are:
   1. Policy-making; or
   2. Arena councils; or
   3. Concerned with internal relationships. (Bailey, 1965:13).

Richards' and Kuper's collection of essays, *Councils in Action* (1971) did not modify this statement in any systematic way although each contributor introduced additional variables which had to be taken into account in particular situations. That a new synthesis was never attempted can be attributed to the complexity of the problem, a fact which Bailey recognized (1965:14). The present section summarizes variables and problems in the literature to date, the aim being to provide an outline of those aspects relevant to decision-making for the Rajgahr Council.

Beginning with Bailey's distinction between policy and administrative decisions, there are immediate theoretical difficulties in applying it to a multi-purpose, as opposed to a specialized, council/committee. First, the Rajgahr Council is ostensibly an administrative organ, labelled a "local authority" in legal parlance. However, both its legally-defined tasks and structure give it power *vis-à-vis* the population and it therefore, by definition, makes policy decisions. This is true of all the hierarchical levels of local government. The ministry, the board, and the district commissioner are each legally administrative in relation to the next higher level. In relation to the next lower level, however, the decisions of each involve policy. The entire 'administrative hierarchy' embodies both policy and administration. Secondly, in strict Weberian terms, administration is not decision-making and from this perspective, Bailey's distinction is untenable. Finally, in actual empirical situations, the distinction is difficult to apply since decisions made by multi-purpose councils embody both elements.

In general terms, pure administration is not decision-making, and administrative organs make policy decisions. Others have found difficulty with the administration-policy distinction: Richards and Kuper (1971) note that the dichotomy does not allow for a major council function – dispute settlement – and the subsequent case studies in their book ignore the policy-administration distinction but distinguish the general type from dispute settlement. The Rajgahr data support this methodological alteration.

Another problem relates to sanctions and administrative staff. According to Bailey, compromise ensues when a council has to take action, especially if there is no separate executive machinery of sanctions to enforce the decision. Three inclusive levels of variability are thereby introduced: the fact that action is required, the presence/non-presence of executive machinery, and the presence/absence of sanctions. However, it becomes clear that each level introduces considerable complexity. For example, sanctions are dependent on their source(s) and on the manipulability of these. Additionally, the administrative staff involves personnel with network involvements, a particular pattern of accountability (Spencer, 1971), and the independent power to turn administrative actions into policy formulations. The issue cannot then revolve solely around sanctions and administrative staff, but more importantly around their particular characteristics.

In the Rajgahr context, sanctions derive ultimately from the council's legal status. The council has access to the courts and higher governmental levels to enforce its decisions. The existence of enforcement sources does not mean, however, that they will be used or that their use will even be contemplated. They exist as a broad parameter, but at high cost (financial and political), and their relevance is situationally rather than absolutely specific.

Similarly, the administrative staff of the Rajgahr Council, particularly the overseer, is theoretically accountable to the council and engaged solely in administration and the execution of predetermined tasks. However, like the council (an administrative organ), the staff takes decisions and therefore, policy formulation is involved. This not only alters the administration of an actual decision, but it also affects the council's perception of what can be administered and hence, the decision-making process. This interpretation/extrapolation as to the behaviour of the administrative staff is also, by implication, situationally specific. Thus, the existence of sanctions and staff does alter decision-making patterns; the direction of alteration, however, is extremely problematic, and the context/character of sanctions and staff must be investigated, not simply noted.

It is proposed that the nature of sanctions and staff also affect the decision-making process *vis-à-vis* the other variables, council structure and internal-external relationships. In the case of council structure, there are additional difficulties. Kuper takes issue with the polar distinction between arena and elite on the grounds that a decision-making elite may develop within a council as a structural attribute affecting the decision-making process. Further, Bailey's distinction rests on two assumptions: that the public is a uniform mass and that the council is accountable to its support from one direction only, above or below, at any given time. In fact, the public is seldom undifferentiated internally, but rather, is more often cross-cut by vertical interest groups and horizontal classes. Contradictory and cross-cutting supports render both the pure elite/pure arena council ideal, a situation further complicated by demands/responsibilities to higher-order entities which may conflict with the support relations to lower-order entities. Bailey does note that the arena/elite distinction is ideal: "We need to ask of actual councils not which of the two types they are, but rather, to what extent or on what occasions they are one rather than the other and whether there is any sustained move from one pole towards the other" (1965:12). Unfortunately, criteria for dealing with this issue are not given; rather one must look at particular situations with the additional implication that the elite/arena distinction is a *post facto* derivation and therefore, not predictive.

The final determinant of decision-making is again the nature of the issue as it concerns internal or external relations. There are, however, levels of 'externality': external to the council elite, the council, the village elite, the village geographically, the village administratively, and to the village as an arena of political competition. All these can in turn be cross-cut by externalities relating to different interest groups which may or may not cross-cut class lines.

A final difficulty is the dichotomy between consensus and voting. Kuper suggests that some decisions depend simply on whether an outside body is available to make the decision. Furthermore, there are three types of decision: the ceremonial, the ambiguous, and no decision. In a similar vein, one can add the consensual decision to defer a decision. Kuper also raises a distinction between repetitive and crucial situations which affect the decision-making pattern. Again one must return to the situation: "To understand the decision-making process, we must fasten on the immediate situational determinants, and these I believe [Bailey] identified correctly –

the structure of the council, the nature of its tasks and resources, and the relationship of the council to its political environment [the lines of support and demand]'' (Kuper, 1971a:20).

IV. DECISION-MAKING ON RAJGAHR VILLAGE COUNCIL

(a) *The Decision-making Process*

The aim of the present section is to show the pattern of decision-making utilized by the Rajgahr council, to specify the situational factors, and to derive regularities in council behaviour. During the period June 2, 1969 to February 16, 1970, seventy-six decisions were reached in council.[6] Nineteen were reached by a motion and the remainder seemingly were decisions by consensus. What, however, is the meaning of a motion and consensus in the Rajgahr context?

The Local Government Ordinances stipulate that all council motions must be reported to the Board via the District Commissioner. The Board then rules on the motion's legality in terms of two criteria: the laws of the country and the precedents which the council itself has established through previous motions. A motion passed cannot be rescinded formally, nor ignored informally, until six months have passed and the motion is rephrased or withdrawn via another motion.[7] A motion thus binds future action and brings in outsiders. In contradistinction, a consensual decision, although theoretically binding, can be reversed, ignored, manipulated, and differentially interpreted. Councillors argue that the minutes are incorrect or assume that a decision can be "remitted."

Under such circumstances, it is not surprising that the vast majority of decisions are non-motion decisions. Does this therefore imply that they are consensual? The data indicate that some decisions are genuinely consensual; that is, all parties agree and discussion is limited. Some decisions are consensual only after a lengthy discussion, a presentation of opposing views, and perhaps ultimately, the lack of desire to phrase or force the decision as a motion. In other cases, the issue may be consensually deferred either to a special meeting or to obtain the advice of the District Commissioner. Another variation is for consensus to be reached only after an explicit compromise has been made.

Six variations appear: (1) consensus; (2) consensus to defer; (3) consensus after compromise; (4) a motion in which split voting occurs; (5) a motion to merely legalize a decision with consensus having been reached beforehand; and (6) a motion to defer. To investigate the conditions under which each type occurs, it is necessary first to associate kinds of decision with corresponding issues. The latter were coded as follows:

(a) Dispute settlement between:
  i. the council and an elite villager
  ii. a councillor and an elite villager
  iii. a councillor and the council
  iv. the council and contracted labour
  v. the council and a villager (non-elite)

(b) Policy/administrative decisions relating to:
  i. procedures within the council itself
  ii. the village elite
  iii. the village public (non-elite)
  iv. the administrative staff of the council
  v. land allocations within the village
  vi. rates/rents/tolls
  vii. common lands within the village
  viii. disposition of the village dragline services
  ix. public works in general
  x. external, non-political agencies (University, Association of Local Authorities)
  xi. public relations with the Prime Minister
  xii. relations with other villages
  xiii. the Race Club 'arena'
  xiv. the Sanatan Hindu 'arena'

The distinction between dispute settlement and policy/administration has been noted elsewhere (Richards, 1971; Kuper, 1971a). The sub-categories can be grouped according to the arenas to which the decisions refer: there is the intra-council arena (b. 1); the village arena in terms of popular support lines (b. ii–iv); the village arena in terms of physical resources (b. v–ix); the arena outside the village, that is, the council's relations with external entities (b. x–xii); and finally there is the council's relations with other competitive arenas within the village (b. xii–xiv). The results of associating these categories with types and number of decision-making procedure are found in Table 1, below.

Clearly, the majority of decisions were consensual, although a large proportion involved consensus to defer, that is, non-decisions. Almost one-third were based on formal motions. Also apparent is that when the council was dealing with external agencies and viewing itself as the representative of the village, it exhibited a definite emphasis on consensus. The unanimous motion, an objection to an adjacent village's trespassing on Rajgahr's dams, was a definitive statement of unanimity and a strategy to have the decision noted by outside authorities. All further decisions in the category of 'external entities' were by consensus, and concerned the council's and village's public image in the national arena. Another observation was the trend toward consensus when dealing with both human and physical resources within the village. Thirdly, dispute settlement was characterized by consensus, but a consensus in which decisions were not being made. Further, internal issues within the council were subject to an inordinate amount of split motions as compared with other categories.

TABLE 1

Distribution of Decisions According to Type of Issue and Process

	Consensus Types			Motion Types		
	Consensus	Consensus to defer	Consensus with compromise	Split Motion	Unanimous motion	Motion to defer
Issues						
Dispute Settlement	1	8	3	2		1
Intra-council		1	1	4		1
Village Support	13	5		3		
Physical Resources	13	3		4		
External Entities	6				1	
Other Arenas		3		2		1
Total Decisions	33	20	4	15	1	3

Finally, decision-making on issues which concerned other competitive arenas within the village seemed to be characterized by consensual deferrals and motions.

In general, the council moves toward consensus. However, the large proportion of deferrals, albeit by consensus, raise the following questions: Do the deferrals represent genuine consensus, or a desire of the council not to be involved, or simply a decision not to consume extensive meeting time on a difficult decision? Furthermore, many decisions are reached by motion. Except for the general associations noted above and the one explicit relationship with external non-political agencies, an analysis of issues according to general/gross categories is insufficient to explain the decision-making patterns of the council. One must therefore ask: dispute settlement between whom? Whose support within the village? Which physical resources? Which competitive arenas?

Table 2 uses the original categorization of issues and associates these with decision types. Dealing first with dispute settlement, the decision involving council versus labour (a. iv) was the case of a contractor suing the council for underpayment on works done. The council agreed to hand the matter to a lawyer for settlement. The three decisions relating to disputes between councillors and elites (a. ii) involved two distinct disputes. All three decisions, and hence the settlement of the disputes, were deferred.

Related to these were six *disputes between the council and elite villa-*

TABLE 2

Decision-making Patterns, Types of Issues, and the Distribution of Decisions

	Types of Decisions						
	Motion Types					Consensus Types	
				No Decision Deferral to		Consensus	Compromise (Consensus)
Issue	Split	Unan.	To defer	D.C.*	Another meeting		
(a) Dispute settlement, between:							
i. council vs. elite villager	2	–	–	1	2	–	1
ii. councillor vs. elite villager	–	–	–	–	3	–	–
iii. councillor vs. council	–	–	1	1	–	1	1
iv. council vs. labour	–	–	–	1	–	–	–
v. council vs. non-elite villager	–	–	–	–	–	–	1
(b) Policy/administration re:							
i. intra-council	4	–	1	1	–	–	1
ii. village elite	1	–	–	–	2	–	–
iii. village public (non-elite)	–	–	–	–	–	9	–
iv. administrative staff	2	–	–	1	2	4	–
v. land allocations	–	–	–	1	–	3	–
vi. rates/rents/tolls	–	–	–	–	1	4	–
vii. common lands	2	–	–	–	1	–	–
viii. dragline services	2	–	–	–	–	4	–
ix. public works	–	–	–	–	–	2	–
x. external, non-political agencies	–	–	–	–	–	4	–
xi. relations with the P.M.	–	–	–	–	–	2	–
xii. relations with other villagers	–	1	–	–	–	–	–
xiii. Race Club "arena"	2	–	–	–	3	–	–
xiv. Sanatan Hindu "arena"	–	–	1	–	–	–	–

* District Commissioner.

gers (a. i) *characterized by three decision-making processes. Three of the disputes involved elite villagers committing three similar public delicts although two different methods for censure were utilized.* Two were held for prosecution, with the decisions phrased as motions. The third offender was called to the next meeting to explain his actions. This was a consensual deferral.

Before commenting further on the above, it is instructive to look at those policy/administrative decisions which concerned the village elite (b. ii). There was one motion and two deferrals on three different issues. In contradistinction, the council reached easy unanimity on policy/administrative decisions in relation to the public (b. iii and b. ix). These involved individuals, general policy decisions, and public works projects. There were no motions taken on public issues. *There was, in short, an elite council in relation to the public and an arena council in relation to the elite.*

This pattern is further borne out by the decision patterns on policy/administration within the council (b. i). Important issues such as declaring councillor Rasool's seat vacant were phrased as motions. The deferral involved a procedural point, and the compromise was related to the circulation of minutes. *There was a definite trend towards decision by motion, a clear characteristic of arena councils and of councils concerned with internal relationships* (see Bailey, 1965).

These trends are further borne out by inspection of the sub-categories within the type labelled 'administration of physical resources' (b. v–ix). It has already been noted that dispute settlement and policy/administration in relation to the general public (a. v; b. iii; and b. ix) were all based on unanimity and/or compromise, as compared with dispute settlement and policy/administration *vis-à-vis* elite villagers (a. i and b. ii) which were characterized mainly by motions. Does this pattern follow through with the allocation of physical resources?

The consensual approach to decision-making has already been noted in relation to public works (b. ix). What of the categories involving land allocations (b. v), rates/rents/tolls (b. vi), the use of the common lands (b. vii), and the hiring of the dragline (b. viii)? Although these issues are scattered throughout the types of patterns, detailed inspection of particular issues indicates regularity.

Both land allocations (b. v) and rates/rents/tolls (b. vi) are characterized by concensus and consensual deferral. The one deferral was made to the Local Government Board and ensured that the council removed itself from legal responsibility. In the case of rates/rents/tolls (b. vi), five decisions were taken, four of them by consensus. The one deferral was made to a special council meeting, a common procedure after harvest for rent reduction applications.

The disposition of dragline services (b. viii) and decisions on village common lands (b. vii) exhibit more complex processes. In the case of the former, four consensual decisions concerned hiring out the dragline to a lone applicant and allocating watchmen to the dragline. The two motions again show the pattern of elite competition which has been associated with decisions by motion. One was associated with the fact that councillor Amin had applied for the dragline services, while the second was associated with several elite families requesting the services at the same time. *When allocation* of the dragline *is a mere 'administrative' decision, consensus is easily reached. When, however, it is a resource for elites, the council moves toward decision-making by motion.*

The nature of decisions in relation to policy/administration of the common lands (b. vii) should predictably be toward consensus, given the assumption that these lands lie in the public domain over which the council takes on the attributes of an elite council. The decision process, however, is more complex as a result of a thirty-year dispute between council and government over the legal status of these lands. The village claimed they were part of the original land allocation to East Indian settlers; the government claimed they were crown lands. For the most part, *the jurisdictional issue remained latent, emerging only when its allocation for particular purposes or to particular groups became relevant.*

All common lands in the centre of the village had been allocated to the various village churches. The lands to the north of the village, however, had been left vacant mainly because it could never be decided how they should be distributed. In 1969, five parties were especially interested in the land: first, there was councillor Premsingh, priest of the Christian Catholic Church which required land for a building, having never been allotted land in the central area. Secondly, councillor Deoroop, chairman of the regional Rice Marketing Board since his defection to the PNC, decided that he needed an office and that the common lands would be the ideal place. Thirdly, the Maha Sabha Sanatan Hindu Organization wanted land for a school. The Gandhi Youth Organization, also Sanatan and claiming to represent the Hindu community, also wanted land for a school and office. Finally, because all available house lots were held in freehold ownership, villagers wanted the common lands surveyed and made available for this purpose.

The land issue first arose during the present period when the Maha Sabha made its request to council for three acres at the same time as the Gandhi Youth asked the government for land. Competition in another arena raised the wider issue of the right of disposal. The issue kept arising throughout the next few months. First, in response to the Gandhi Youth tactic, a motion was passed to apply to government to have the area surveyed for house lots. Only Rasool dissented. His reasons became clear at a special meeting several weeks later when the District Commissioner pointed out that to apply for government intervention meant the council was abandoning its jurisdictional claim. Partially to ensure legality, a motion was put to send a delegation to the Prime Minister. Sultan, Rasool, and Deoroop voted against. At that point, the Public Health Inspector's report indicated that Deoroop had illegally erected his RPA office on the common land. Rasool asked the District Commissioner why his protest against Deoroop had not been forwarded to the Board and the Commissioner several weeks before. Insulted, the District Commissioner left the meeting. Dagleish moved that the matter be deferred; four of the seven councillors abstained. At the regular meeting the next month, the council consensually agreed on the amount of rent Deoroop should pay for his office, while applications from two villagers to rent house lots on the common land were deferred.

The two decisions involving Deoroop were coded under council versus councillor dispute (a. iii), and what is again obvious is *the council's difficulty in dealing with elites/councillors. Its solution was simultaneously to close ranks* (setting the rent, thereby accepting Deoroop's encroachment) *vis-à-vis outside authorities and the public* (the deferred house lot applications). Further, the split motion on the deputation to the Prime Minister indicates that councillors compete for the political credit which can be obtained by publicly showing direct access to the national arena. In brief, the common lands issue points out *the different roles of the council even when a series of decisions occurs on the same basic issue*.

In policy/administration *vis-à-vis* staff (b. iv), a total of nine decisions were taken using three types of decision-making. Why the variation? Four consensual decisions concerned straightforward issues; for example, increasing the assistant overseer's salary to the level set by the Board. Three decisions involved the dragline watchman, Mattai, who was accused by Sultan of having left his watch. The matter was deferred until a witness was brought forward at the next meeting who confirmed Mattai's explanation; the council consensually agreed to pay him. Several months later, Sultan claimed he saw Mattai working on a combine instead of operating the creek gate. He insisted, and the council agreed, that Mattai be suspended until the "matter is clarified."

Another decision had to be made concerning the appointment of an additional ranger. Two motions were put – one for Madramootoo, the other for Mattai. Madramootoo won and Premsingh declared he would protest to the Board. This election occurred after the two decisions were taken on Mattai and one week before the final accusation by Sultan. This on-going process revealed that *the council reaches unanimity when decisions have to be made in situations where the lines of support and demand are not viewed as critical nor the objects of the decisions (human and/or physical resources) regarded as important*. In the case of staff support, partisanship is ensured prior to and on the occasion of appointments being made. The council becomes an arena council in such situations.

The final issues concern decision-making patterns in relation to competitions in other village arenas. During the present period, two are relevant: the race club arena in which two clubs competed for resources (b. xiii) and the aforementioned split in the Hindu community (b. xiv). In the case of the former, the first motion centred on whether the council should contribute one hundred dollars to improve the race track. Amin, president of one of the two clubs, abstained. It was then consensually decided to call both clubs to a meeting to effect a merger. This did occur, and at another council meeting, the united club applied for control of the common lands during the race meet, a usual procedure. The decision, necessarily phrased as a motion, was voted against by Amin, Rasool, and Taharally. Before unification, Amin had been ousted as president of his club and at the merger meeting he agreed to unification to undercut his former club. He then refused a nomination for the vice-presidency of the united club. His negative vote on the meet also reflected his recalcitrance. Rasool disagreed in principle with any allocation of the lands, while Taharally's vote was, at the moment, inexplicable. In the end, it was consensually decided to defer the issue to a special meeting, a common procedure. In sum, *the council performed as an elite council in relation to this arena, except in the case of councillors whose immediate vested interests were involved.* This view is borne out by Mangal's statement at the special meeting: "Ratepayer's money was spent on the track, and the council, as village fathers, should demand that the two clubs be united so that better racing would be promoted in the village."

A similar situation was apparent in the Hindu split. The council decided to see a solicitor (and thus deferred) on the legality of the Gandhi Youth's application to government. Only Rasool dissented. At the meeting, however, all councillors spoke on the issue and the general feeling was that the two associations should unite. The council had in fact attempted to call in representatives of both groups, but they did not appear. *In failing in the role of conciliator as an elite council, the council then proceeded to defend its own jurisdiction.*

(b) *Regularities in Decision-Making on Rajgahr Village Council*

From the above description, several patterns may be summarized. These include both methodological and theoretical deductions on decision-making in councils with specific reference to Rajgahr Village, and perhaps, more generally.

Methodologically, analysis in the previous section involved categorizing council's tasks/issues according to the arena of reference and then associating these with a typology of decision-making processes. It was found that the initial categories of tasks yielded only general trends, with the exception of those decisions relating to 'external non-political arenas' which were, predictably, consensual.

Subsequent categorization of tasks into smaller units and their association with decision-making still left anomalies. This lead to an investigation of certain individual issues and decisions which enabled the linking of particular decisions into a logically related 'series' based on common personnel or content; at this point particular patterns emerged.

In methodological terms, an investigation of council decision-making must examine the following:

(1) the meaning of a motion and consensus in particular contexts, and the legal and non-legal implications, the formal and informal constraints/sanctions in each type of decision.

(2) Types of decision-making processes are more complex than a simple dichotomy between consensus and voting. It is important to note that a vote may be split or unanimous. Further, the processes may include a "no-decision" category (Kuper, 1971a and b). In the Rajgahr context, this is phrased as a "deferral" which may in turn be a product of a motion or consensus. Additionally, consensus can sometimes be reached only after explicit compromise.

(3) There is a definite methodological problem in developing a categorization of tasks. For example, the council decides on the tolls to be charged outsiders' *padi* brought in to an elite villager's mill. In terms of the arena to which the decision will refer, one is dealing simultaneously with *padi* in general (the public), the mill owners (elite), non-villagers (outsiders), and both physical and human resources. Categorization thus has to be made *via* an intuitive awareness of the major issues within a particular context. In the Rajgahr case, this issue was typed as 'relations with elite' because of Rajgahr history and the role which the milling family played, and is playing, in village political affairs. The point is, however, that micro-investigation of each issue, individually, and of the series of issues is a critical methodological step.

The theoretical findings are also relevant. When councillors are enmeshed in relationships with constituents through their roles as both councillors and villagers, the general trend will be toward consensus under the following conditions: when the council acts as a body and views itself as representing the village interests *vis-à-vis* outsiders, and when such outside interests do not themselves contain, in the particular context, resources for which councillors are competing as individuals or as a group. This situation also occurs under the same conditions *vis-à-vis* other competition occurring within the village and finally, in the council's relationship to the general public. In short, *when distance is possible, regardless of task* – be it administration/policy or dispute settlement – *the council achieves consensus*. Conversely, in situations containing vested interests for the council or councillors, the decision-making process becomes more complex than a vote or consensus. *In relation to elite villagers*, that is, to councillors' peers, *and in relation to scarce resources, motions and deferrals characterize decision-making*. In Bailey's terms, the council is an elite council in relation to the public, outsiders, and other competitors – in other words, in relation to 'apolitical contexts'; the council is an arena council in relation to scarce resources, whether human or physical.

Task is therefore not predictive of council behaviour, as for example, when dispute settlement becomes part of the competitive political process. This is clearly demonstrated when a series of decisions, ostensibly on the same issue, involve different decision patterns. What is critical is whether the council can distance itself from the issues. *The basic determinant of council decision-making is the council's actual relationship to physical resources and human support*.

V. THE COUNCIL AS AN ARENA: THE ISSUE OF FACTIONALISM

(a) *The Nature of Factionalism on Council*

Factional politics have been the mainstay of the local political organization for decades. It is therefore suggested that when the council exhibits 'arena-council' features which render councillors unable to distance themselves from the resources embodied in issues, the resulting internal organization will be a product of the factional politics which characterize the village.

The data for this analysis are the voting patterns of those issues in which decisions were reached by motion. The following questions are relevant: do voting patterns exhibit factional alignments? Does the definition of factionalism presented in Section II fit Rajgahr council politics?

Nineteen motions were raised during the period under discussion. With the exception of the voting on five motions, there were no direct confrontations between any two factions in terms of one faction membership consistently opposing the members of the other. However, an association can be shown between the five explicit factional alignments and the contents of the motions. Four motions were so phrased because of legal requirements: the election of the chairman and deputy chairman and the appointment of two rangers. The final motion set up a delegation to the Prime Minister on the issue of the common lands jurisdiction. It is suggested that when a decision involves explicit access to resources for councillors, factional alignments emerge in sharp relief and are reflected in the voting pattern. Under these conditions, factionalism becomes the idiom through which competition is expressed. Why can these five issues be phrased as involving 'explicit access'?

The chairman and deputy positions involve a great deal of power with

TABLE 3

Factional Leadership and Support on Council

Leaders:	Sultan	Premsingh	Neutral
Supporters:	Amin (until December, 1969)	Dagleish	Bharat
	Jaikarran	Amin (after December, 1969)	
	Deoroop	Mangal	
	Taharally (until December, 1969)	Nagassar	
	Rasool	Taharally (after December, 1969)	
	Brijlall		

access to the informal prerogatives of power. Also, the chairman controls communication links with the formal hierarchy, and after the PNC infiltration, the chairman controlled the informal broker role with the PNC party also (providing he were able to establish and maintain credibility). On that basis, Premsingh and Sultan were both nominated for the chairmanship. Taharally and Brijlall ran against each other for the deputy chairmanship. Each leader had put forward its candidates and Taharally's defection to Premsingh was paid off by his nomination for deputy chairman (see Table 3).

With regard to the administrative staff, their support was critical for maintaining the everyday administrative functioning of the council. A recalcitrant officer meant not only negligent, but also subversive administration. Since officers were villagers with networks of alliances and supports, their partisanship was crucial.

Finally, the delegation to the Prime Minister would indicate to the PNC who were the 'big men' of the village. Ostensibly, the councillors selected for the delegation would be representing village interests. Simultaneously, however, they would be representing themselves, as the chosen few, to the national arena. When the village visits the Prime Minister, the political implications are not analogous to those of the Prime Minister visiting the village.

In short, *those decisions in which factional confrontations emerged in clear, explicit relief were also those situations in which the payoffs were high and, importantly, immediate.* It is further suggested, and discussed later, that in these critical situations, the idiom of factionalism becomes the best strategy. What of the other motions and the seemingly random pattern of voting behaviour?

To see if further regularities existed, correlation coefficients were obtained for all possible two-person voting combinations and their rank ordered from high to low. Intra-factional voting appears to be the norm and cross-factional correlations occur only at a low point in the rank ordering – initially via the association of Sultan and Nagassar – with a correlation index of .057. However, Ramsaroop had associations with Sultan and Rasool that were greater than his associations with Mangal and Dagleish, two important supporters of Premsingh. This was a major anomaly further complicated by the actual numerical coefficient. The coefficient for Dagleish-Nagassar was – .009, a negative correlation.

In general, then, council voting patterns tend to follow factional alignments in terms of all possible intra-factional combinations. However, the anomalies indicate that either the association of factional membership with the voting pattern is not totally justified for the present data or that factions are not simply a "coalition of individual members with common interests," but that perhaps they cluster around a focal point, a leader. Assuming that the latter may be so, a rank ordering of correlations done solely in terms of the two leaders, Premsingh and Sultan, indicates *a perfect fit between voting patterns on council and factional alignment defined in terms of leadership*. The previous anomaly of a cross-factional correlation being higher than an intra-factional correlation disappears, as do any negative correlations within a particular faction. The Sultan-Nagassar association remains positive, but it becomes the lowest positive correlation (.057) since the next association in the ranking, Premsingh-Brijlall, is negative (– .032). Not only then is there a perfect fit between the leader-supporter relationship and the voting pattern, but also, with one exception (Sultan-Nagassar), each leader is negatively correlated in voting association with all those who are not followers.

Of interest, as well, is the fact that although the general trend is – the higher the association with one leader, the lower the correlation with the other – there is no perfect association between an individual's voting with one leader and, by implication, casting a vote against the other. The previous discussion indicates there were only five situations in which this perfect association occurred and these situations had exceptionally high spoils. Furthermore, anomalies in the ranked correlations on all-councillor voting combinations can be construed as another index of this general point.

In theoretical terms, the implication is that factional politics do not necessarily involve "segmentary arenas" (Nicholas, 1965). Nor does factional association have to be exclusive and absolute, and thereby, by implication, pre-defining all supporters' actions by virtue of so-called factional membership. This brings into sharp relief the importance of viewing factionalism as a process, rather than as a competition between two or more competing structures. Conclusive evidence of this point is the fact that the two leaders themselves are not the lowest correlation of all combinations!

A possible explanation for the leaders' voting together – cross-factionally – lies in the hypothesis of collusion between the two leaders as a factional alliance (Nicholas, 1965), or as an elite within the council (Kuper, 1971a). However, because this hypothesis sees each faction as dependent on leaders rather than on supporters, it (the hypothesis) necessarily implies that each leader manipulates his factional structure as a single entity. Instead, given that these 'collusive' leaders vote together cross-factionally more often than supporters vote cross-factionally, and given that the pattern is not symmetrical (that a vote for one leader is not necessarily a vote against the other), the utility of a collusion or elite hypothesis is limited since each leader is manipulating, not a faction, but the various linkages in his partial network/political set for particular issues. The collusion and elite hypotheses would further obscure the possibility that supporters may not wish to be, and are not, manipulated at all times on all issues. Can leaders collude while support goes its own way? The answer is a qualified 'yes' – qualified by the fact that one is thereby accepting that followers manoeuvre. This necessarily involves the acceptance of an action-set notion of factions, and by implication, the limited scope of 'structure'/'faction' in the analysis of factionalism.

The next logical question is when do leaders collude? Why do supporters bolt? Phrased another way, what is the process called "factionalism," or what is its sociological context? In other words, factionalism is not a series of structures analysable through the mere tracing of changing alignments. It is a process, and in the Rajgahr context, the process of leaders' action-sets is occurring within a context which is providing constraints and resources. What are these?

An answer lies in the issues with which the council was dealing. When viewing how supporters vote on particular motions as compared with the leaders, an obvious hypothesis is that supporters tend to vote with leaders – including those instances when leaders themselves vote together. The data, however, indicate some anomalies – votes cast on particular motions which depart from the leaders' votes. There are thirteen such 'misvotes' out of a total of eighty-three and they occur on eight motions. What were these issues and why did this occur?

One motion, in which Nagassar and Amin 'misvoted,' concerned the prosecution of an elite villager, Taharally, for an illegal water connection. It was one of the three public delicts mentioned previously in which there appeared to be a differential treatment of elites. In this case, Taharally was the nephew of Councillor Taharally, who was absent from the particular meeting. Premsingh and Dagleish voted with Amin against the motion. Basically, Premsingh and follower Dagleish were indebting Taharally, while Amin was becoming disillusioned with Sultan; as a prelude to his and Taharally's defection, he supported Taharally. Nagassar's motives in voting for the motion are unknown.

The second motion was a surprising situation in which Premsingh attempted, with Deoroop's support, to have Rasool's seat declared vacant on a technicality. The majority of councillors did not regard this as 'fair play.' Yet Premsingh chose to pursue the matter; Deoroop, for an unknown reason, disliked Rasool intensely and therefore supported the motion. Dagleish, Bharat, Sultan, and Amin, given Premsingh's valid legal point in relation to Rasool's seat, had no alternative but to abstain. Personal enmity accounts for Deoroop's vote; good conscience and/or elitism account for Dagleish's, the other 'misvote' on the issue.

On the third motion, to improve the race track, Amin departed from the rest of the council's unanimity. The recent coup deposing him as club president resulted in his refusal to countenance or take part in any further race meets. His abstention reflects the outcome of competition in another arena.

Two motions involved Rasool's departing from the council's consensus on the common land issue. Already noted was Rasool's disagreement over the council's handling of the issue. At the particular meetings, about twenty proprietors heard him denounce the council. As a councillor who could have lost his seat at any time on the technicality which Premsingh raised, that he was not a proprietor and hence not entitled to a council seat, the political credibility and popular support which Rasool received was great.

The seventh motion was to rent the dragline to councillor Amin. His misvote, an abstention, was formal recognition that the council did occasionally have to take into account the notion of 'interested parties.' Rasool's negative vote reflected his preference for having the dragline rented to an outsider and his dislike of Amin. However, with the two leaders jockeying for Amin's support just after the chairman elections in which Amin defected publicly by casting his vote for Premsingh, the council rented Amin the dragline.

The eighth motion had three Premsingh supporters voting against him; or phrased another way, Premsingh voted with Sultan on a motion to defer the issue of Deoroop's office on the common land after the meeting in which Rasool insulted the District Commissioner. Premsingh, like Sultan, Deoroop, and Rasool, abstained. Premsingh did not want the matter deferred since the sooner it was settled, the sooner he could obtain land for his church. With the District Commissioner gone, however, discussion could not proceed, and Premsingh's abstention reflects this awareness without his sanctioning the deferral. At the same time, Premsingh followers Dagleish, Nagassar, and Amin saw no point in continuing and hence moved to defer. Meanwhile Sultan and Deoroop had to support publicly Rasool's recalcitrance toward the District Commissioner, but because the issue had to be deferred, they simply abstained.

On the final motion, the draft estimate for 1970, Rasool again attempted to make public points by insisting that the collectable percentage of rents in arrear be lowered.

To summarize, councillors' apparent 'misvotes' were motivated by a variety of factors directly related to their particular interests. Ali desired public support for a vulnerable legal position on council and became the watchdog of council ineptitude. Premsingh was motivated by personal dislike for Rasool's style, for his church, and his need to maintain the support of Amin and Taharally. Dagleish was motivated by a concept of fair play, Deoroop by personal enmity, and Amin by his vested interests and the outcome of competition in another arena.

(b) *Regularities of Factionalism in Rajgahr Village Council*

The previous section traces factional alignments as they affect council deliberations and decision-making in those situations in which the village council is defined as an arena council. Three levels of factional involvement on the council are delineated.

First, factionalism involves segmentary and exclusive alignments only in those situations in which the spoils are immediate, exceptionally high, or involve consolidating a position which would result in access to additional resources. Such is the reasoning behind efforts to control the executive positions of the council, its administrative personnel, and the informal nexus between village and national arena. Under such circumstances, factional alignments manifested through 'exhaustive structures' become apparent.

At a second and more inclusive level, alignments are not clear-cut, and the faction as a bounded entity is no longer perceivable. Indeed, factional structures no longer exist, in that voting patterns cannot be explained by reference to a faction, since relationships among followers are not necessarily predictive of voting patterns. Rather, in lieu of structures or factions, leader-focused action-sets provide a perfect fit between ranked coefficients on voting patterns and factional alignments on council. Factionalism exists only in relation to leadership; there are no factional structures. In Rajgahr, factions are thus factionalism – the activation of leader-centred action-sets.

At a third level, it has been noted that despite correlations in voting behaviour, there are individual departures from leaders' positions. Although these do not occur in sufficient numbers to affect the correlation matrix, they do require explanation and have been traced to other interests which individual councillors have. Individuals can and do depart from their leaders in order to defend or maximize these interests. At this level of analysis, factionalism does not explain the council as an arena council.

In short, factionalism is best seen as a strategy in relation to particular resources; it is a political means for maximizing resources and access to resources carried out with reference to leadership as opposed to membership in a group *per se*. It is a mobilization of personnel which may or may not be used in particular situations according to particular issues. The leaders themselves recognize this fact, as evidenced by their own departure from their followers' positions on issues which concern their own personal vested interests.

With factionalism defined as a political strategy involving the deployment of leader-centred action-sets, there still remains the need to explain the wider sociological context. Why, in specific issues, were there departures from leaders' positions? The answer lies in the vested interests of individual supporters which were more important than was loyalty to the leader. Why should this occur? Why should supporters not support their leader, build credit which the leader would have to repay at a later time and in that way, defend their personal vested interests? In other words, why is factionalism not regarded as a sufficient strategy for all political manoeuvring?

It is suggested that a parallel exists between this question on the extensiveness of factionalism and the findings on council decision-making patterns. As will be recalled, "the basic determinant of council decision-making (consensus vs. voting) is the council's actual relationship to physical resources and human support." It is suggested that the same pattern characterizes the use of *factionalism as a political strategy*. That is, its use *is conditioned by the leaders and supporters' individual relationships to physical resources and human support*. Depending on the issue involved, "particular lines of support-demand" (Kuper, 1971a) become relevant. Decisions in relation to both the issue and to the relevance of the factional strategy become circumscribed by a 'cost analysis' of various strategies. A choice is then made. The fact that a choice is available necessarily leads back to the nature of Rajgahr village itself, the differential allocation of resources which exists, and the means of competition in this larger context.

VI. THE BASIC DETERMINANT OF COUNCIL DECISION-MAKING AND FACTIONALISM

Factionalism is a game played by elites. All Rajgahr councillors are elites in financial and/or prestige terms. As elites, they compete with each other and by implication, they compete with the majority of villagers when necessary. The situation of scarce resources in the Rajgahr context makes such competition inevitable. As such, the context is clearly not one of the disorganizing effects of social change, but rather one of a constantly changing political and economic environment in which every new resource must be allocated and in which the possibility of old resources being re-distributed is not unlikely. Council decision-making occurs in such a context and factionalism provides a possible strategy for competition within it. Factionalism in turn is reflected, given particular conditions, on the council. Also reflected, however, is the councillors' elite position in the village in general. Their self-perception as 'village fathers' indicates the dual aspect – elitism and competition – of the processes of decision-making and factionalism. It is an elite prerogative; it is competition for resources within this larger pattern of stratification.

My conclusion is that whenever a village is stratified and whenever resources are selectively available:

(a) local councils will reflect the stratification pattern by being composed of elites;
(b) the decision-making process on council will oscillate between consensus *vis-à-vis* the public and voting *vis-à-vis* the elite;
(c) the voting patterns will tend to be organized by strategies of factional politics;

But: (d) the wider explanation for both decision-making patterns and factionalism lies in the fact of stratification and scarce resources;
(e) these in turn are a product of the resource allocation in the larger society. In the Rajgahr context, this is an encapsulation policy ('incorporation') which not only favours elites, but systematically seeks them out as part of a process of political and economic cooptation in the interests of maintaining intact the structure of the national arena.

NOTES

1 The field research for this paper was carried out in 1969–70 under the auspices of a Canada Council Doctoral Fellowship with additional grants from the Centre for Developing-Area Studies, McGill University and the Research Institute for the Study of Man, New York. In writing this paper, I am indebted to Malcolm Blincow, Lecturer, York University, for his detailed and insightful comments.

2 The distribution of acreage in 1969 was as follows:

Acreage cultivated	% of farming population
1–10 acres	55.4%
11–20 "	25.9
21–30 "	6.6
31–50 "	6.9
51+	5.2

3 In 1900, the village area was surveyed and divided into depths or sub-areas which were further subdivided into house and cultivation lots, the former clustering around the public road which runs the length of the Guyanese coast, and the latter lying behind the house-lot

area in plots of three-quarters of an acre. Each house-lot owner has a cultivation lot. Behind these are approximately 2,000 acres of crown land, leased by the local authorities (as represented by the village council) and rented to proprietors (house-lot owners) in 2–20-acre lots. The Abary crown land is located behind the village crown lands across the Abary River.

4 From the council membership, a chairman and deputy are elected each year by the members. They exercise 'executive control'; that is, they make decisions in between the monthly statutory meetings and have the prerogative of calling special meetings should the need arise.

5 A strategy which exploits the divisions caused by factional competitions, religious affiliation, and economic differentiation in order to infiltrate a village. The tactic is to designate local middlemen/activists through whom the patronage of the party for subversion efforts is selectively filtered and whose continued position becomes dependent on their success in the local arena.

6 Data on council deliberations come from formal minutes recorded by the assistant overseer, and from extensive notes taken at all meetings which I attended, from both of which were abstracted council decisions – their content, whether consensually decided, whether deferred or phrased into a motion, and if the latter, the voting patterns.

7 The best example of this process is in the formulations of the draft estimate, that is, the village's projected budget for the year prepared early in the new year. Its passing by the council, after being prepared by the overseer and interested councillors, is phrased in terms of a motion in which a vote must be taken. It is called a draft because the estimate must be passed onto the District Commissioner and ultimately the Local Government Board which accepts it or suggests changes, and then back to the District Commissioner, who in turn, sends it back to council with the recommended changes, which the council must then pass again as a motion. The 'draft estimate,' through this process, becomes the 'estimate.'

REFERENCES

Bailey, F. G.
1965 "Decisions by Consensus in Councils and Committees: With Special Reference to Village and Local Government in India." In M. Banton (ed.), *Political Systems and the Distribution of Power*. ASA Monograph 2, London, Tavistock.

Bailey, F. G.
1968 "Parapolitical Systems." In M. J. Swartz (ed.), *Local Level Politics*. Chicago, Aldine.

Bailey, F. G.
1969 *Stratagems and Spoils*. Toronto, Copp-Clark.

Barnes, J. A.
1968 "Networks and Social Process." In M. J. Swartz (ed.), *Local Level Politics*. Chicago, Aldine.

Blok, A.
1973 "Coalitions in Sicilian Peasant Society." In J. Boissevain and J. C. Mitchell (eds.), *Network Analysis: Studies in Human Interaction*. The Hague, Mouton.

Boissevain, J.
1964 "Factions, Parties and Politics in a Maltese Village." *American Anthropologist*, 66:1275–87.

Boissevain, J.
1968 "The Place of Non-groups in the Social Sciences." *Man*, 3(4):542–56.

Boissevain, J.
1971 "Second Thoughts on Quasi-Groups, Categories and Coalitions." *Man*, 6(3):468–72.

BOISSEVAIN, J.
1974 *Friends of Friends: Networks, Manipulators and Coalitions*. Oxford, Basil Blackwell.
BUJRA, JANET
1973 "The Dynamics of Political Action: A New Look at Factionalism." *American Anthropologist*, 75(1):132–52.
COMITAS, L.
1964 "Occupational Multiplicity in Rural Jamaica." In L. Comitas and D. Lowenthal (eds.), *Work and Family Life: West Indian Perspectives*. New York, Doubleday.
GRAHAM, B. D.
1968 "The Succession of Factional Systems in the Uttar Pradesh Congress Party, 1937–66." In M. J. Swartz (ed.), *Local Level Politics*. Chicago, Aldine.
GULLIVER, P. H.
1971 *Neighbours and Networks*. Berkeley, University of California Press.
JAY, E.
1964 "The Concept of Field and Network in Anthropological Research." *Man*, Sept.–Oct.: 137–39.
KUPER, A.
1971a "Council Structure and Decision Making." In A. Richards and A. Kuper (eds.), *Councils in Action*. Cambridge, Cambridge University Press.
KUPER, A.
1971b "The Kgalagari: 'Lekgota.'" In A. Richards and A. Kuper (eds.), *Councils in Action*. Cambridge, Cambridge University Press.
LANTZ, C. C.
1971 "Yadava and 'Quasi-Groups': A Comment." *American Anthropologist*, 73(3): 803–04.
MAYER, A. C.
1966 "The Significance of Quasi-Groups in the Study of Complex Societies." In M. Banton (ed.), *The Social Anthropology of Complex Societies*. ASA Monograph 4, London, Tavistock.
MITCHELL, J. C.
1969 "The Concept and Use of Social Networks." In J. C. Mitchell (ed.), *Social Networks in Urban Situations*. Manchester, Manchester University Press.
MITCHELL, J. C.
1973 "Networks, Norms and Institutions." In J. Boissevain and J. C. Mitchell (eds.), *Network Analysis: Studies in Human Interaction*. The Hague, Mouton.
NICHOLAS, RALPH W.
1965 "Factions: A Comparative Analysis." In M. Banton (ed.), *Political Systems and the Distribution of Power*. ASA Monographs 2, London, Tavistock.
NICHOLAS, RALPH W.
1966 "Segmentary Factional Political Systems." In M. J. Swartz, V. W. Turner and A. Tuden (eds.), *Political Anthropology*. Chicago, Aldine.
RICHARDS, A.
1971 "Introduction: The Nature of the Problem." In A. Richards and A. Kuper (eds.), *Councils in Action*. Cambridge, Cambridge University Press.
RICHARDS, A. and A. KUPER (eds.)
1971 *Councils in Action*. Cambridge, Cambridge University Press.
SILVERMAN, M.
Forthcoming "The Role of Factionalism in Political Encapsulation: East Indian Villages in Guyana." In F. Henry (ed.), *Ethnicity in the Americas*. Proceedings of the IXth International Congress of Anthropological and Ethnological Sciences, Chicago, 1973. Mouton.

Spencer, P.
1971 "Party Politics and the Processes of Local Democracy in an English Town Council." In A. Richards and A. Kuper (eds.), *Councils in Action*. Cambridge, Cambridge University Press.

Spiro, Melford E.
1968 "Factionalism and Politics in Village Burma." In M. J. Swartz (ed.), *Local Level Politics*. Chicago, Aldine.

Swartz, M. J. (ed.)
1968 *Local Level Politics*. Chicago, Aldine.

Van Velzen, H. U. E. T.
1973a "Coalitions and Network Analysis." In J. Boissevain and J. C. Mitchell (eds.), *Network Analysis: Studies in Human Interaction*. The Hague, Mouton.

Van Velzen, H. U. E. T.
1973b "Robinson Crusoe and Friday: Strength and Weakness in the Big Man Paradigm." *Man*, 8(4):592–612.

Yadava, J. S.
1968 "Factionalism in a Haryana Village." *American Anthropologist*, 70(5):898–909.

Of Men and Marbles: Notes Towards a Reconsideration of Factionalism[1] **5**

Jeremy Boissevain

INTRODUCTION

There is a pervasive, and to my mind incorrect, view which holds that some conflict, while full of sound and fury, is socially insignificant. Factionalism, it is argued, despite being a *product* of rapid social change, is not *about* change. Rather, faction fighting is viewed by many as a game, and hence scarcely worth the attention of today's social scientists. Instead, they prefer to focus on conflict that is socially significant – on class conflict. As one aggressive seminar discussant recently put it, "Factional leaders, like Wilson and Heath, only play games for marbles!"

Related to this view that factional and class conflict are logically different types of conflict are a number of assumptions that have become commonplace in political anthropology. These include the notion that factions are vertically organized rival coalitions that cut uniformly across socio-economic classes; that faction leaders recruit support through structurally diverse linkages, and that competing factions are structurally similar. In short, factions are seen as competing in balanced opposition. It is further held that factionalism does not have an ideological expression because rival factions compete for control over power, status, and resources which are available within the existing framework of society. Hence they do not attempt to change the social order. Factional conflict is consequently viewed as segmental rather than class-based (see Firth, 1957; Boissevain, 1964, 1969, 1974a; Nicholas, 1965; Siegel and Beals, 1966; Bailey and Nicholas, 1968; Bailey, 1969; and Bujra, 1973).[2]

The purpose of this discussion is to place several question marks behind a number of these comfortable, time-worn assumptions. In fact, I shall argue that most of them are false. It makes more sense to regard factionalism not as a separate, exotic type of conflict, but simply as small-scale conflict, usually at a face-to-face level. Factionalism, as will become apparent, is not necessarily a product of or even associated with rapid social change. Factional conflict, on the other hand, seems always to be about changes in power balances and thus about those whose way of doing things is to be 'accepted' as 'normal.'[3] Rival factions, far from being in balanced opposition, are structurally and organizationally asymmetrical. Moreover, they are not invariably ideologically neutral. In short, my general conclusion is that it is not possible to draw a categorical line between factionalism and class conflict.

It should not surprise us that the validity of the categorical distinction between faction and radical or class conflict is raised, historically speaking, at this time. After all, this distinction was fundamental to the structural-functional view of the relation between conflict and change. Factions (and rebellions) were seen as 'normal' conflict that did not threaten the equilibrium of the system. They were contrasted to class-based conflict (revolution) that did threaten the systemic equilibrium. In short, on logical grounds, the structural-functional notion of equilibrium required a category of conflict that would not endanger the system. It is thus quite understandable that since structural-functionalism is increasingly being called into question, the notions of conflict which are an essential part of it should also be questioned.

Let me now be more explicit by trying to answer two questions: What is the relation between factionalism and social change? Are factions symmetrical groups in balanced opposition?

FACTIONALISM AND SOCIAL CHANGE

More than fifteen years ago Siegel and Beals stated that pervasive factionalism is "essentially a phenomenon of socio-cultural change" (1960:399). They argued that it is the result of interaction between internal "strains" and external "stress." Epstein, too, noted that "... factions are informal pressure groups which act as mechanisms whereby gains in economic status might be realized also in terms of political and social mobility" (1962:289, 128). In the Indian village she examined, economic, political, and ritual status no longer coincided after the introduction of irrigation. Nicholas also pointed to the influence of change on factional dispute. He commented that "... factions, in the absence of conventional political divisions perform necessary functions in organizing conflict" (1965:47). He went on to observe that "If we distinguish between the social disruption brought about by social change and the social order brought about almost any kind of political systems, our attentions will be drawn to the functions of factions" (*ibid.*:57). Bailey, too, observed that "Factions may arise when the environment provides some new kind of political resource, which existing groups cannot exploit" (1969:52). Finally, after reviewing a number of studies, Bailey and Nicholas commented that "It is helpful to think of a faction as a group of enterprising and self-interested men who have realized that there are new political resources available and wish to make use of them before others do ... . Factions, therefore, seem like a stopgap to fill a void that occurs when existing groups are proved ineffective in gaining political ends; in fact, they may act so as to further the decline of older political groupings" (Bailey and Nicholas, 1968:278).

These statements have two characteristics in common. First, they stress the functional, system-maintaining character of factions. Factions arise because the equilibrium of the system has been disturbed. Factions work to restore the equilibrium. Factionalism is thus a form of cybernetic activity symptomatic of systems undergoing change. Second, the change to which they refer is externally introduced. It comes from outside the system. It is not a product of tensions inherent to the societies under examination. Moreover, although many of these writers provide certain data indicating that rival factions are asymmetrical, in their analysis, they treat them as though they were more or less evenly matched teams competing in a game. The notions that conflict is system-maintaining, that change comes from outside the system, and that conflict groups are in balanced opposition are dominant assumptions of functionalist social science (Gouldner, 1960).

Despite the case made to link factionalism to external change, this relation is notably absent in several societies in which factions have been studied. For example, there is no apparent connection between externally introduced economic or political change and the factionalism described in the Akwe Shavante village, Sao Domingos (Maybury-Lewis, 1967), the Orissa village, Bisipara (Bailey, 1957), the Ndembu village, Mukanza (Turner, 1957), and in the Bengal village, Govindapur (Nicholas, 1965). *It appears that factionalism is not necessarily a result of change*. Alavi made much the same point: "... typically, factional politics are found in peasant societies, such as those in South Asia, which have not been subject to rapid social change," (1973:47). In fact, he went on to note that "... rapid social change, associated with the 'Green Revolution' in those societies, has tended to replace the factional mode of politics by class conflict" (see also Sharma, 1973). Obviously, the relation between factionalism and social change is more complex than most authors indicate.

On the other hand, if factionalism is not always a *result of* changes, all factional conflict seems to be *about* changes in power changes, ideology, ways of doing things, and so on. Faction leaders seek to change or to protect threatened power balances or prestige ratings. Factional conflict would appear to be about attempts to change the normative concepts of who is boss, about which way of doing things is correct, about whose views will prevail, about whose ideas will be called 'normal' and 'right.' Factions compete about those persons who will dominate, and thus about those who will be able to impose their rules. It is this element which distinguishes politics from games. Politics seem always to be about those who will rule, and hence about those whose rules will prevail. Games are not about rules. Political competition, consequently, is never a game.

FACTIONS, SYMMETRY, AND BALANCED OPPOSITION

When factions are examined closely and with an open and enquiring mind they are usually found to be unlike in many ways. Far from being in balanced opposition, rival factions usually differ with respect to access to resources and strategy, internal organization, ideology, social composition, and symbolism.

Access to Resources and Strategy

Conflict groups often form in opposition to some pre-existing locus of authority and power in a community (cf. Bujra, 1973:138). The view that factions are coalitions competing for power changes in order to dominate their rivals helps to explain why they so often appear in pairs.[4] The distribution of power chances (resources) is by its nature dichotomous. Some have more, and some have less. One coalition is associated with the dominant power configuration in a community. This most often is focused on the headman, chief, mayor, wealthiest landlord, chairman, club president, parish priest, and the like. Ranged against this power bloc is a category of persons who are dissatisfied with the way they, who have superior power, wield it. Initially they may be merely disgruntled, but later they may organize themselves into a rival coalition (faction) to challenge or unseat those more powerful. Those who wield relatively more power are often referred to as the establishment; those who oppose them form an anti-establishment category: the opposition.[5]

The local establishment usually defends tradition and the *status quo*. The opposition faction attacks, seeking to unseat its rivals, who because they defend the established order, are regarded and often labelled as conservative. The opposition faction thus becomes the 'progressive' faction. There is a further reason why opposition factions are more often viewed, in local terms, as progressive. In their struggle to dominate their rivals, competing factions make use of various resources available to them to increase their power chances. In very slowly changing societies, these will be known and are, therefore, traditional resources. But in rapidly changing societies, new resources such as offices with development, commercial or political agencies, education, new laws, ideologies, and so on become available. These can also be used by competitors to increase their relative power.

The new resources tend to change the balance of power rapidly. Thus factions do not necessarily result from the availability of new resources, as Bailey seemed to suggest. Rather, new resources are used in ongoing competitions for power and prestige and tend to escalate them. This is also why some authors speak of 'conservative' and 'progressive' factions (for example, Nicholas, 1965 and Epstein, 1962, 1973). The use of new resources is not random; it is structured. A faction will make use of new resources when it becomes apparent that by doing so its position will be strengthened. It is then labelled progressive, in the sense of favouring change of the *status quo*. Thus Nicholas noted that the wealthy young entrepreneurs among the Iroquois seized upon the principle of elective leadership advocated by the larger American society to unseat the local establishment of hereditary chiefs. "... The political aspirations of socially successful and economically mobile individuals had, before 1924, been frustrated by hereditary government. For the progressives there was no course to political power other than changing the system" (1965:52).

Internal Organization

There is some evidence that conflict groups – whether faction, ritual moiety, or political party – differ organizationally. When the opposition consists merely of a category of persons jealous of or disgruntled with the local big shots, they are patently less well organized than the establishment. The organization of the establishment will consist of, at the least, a better developed exchange circuit (Thoden van Velzen, 1973). But if the conflict persists over time – for example, because it concerns an office such as headman or parish priest – it is quite likely that the opposition will become better organized than its rival. In Malta, opposition groups, whether parish factions or national political parties, were more tightly focussed around a single leader, were less prone to internal factionalism, and had a more clearly demarcated bureaucratic structure than their establishment rivals (Boissevain, 1974b:31–2; 38–9). Bailey has also noted that the smaller opposition parties were better organized than the larger dominant parties in Orissa (1968:xi; and personal communication).

It seems logical for opposition coalitions to concentrate more than their rivals upon certain organizational characteristics. One of the ways an opposition coalition can successfully compete with its stronger rival is to tend its internal housekeeping. It must fashion itself into an instrument which can successfully challenge its rival. It is thus more open than the establishment to organizational innovation such as creating an efficient bureaucracy, keeping records, stimulating grass roots growth, and so on. Furthermore, because of its superior position, based on a relative surplus of resources, an establishment coalition tends to be more wasteful in its organizational housekeeping. It does not need to administer (in the sense of husbanding) its resources to the extent that the opposition does.

Ideology, Social Composition, and Symbolism

Many authors have noted an apparent lack of ideological commitment in factional disputes (Siegel and Beals, 1966:127; Bailey and Nicholas, 1968:278). Bujra (1973:136) even raps Friedrich (1968) on the knuckles because he pointed to the ideological differences between the factions he studied. She accused him of confusing "class conflict" and "factionalism" (1973:138).

There are several good reasons why factions are not necessarily ideologically neutral. The dichotomies between establishment and opposition, and between conservative and progressive, are not random and have ideological implications. It is understandable why those who form part of the establishment local-power elite often hold conservative ideologies, and why their rivals are more radical. Bujra, for example, noted that it is in the interest of village headmen to give at least nominal support to the external political establishment. In India this is dominated by the Congress Party. Thus opposition factions usually support parties opposed to Congress (Bujra, 1973:138). These will usually be ideologically to the left, although occasionally they are to the right of the ruling regional party and thus of the dominant village faction. Nicholas also used his data on Govindapur to illustrate the ideological polarity that factional conflict brings about (1965:40). It could be argued that the consequence of this is a sort of 'tit for tat' alignment between the strongest village faction and the dominant (usually conservative) national political party, and between the weaker faction and the corresponding (usually radical) national party. Implicitly at work is the transactional principle, "the enemy of my enemy is my friend."

There is a further, more pregnant relation between faction and ideology. There is considerable evidence that opposition factions recruit more support than their rivals from weaker or even marginal social categories. The strength of a faction is often a function of its size. An opposition leader cannot afford to be too particular about the nature of his support if he is to topple his rival. Just as they often turn to new ideologies and techniques which are not always socially acceptable to their rivals, opposition leaders also recruit support from those who for various reasons are less influential or are regarded as social or moral inferiors. Supporters are supporters.

Turner, for example, describes how Sandombu, the aggressive opposition faction leader in Mukanza, recruited social outcasts to swell his following. These included a sorceror who had been banned from the village, a prostitute, and a juvenile delinquent. Epstein, too, has described how the leader of the progressive faction in Dalena protected a washerman, boycotted by his faction (conservative) for incurring ritual pollution, by striking a higher caste peasant who had been cuckolding him (1962:285 f.). In Malta, the opposition faction that formed after the middle of the last century to celebrate saints in competition with the established parish patron saints were largely composed of poor people, young persons, and others at the bottom of the social hierarchy. The economic class bias is still reflected in the ritual moiety-like conflict groups (*festa partiti*) that grew out of these factions: 83 percent of the professionals and white collar workers of Hal-Farrug, the village I studied closely in 1961, belonged to the establishment *festa partit* celebrating the parish patron, St. Leonard. In contrast, 62 percent of the farmers who were at the bottom of the social totem-pole were members of the opposition *partit* celebrating St. Joseph (the patron of the working classes) (Boissevain, 1965:74–96, 1974b). Thus it is not surprising that when Malta Labour Party became more firmly established, it received more support from opposition than from establishment *partiti*. Alavi, too, in re-analysing data provided by Nicholas (1965:45, Table 1) demonstrated a definite economic class bias in factions formed to contest an election in Govindapur (Alavi, 1973:49). The way in which factional leaders recruit support may be diverse, as Firth and Nicholas have argued, but it is not structurally random, as they suggest.

Having recruited socially weaker persons, it is understandable that an opposition leader reflects, develops in dialogue, or adopts an ideology and aligns himself with a political party that defends the interests of his supporters (or those whose leader he wishes to become), whether they be poor, women, children, of lower caste and so on. Moreover, given the disparate nature of those in opposition, a potential leader often must develop an over-arching ideology or symbol that will weld them into a unity. This is what appears to have happened one hundred years ago in Hal-Farrug. The new parish priest established a devotion to St. Joseph in order to unite anti-establishment elements against the clique of local big shots who had been running parish affairs, including the annual *festa* of the parish patron, under his predecessor (Boissevain, 1974b). Once an ideology or moral element has been introduced, it tends, in time, to become self-fulfilling. The leader must continue to express it or lose followers. Consequently, if the conflict groups persist – and many, for various reasons, do not – moral or ideological ties will probably be more important as linking elements between opposition leaders and followers than between their rivals (although much more systematic research must be done in this area). On the other hand, because leaders representing vested interests generally dispose of more resources, economic and political calculations are probably more prominent in the way they are linked to their supporters.

This difference in leader/follower linkages appears to be supported by further analysis of the Govindapur electoral factions already referred to. Of the relations between the voters for the dominant Congress party and their faction leaders, Nicholas has characterized no less than 74 percent of the party as economically or politically motivated (they are economically dependent, the leader is neighbourhood headman, the leader opposes mutual enemy). In contrast, 71 percent of the pro-Communist voters are linked to their faction leaders by ties of kinship and caste solidarity. These figures are set out in Table 1 below.

Finally, in many societies whose factions have become ritualized, like Maltese *festa partiti* and the more primitive dual organizations or moieties described, among others, by Lévi-Strauss (1956), dominant factions claim the most important symbols. Thus, in Malta, the symbols which are impor-

TABLE 1

Bases of Factional Alignment of Govindapur Voters

Basis of Support	Congress Voters	Communist Voters
Economic and Political	74	29
Kinship and Caste	26	71
Total %	100%	100%
Number	191	133

Sources: Nicholas, 1965:42, Table 1; Alavi, 1973:49, Table 1.

tant to the people of Hal-Farrug, for example, are aligned in a manner congruent with the strength of the rival *partiti*. These are as follows:

Establishment	Opposition
(St. Leonard)	(St Joseph)
• Titular Saint	• Secondary Saint
• Statue stands on right hand (Evangel) side of parish church	• Statue stands on left hand side of church
• Main altar dedicated to Saint	• Side altar dedicated to Saint
• Principal celebrating confraternity (Blessed Sacrament) walks last in procession (highest prestige)	• Principal celebrating confraternity (St. Joseph) walks first in procession (lowest prestige)
• *Partit* colour: red (most important liturgical colour)	• *Partit* colour: blue (colour unimportant liturgically)
• Representatives of all the parish confraternities carry statue in procession	• Only representatives of the St. Joseph confraternity carry statue in procession
• *Partit* symbol: star	• *Partit* symbol: eagle[6]

In short, it cannot be seriously sustained that conflict groups – whether village factions or political parties – are structurally symmetrical or in balanced opposition. Coalitions in conflict have been shown to differ in respect to (1) access to resources (the establishment faction represents the vested interests, the opposition, the underdogs); (2) strategy (the establishment defends the present order, the opposition attacks it, often by means of new techniques and resources which earn it a progressive label); (3) internal organization (opposition groups which persist over time are more tightly organized than their rivals); (4) ideology (factions representing establishment interests are more often conservative, and their opposition rivals more often progressive or radical); and (5) social composition and symbolism (relatively speaking, opposition coalitions contain socially weaker persons than establishment ones do, and 'own' less favoured social and ritual symbols).

Why the obvious asymmetry of conflict groups should have escaped the theoretical attention of two generations of social anthropologists is an interesting question. Twenty years ago Levi-Strauss also argued that moieties or dual organizations, long characterized as both static and symmetrical, were in fact dynamic and asymmetrical. His explanation of the reason they were mistakenly characterized this way is so relevant to the question just posed and to the foregoing analysis, that I quote him *in extenso*:

> "... I have tried to show that the study of so-called dual organizations discloses so many anomalies and contradictions in relation to extant theory that we should be well advised to reject the theory and to treat the apparent manifestations of dualism as superficial distortions of structures whose real nature is quite different and vastly more complex. Yet these anomalies in no way escaped the attention of Rivers and his school – the originators of the dualist theory. They were not perturbed by them because they saw dual organizations (on the basis of the anomalies) as the historical result of the fusion of two populations differing in race, in culture, or simply in power. In such a formulation, the social structures considered could be both dual and asymmetrical at the same time – and indeed they had to be.
>
> First Marcel Mauss, then Radcliffe-Brown and Malinowski, revolutionized anthropological theory by substituting a socio-psychological interpretation, based on the concept of reciprocity, for the historical interpretation. But as schools grew up around these masters, *asymmetrical phenomena faded into the background, since they were not easily integrated into the new perspective*. The inequality of the moieties came to be treated as an irregularity of the system. And – much more serious – *the striking anomalies that were discovered later were completely neglected*. As often happened in the history of science an essential property of an object was first taken by researchers to be a special case; later on, scientists were afraid to jeopardize their conclusions by submitting them to more rigorous proof" (1956/68:161–2; my emphasis).

CONCLUSION

If factionalism is not necessarily a product of social change, it appears always to be about change, for factions are groups that compete for power to determine, and thus to change, what is to be accepted as normal. Because they have different access to power chances, rival factions are not evenly matched, structurally similar groups. Their structural asymmetry is fundamental to understanding the nature of their rivalry.

Structural asymmetry and competition for power to effect change are also attributes of class-based conflict groups. This suggests that the line of cleavage between conflict groups – whether faction, class, or party – cuts across moral categories and socio-economic classes, not at right angles, as most functionalists and many marxists postulate, but diagonally. Where the line approaches the vertical, forming conflicting coalitions with a reasonably even spread across socio-economic classes, it is reasonable to speak of factionalism (in the case of face-to-face groups) and party conflict (in the case of conflict on a broader scale). Where the line of cleavage approaches the horizontal, forming conflict groups that are more clearly differentiated according to socio-economic criteria, the term class conflict seems appropriate. But the axis of cleavage in every case must be determined by empirical investigation. It should not be assumed. I suggest this axis will always be found to be diagonal, and that symmetrical coalitions and pure class conflict groups are the product of wishful scientific and/or political thinking. To argue about whether rival coalitions are engaged in factional, party or class conflict is ultimately sterile and can lead to such politically and scientifically naive statements as "Faction leaders like Wilson and Heath only play games for marbles." Rigid classification usually results in pigeon-holing in the course of which important attributes are ignored in the interest of a tidy decision.

This, of course, leads to a sense of bafflement when it is discovered that one of the players has run away with all the marbles.

Family, faction, party and class conflict, rebellions, revolutions, and other uprisings always appear to be about who is to decide what is normal. All are thus sub-species of the genus conflict. That they consequently share structural characteristics is not surprising. These common attributes include the fact that competing units differ in respect to access to economic and social resources, strategy, internal organization, ideology, social composition, and symbolism. The degree to which structural attributes are similar and different varies, consequently, as does the scale of changes which the competitors seek to introduce or prevent and their ability to do so. We can only increase our understanding of social conflict if we abandon dogmatic categorizations and begin to examine seriously the real similarities and differences of conflict groups and the conditions affecting these.

NOTES

1 The first draft of this paper was prepared while I was a visiting fellow at the Institute of Development Studies, University of Sussex, in March 1975. Various versions were discussed at the University of Sussex in March 1975, at a conference on "The Anthropological Study of Factional Politics" organized by York University at Orillia, Ontario in April, 1975, at seminars at the State University of New York, Binghamton in April, 1975, and at the University of Stockholm in October, 1975. I am most grateful to the many discussants, and especially to Jojada Verrips and Roderick Aya, for trying to help me clarify what I wish to say.

2 Alavi criticizes many of these assumptions. But he, in turn, assumes a continuum at one end of which are factions that "are structurally similar" (1973:44), thus meeting the above criteria, and at the other end of which are groups in conflict containing elements of class conflict. He examines only the latter in detail. I disagree with him only in that I reject the notion of structurally similar conflict groups.

3 'Accepted' and 'normal' are used advisedly. I do not wish to suggest a necessary consensual notion of legitimacy. Norms may be and very often are imposed upon a weaker party. They are accepted not because they are viewed as correct or just, but because there is force behind them. "*Chi commanda fa la legge*." "Might is right." "Justice comes out of the barrel of a gun." "To disobey the natural law of the word of God is to risk eternal damnation." These are statements about acceptance of action that is defined by the dominant party as lawful, right, and just. Leaders of conflicting groups compete to be able to define the norms – hence to effect changes.
4 For further discussion of the reason why conflicting coalitions are often paired, see Caplow, 1968.
5 Thoden van Velzen (1973) talks about the "interest" coalitions of local elite and government experts in Tanzanian villages and the "levelling" coalitions of anti-establishment elements who combine periodically to attack the resources of the elite and try to pull them down to their level.
6 The relative prestige of these two symbols is set out neatly in the couplet often declaimed by St. Leonard supporters during the feast of St. Joseph, and during the secondary feasts in other parishes (most have the eagle as their symbol):

"It is true that the eagle soars high;
But it will never reach the star."

REFERENCES

ALAVI, H.
1973 "Peasant Classes and Primordial Loyalties." *Journal of Peasant Studies*, 1:23–62.
BAILEY, F. G.
1957 *Caste and Economic Frontier*. Manchester, Manchester University Press.
BAILEY, F. G.
1968 "Parapolitical Systems." In M. J. Swartz (ed.), *Local Level Politics*. Chicago, Aldine.
BAILEY, F. G.
1969 *Strategems and Spoils*. Oxford, Basil Blackwell.
BAILEY, F. G. and RALPH W. NICHOLAS
1968 "Introduction to Part Four." In M. J. Swartz (ed.), *Local Level Politics*. Chicago, Aldine.
BOISSEVAIN, J.
1964 "Factions, Parties and Politics in a Maltese Village." *American Anthropologist*, 66:1275–87.
BOISSEVAIN, J.
1965 *Saints and Fireworks: Religion and Politics in Rural Malta*. London, Athlone.
BOISSEVAIN, J.
1969 *Hal-Farrug: A Village in Malta*. New York, Holt, Rinehart and Winston.
BOISSEVAIN, J.
1974a *Friends of Friends: Networks, Manipulators and Coalitions*. Oxford, Basil Blackwell.
BOISSEVAIN, J.
1974b "Conflict and Change: Establishment and Opposition in Malta." In John Davis (ed.), *Choice and Change: Essays in Honour of Lucy Mair*. London, Athlone.
BUJRA, JANET
1973 "The Dynamics of Political Action: A New Look at Factionalism." *American Anthropologist*, 75(1):132–52.

Caplow, Theodore
1968 *Two Against One: Coalitions in Triads*. Englewood Cliffs, N.J., Prentice Hall.
Epstein, T. S.
1962 *Economic Development and Social Change in South India*. Manchester, Manchester University Press.
Epstein, T. S.
1973 *South India: Yesterday, Today and Tomorrow: Mysore Villages Revisited*. London, Macmillan.
Firth, R.
1957 "Introduction: Factions in Indian and Overseas Indian Societies." *British Journal of Sociology*, 8:291–95.
Friedrich, Paul
1968 "The Legitimacy of the Cacique." In M. J. Swartz (ed.), *Local Level Politics*. Chicago, Aldine.
Gouldner, A.
1960 "The Norm of Reciprocity: A Preliminary Statement." *American Sociological Review*, 25(2):161–78.
Levi-Strauss, Claude
1956 "Les Organisations Dualistes Existent-Elles? *Bijdragen tot de taal-, land- en Volkenkunde*, 112:99–128.
Maybury-Lewis, David
1967 *Akwe-Shavante Society*. Oxford, Clarendon Press.
Nicholas, Ralph W.
1965 "Factions: A Comparative Analysis." In M. Banton (ed.), *Political Systems and the Distribution of Power*. ASA Monographs 2, London, Tavistock.
Sharma, Hari
1973 "Green Revolution in India: A Prelude to a Red One? In Kathleen Gough and Hari Sharma (eds.), *Imperialism and Revolution in South Asia*. New York, Monthly Review Press.
Siegel, Bernard J. and Alan R. Beals
1960 "Pervasive Factionalism." *American Anthropologist*, 62:394–417.
Siegel, Bernard J. and Alan R. Beals
1966 *Divisiveness and Social Conflict: An Anthropological Approach*. Stanford, Stanford University Press.
Turner, V. W.
1957 *Schism and Continuity in an African Society*. Manchester, Manchester University Press.
Van Velzen, H. U. E. T.
1973 "Coalitions and Network Analysis." In J. Boissevain and J. C. Mitchell (eds.), *Network Analysis: Studies in Human Interaction*. The Hague, Mouton.

Transactional Politics: Factions and Beyond

6

Richard F. Salisbury

When a theorist first clearly defines a new concept that has emerged vaguely in earlier empirical work, the usual reaction of other theorists is to elaborate the concept, to describe variant sub-types, and to proceed with what Leach (1962) called "butterfly collecting." When Nicholas (1965) defined what distinguished *factions* as units in political conflict, this process did not occur. No great consideration was given to documenting the variety of factional forms or processes, or to constructing typologies of factions on the basis of induction from empirical cases. Such study is still needed, but the decade 1965–1975 has seen the emergence within anthropology of a more general approach to politics that may be called *transactional politics*. This approach is sufficiently productive to permit one to derive hypothetical typologies of factions and factional processes from it, by deduction. The present paper attempts to develop such a typology, to compare it with some empirical data, and to suggest where future research studies could be profitably directed.

Transactional politics is the study of how individuals, within particular institutional systems, exercise political power through transactional behaviour which may be described as the transmission of goods and services by leaders in exchange for acceptance of their power by supporters who grant them authority. Factions, by Nicholas' definition, are *ad hoc* political groupings, linked to a leader in relation to specific conflict issues, that is, in terms of what followers can obtain through the leader's action. They are thus special groupings that emerge in transactional politics, despite the individualistic basis of transactions.

However, this general definition leads us to ask other questions of factions. How do different institutional contexts affect the nature of factions and factionalism? Are there particular institutional environments within which politics tend to take a factional form? How does the wider availability of goods and services affect the strategies of leaders, and the responses to them of potential followers? How does the value of the support of different followers vary, and how does this variation affect the behaviour of leaders? While many other questions also come to mind, these few provide the basis for our abstract analysis of the game of factioning, for a consideration of some variations in it, and for some added understanding of the ethnography of factionalism.

Factions and Corporateness

All definitions of factions agree that they are political groupings that are not corporate. But this does not mean that the societies within which factions occur are devoid of corporate groups, or that those corporate groups do not affect the factions. I would go so far as to assert that factional groupings always emerge within the framework of a wider 'political community' that is corporate – a nation state, a village, a commune, or a tribe – and that although the factions may be composed of leaders and individual supporters, those supporters are commonly members of smaller corporate groupings, such as households. Does the nature of the circumscribing corporate groups (CCG) affect the nature of factons? Does it matter whether the members of factions are single individuals, or representatives of smaller corporations?

Bailey (1969) sees the pursuit of "offices" as the aim of politics. The concept of an office, however, implies that there be some corporate entity which provides resources to the office and whose members recognize the office. In defining what those offices are, and in setting limits on the means that may be used to attain those offices, the CCG provides the parameters within which factional competition occurs. As Bailey and others have noted, however, factionalism is rarely, if ever, normatively prescribed as a means of political action; it emerges as a pragmatically productive "strategy" (Salisbury, 1968) that can be described (or what Bailey [1969] would term "a pragmatic rule"), and derived from the parametric conditions of the cultural rules of the CCG. The question to answer is what characteristics of the CCG produce and affect the nature of the emerging factions.

At the same time, it must be recognized that factions are not the only type of competing group which may be engaged in trying to obtain an office for its leaders, and by derivation, benefits for its supporting members. The competing groups may well have a corporate identity. For example, in New Guinea the corporate groups such as clans, landowning lineages, or village groups, who now compete for elected offices in the local councils or national legislature (Bettison, Hughes and van der Veur, 1965) are the same groups who competed for prestige, pigs, and valuables in earlier times. "Big man" techniques of gaining support through transactions have continued to be used by leaders within those corporate groups. The New Guinea groups, which will be returned to later, provide a graphic example of the meshing of factional and corporate group politics, and of changes over time in the balance of one against the other. For the present we should merely note that factions and corporate groups are alternative types of political grouping in supposedly tribal societies.

In peasant societies, particularly in the best reported areas of South Asia (Nicholas, 1965; Bailey, 1960; Islam, 1974; Attwood, 1974a; and others), it is often hard to distinguish from the given descriptions whether the politically active group (Islam uses the Bengali term *dal* and Bailey talks of *dolidoli*) is a corporate lineage, or sub-caste group, or an *ad hoc* factional grouping under a leader with a nuclear cluster of members of a corporate group. Characteristics of both types of grouping can be discerned. In studies of Lebanese village factionalism in the 1950s (Ayoub, 1955), Christian, Moslem and Druse factions were reported alongside factions recognized as surname groups. The Hatfields and McCoys are legendary in the United States, as the Montagues and Capulets are in Verona. The lineages had clear corporate identities even if their boundaries were not clear. In modern Malta Boissevain (1965) explicitly showed how the competition for offices may be between factions, or between corporate political parties – again with unclear demarcation. Frankenberg (1957), without using the factionalist idiom, showed how manoeuvring for power in a Welsh village involved organized corporate groupings such as football clubs or church groups in some contexts, and non-corporate groupings in others. The question becomes widened. Do characteristics of the CCG similarly affect both corporate and non-corporate competing groupings? Does the nature of the CCG affect the probability of factionalism occurring at all?

A first characteristic of CCG's to be considered is their degree of multifunctionality, since transactional propositions can be derived from this multifunctionality.

Many studies of factionalism are of single villages, as are those of Silverman (1973) and Islam (1969), in which the village is treated as a corporate administrative unit by the bureaucratic structure of the surrounding nation-state; although many types of sub-units are recognized by the local people, they are predominantly ignored by the nation-state. The village is also a significant unit for various other activities of a religious, economic, and recreational nature, to mention but a few. Benefits defined as flowing from the nation-state to 'the village' predominantly flow through the office of village representative (or council president), whether these benefits relate to subsidies for irrigation, education at government schools, or prestigious offices in religious assemblies. The primary axis of factionalism is therefore the competition between aspirants for the office of village representative to the nation-state. Though the same individual may not be the representative in every activity, the faction that has control of the major office is in a position to obtain control of all offices. Since the government recognizes only the village unit, there is no legal way for individuals to obtain access to benefits from government, except through factional competition. Short-circuiting this competition by personal appeals to higher authorities is common, but theoretically illegitimate.

Once in power (and assuming that no parameter changes occur), the faction with control over benefits from the nation-state has the means to retain power indefinitely through transactions. It can distribute patronage to enough individuals to give itself majority support. A majority faction has almost absolute power, subject largely to the readiness of the CCG to intervene. It may be called on to intervene should the majority seek to eliminate its minority (something of which anglophone Quebeckers became aware at the moment when the Prime Minister refused to extend them protection in linguistic matters at the provincial level; yet Canadian Indians had long been aware of how a federal CCG protected them in conflicts with non-Indian neighbours). The minority can also seek CCG intervention should the majority faction become too blatant in its exercise of patronage.

The multifunctional CCG, I argue, tends to produce a dualistic set of opposing sub-groupings – the powerful in-group and the weak out-group – with a relatively permanent in-group or establishment and an opposition out-group which may appear and disappear. Within such a system it also makes a great difference (in theory at least) whether there exist sub-groupings that are corporate. Southwold (1968) has analysed in game theory terms what happened with corporate sub-groupings in Uganda before 1901. Division among the in-group of the benefits of winning provided less to each winner if the in-group comprised much more than 50 percent of the population, whereas less goods could be extracted from the losing minority if the minority was a small one. What occurred were coalitions of corporate groupings that exceeded 50 percent of the population by only a small margin, and that tried to placate losers after any confrontation. The visibility and relative fixity of corporate sub-units meant that the margin necessary for insurance against miscalculation could remain small.

In factional recruitment, however, the major threat to the leader of the establishment faction is not from a visible opposition but from the secret seduction of individual supporters within his own faction. Both Bailey and Nicholas (1968) have observed that where a single caste group constitutes a majority in an Indian village, factional competition tends to be entirely between members of that caste group. I would derive this empirical finding from the more general multifunctional corporateness of village units, rather than from demographic composition.

If a rival within a faction can divert a significant portion of the benefits that come from the nation-state to the corporate village to his own sub-group within the main faction, and can also secretly gain the support of the opposition, he may well achieve an overall majority within the village. Once a majority has been achieved on one occasion, power is likely to remain with the new faction, and its leader is likely to switch from the majority faction, even if his immediate supporters constitute a minority of the faction. He can always threaten to rejoin the old majority faction, and is the most likely leader to seduce more supporters from the old majority faction; this no other opposition leader of dissenting supporters can do. He has power over the swing-voters, and this is decisive.

If the above is a valid analysis of how factional politics differ from corporate group coalition politics, it has implications for the size of majority factions in apparently stable factional situations. If the majority faction numbered only 51 per cent, a sub-group leader with only one-thirtieth of the faction behind him could swing the balance by defecting to the opposition. If the major faction were 66.7 percent of the total active population, then the defection of one quarter of it would be needed to produce a swing. Although security against all rivals is impossible to guarantee, a faction size in the range of 66 percent would be needed to provide a majority leader with an effective compromise of security with manageability.

A second implication of this analysis – one that has been incidentally indicated and implied by the description of dualistic sub-groupings – is that when the CCG is multifunctional, there is little possibility for an individual to stand aloof from factional disputes. To do so would mean getting none of the benefits of faction membership; the majority leader is little interested in buying individual votes: a non-supporter of the majority faction would become branded as a 'dissenter' and a member of the opposition, willy nilly. The dominant faction may, in many cases, be the only active faction, with the 'dissenters' forming a faction only in the perception of the dominants, and in reality not combining for action nor having a leader. Even so, their potential emergence as a faction, should an appropriate conflict situation develop, is a major factor structuring the behaviour of the dominant faction and its leader. In this sense, everyone is involved in the factional politics of this kind of CCG.

By contrast other types of CCG are illustrated in the works of several contributors to this volume (Schryer, 1974; Attwood, 1974a; Nagata, 1970). The nation-state may provide the only single circumscribing group for all purposes, and for most specific purposes or specific decisions, there may exist a multitude of intermediate groupings, each of which is looked to by different people at the village level for specific decisions. Each specific grouping provides an arena for a distinct factional game. The various games inevitably are interrelated, as both leaders and followers can each bargain independently for support or benefits in one arena in exchange for benefits or support in a different arena. Inevitably there is some tendency for alignments in every arena to parallel the alignments in the arena where the largest volume of benefits are obtainable – the national political level in most cases – but many degrees of freedom exist. Most strikingly the role of the 'independent' is necessarily tolerated, and may become critical in such situations. In any one arena no faction necessarily comprises a majority of participants, and decisions may be made by a minority, often depending on the acquiescence (or at least the non-opposition) of a category of 'solid citizens' – an undistributed middle.

The presence of an undistributed middle provides a role for two kinds of factional leadership. In one direction a leader who appeals to the moral feelings of uncommitted solid citizens has the opportunity to cast himself in the role of community leader. Bailey (1972) has called this the role of *Tertius Numen*, otherwise known to television viewers as *Mr. Clean*, the fighter of corruption. In another direction, where the undistributed middle has previously been politically inactive, the self-appointed spokesman for grass-roots sentiment takes the role which Attwood (1974b) has termed the *group mobilizer*.

The result is an open set of factional games marked by much individual shifting of support, and much wheeling and dealing by leaders active in different areas. Schryer (this vol.) describes such a situation in Mexico where municipios, regions, hamlets, the national PRI party, trade, ranching, and religion provide the different arenas. Oppositions appeared multiple and changing. It is noteworthy that such an open situation also provided the possibility of a united front emerging among competing factional leaders, when non-participants in the factional situation appeared likely to enter the fray – the merchants or even the village peasants. Factionalism could lead to class-solidarities among an elite.

Attwood (1974b; also this vol.) indicates what could happen when there is a multitude of CCGs, each with a different function: state, municipal, and regional administrative units, each with an elected political representative, as well as a series of irrigation and sugar factory cooperatives, religious groupings, caste groupings, school groupings, and charismatic (quasi-political) movements. No grouping at any time has exclusive control of a majority of the benefits, and at any one moment any individual has a choice of several factions he can ally himself with (or, indeed, refrain from alliance). Although Attwood (1974b) shows how the situation he observed put power in the hands of supporters (via their mobilizers), this does not mean that such a situation always locates power at the grass-roots level, rather than in the hands of an elite. It does suggest that under these conditions an open market situation occurs, in which authority and benefits are openly exchanged.

Theoretically, in an open market situation, the rate of exchange between support and benefits should reach an equilibrium, if undistorted by monopolistic pressures from either side. In other words, where multiple CCGs exist, each unifunctional, and where monopolistic pressures are minimal, the exchange rate between support and benefits will depend on the balance of supply and demand – on the volume of benefits provided by the CCGs and the number of supporters available (and needed). Leaders will be effectively controlled by their supporters who will receive benefits from the leadership. But these quantitative aspects of factionalism are the concern of our next section; let us return to corporateness.

We have, at the minimum, established two polar types – factions within multifunctional CCGs which approach a predictable pattern of dualistic opposition, and factions within widely embracing CCGs that may be either specialized or distant, and where the opposition between factions and their patterns of recruitment are those of the multiple distributive oppositions found in a market system. Whether there are other relationships with other types of CCGs remains an open question.

Corporate Groups within Factions

Though Nicholas defined factions as non-corporate groupings, it is clear that in reality all factions are more than purely *ad hoc* alliances of individuals who have no ties outside the factional relationship. As Mayer (1966) and others indicate most factions have a "core" of individuals who have close multiplex relations with the faction leader (and often among themselves), and around this core the bulk of the supporters constellate. The core is quite often a major segment of a corporate group: a caste group, a lineage, a religious group, and so on. In the local folk model of factions it is common for such groups to be referred to as though the faction actually *was* the corporate group to which its core belongs even though this is not the case. I would venture to suggest that if many of the studies of local politics of the 1940s and 1950s were re-analysed in a modern idiom, it would be found that much of what was analysed as "descent group" politics in Africa could be interpreted equally well as factional politics. Where oppositions are described emically as being "between descent groups," they could often be better analysed etically as being between the factional followings of individual leaders. Evans-Pritchard (1940) indicates for the Nuer, for example, how the "descent group" idiom that is used by local people to describe political oppositions masks a much more complex process in which local headmen or "bulls" recruit followings. By contrast, in the study of New Guinea politics, the recruitment of followings by individual "big men" has often been emphasized (see for example, Sahlins, 1964) without adequate recognition being given to the degree of corporateness within the groupings which they then lead (cf. Salisbury, 1964).

In accordance with our initial definition, we concern ourselves in transactional politics with the non-corporate groupings – the factions. But, as indicated, the relationship of factions to corporate political pressure groups is of major concern. Let us look at the advantages and disadvantages of the two types of grouping, for both the leader and the followers. For the leader a corporate following gives him defined obligations towards his followers, but an assurance of free rein and unqualified support in negotiations outside the corporate group (provided, that is, he can live up to his internal obligations). A following that has been recruited transactionally may give the leader less general and more easily fulfilled obligations to his followers, but it also means that his freedom to commit those followers in a conflictual situation outside the faction is unpredictable. For the supporters the immediate transactional benefits may be high, and the immediate cost of obligations to support may appear low; but there is always the possibility that if the leader succeeds, he may desert his erstwhile supporters, whereas if he fails, nothing will accrue to the supporters in any case. In New Guinea the successful leader gets advantages of both kinds. Traditional (Salisbury, 1964; Strathern, 1971:223ff) and modern "big men" (Finney, 1973; Salisbury, 1969) who are successful in their external negotiations can exert almost despotic power over members of their support group. It tends to appear as a corporate unit. For the supporter, again, the demands of the leader are known and the rewards from a successful leader predictable (and high if he lives up to his obligations). The relationship of leader to followers is likely to be strong enough to persist should there be one or two examples of failure, by one side or the other, to live up to defined obligations.

Both leader-follower relations also contrast with the pattern described by Banfield (1958) for Montegrano in Southern Italy, and called by him "amoral familism." One may doubt the empirical validity of Banfield's description (cf. S. Silverman, 1968), but his abstract model may be analysed regardless. It is of a situation where each family unit is so suspicious of any other party exploiting them, should they join to form a faction or enterprise of any kind, that no larger groupings ever cohere. The result is that none of the benefits from wide-scale collaboration ever are produced, and everybody suffers.

In the three-fold contrast of no groupings/*ad hoc* groupings/corporate groupings, factions appear as the middle term – a compromise between the predictable benefits to be obtained from wider-scale collaboration and the unpredictable costs and dangers of exploitation by other parties should long-term relationships develop.

We would expect to find empirically, in any situation of transactional politics, a fluctuating balance. To the extent that major additional benefits accrue from organized group activities, the entropy of interpersonal suspicions will be overcome and groupings will persist; as leaders see external benefits regularly obtainable by entrepreneurial action on the part of their faction, they will try to incorporate their support group to stabilize it, and to make predictable the claims of the followers for a share in the benefits; supporters will also attempt to stabilize and incorporate a group which gives them important benefits in an attempt to control the leader. Against this centripetal tendency are centrifugal forces leading to either no groups, or to *ad hoc* groupings only. These forces include both overall quantitative factors: no benefits resulting from combined action, or benefits received which are lower than those obtained otherwise; and internal conflict factors: dissatisfaction by either leaders or supporters with what they receive from the other party, making them suspect exploitation.

Many variations are possible within this three-category dimension of corporateness of factions. It is clear that a wider study would amplify the range, and would test the value of these theoretical predictions.

The Resource Parameter

This parameter – the nature and quantity of resources which are allocated as a result of factional competition – is one where change can be easily seen. Silverman's study of Guyana (1973), and Attwood's (1974a) study of Maharashtra both sought to show how factional struggles changed when the resources available for allocation by political means also changed. Empirically, of course, the nature of CCGs (most commonly, the degree of involvement in local affairs of the nation state, colonial administration, or large business enterprises) has also changed in any local area studied. It is only analytically, or through the construction of models, that one can separate the effect of resource change from that of a changing political structure. In the sections on corporate groupings we left implicit the assumption that resource availability does not change; in the present section we make explicit that our model construction has to be understood in terms of the unchangeable nature of the CCG.

To characterize leader-follower attitudes to resources and positively desired benefits, I would reverse an old saying: "Enough is enough, but enough is too little." A continuation of the same amount of benefits is recognized as satisfactory, but always leaves the lingering suspicion that through change, a larger amount of benefits could be obtained. (Parenthetically the original saying "enough is enough, and enough is too much" applies to negatively valued acts, so that for positively valued resources, the apparently reversed expression actually has the same meaning). In other words, in real human society the degree of satisfaction is likely to depend more on the *rate of change of benefits received*, than on the *absolute volume* of benefits. We can theoretically envisage four main types of changing rates of benefits: rising, falling, stable, or oscillating volumes of benefits. We could further subdivide each of these types in terms of how long they have been offered, of whether they follow a different pattern, and of whether people anticipate the continuation of these benefits. More generally I would subsume all these latter considerations under the heading of how predictable the current pattern is. And as soon as one talks of predictability, one must clearly include the degree to which the action of the predictor can affect the likelihood of the prediction coming true. There are infinite variations in the rate of change and of predictability of resources available for distribution through factional competition, and each variation could affect factionalism distinctively.

Within such a range one can, however, make some theoretical hypotheses. Easiest are the hypotheses having to do with predictability and stability – conditions which would generally be expected to promote a long-term stability of distribution according to standard terms of exchange. That is, under stable and rising conditions of resource availability, distribution tends to be through corporate groups, within which further distribution tends to be standardized by permanent relationships between leaders and followers. *A priori*, one would expect factionalism to emerge either when an unpredictable increase occurred in distributable benefits and competition ensued over who would receive the benefits, or when unpredictable decreases in distributable benefits made some people band together to ensure that they did not suffer. Oscillation, or unstable variation in rates of increase, presents situations where no *a priori* hypotheses seem immediately evident.

The empirical evidence does contain several findings that can be fitted within this general framework. Silverman (1973) reports a period of factional peace (or, alternatively, a time when aspirant competitors found it better to support a single leader and to emphasize village corporateness) at a time when resources for distribution through the corporate village were rapidly increasing. Attwood (1974a) also reports that at a time when increases in income from sugar were being created by efficient management of the sugar factory, rather than by manipulations of quotas and the like, factional strife did not occur in that arena.

On the other hand although steady increases in available resources may have made factionalism irrelevant in one arena in Attwood's study, it did not eliminate faction in all arenas. Given a situation of multiple CCGs, the switch from factionalism to stable allocation as a means of distributing benefits within one CCG has little effect on other CCGs. The overall impression given by many studies in which there has been a major increase in the volume of resources available to the local community through political channels is that factionalism (together with other processes of transactional politics such as patronage, coalitions, and others), *expands* its scope proportionately with their resources. Even if the corporateness of the main CCG is stabilized, factionalism becomes an important process for benefit allocation *between* subgroupings and on issues of a more personal kind, during a time of expansion.

These two divergent empirical findings are reconcilable if one assumes that a *long-term* increase of resources allocated by a CCG will decrease the incidence of major internal conflicts (until the increase slows and competition emerges); however, short-term increases requiring distribution by smaller sub-groups provoke the emergence of factionalism. The factional sub-groups become functionally specialized, and then further encourage the emergence of multiple-opposition 'open market' factionalism.

Factional behaviour within situations of oscillating or declining availability of resources for transactional political distribution is less commonly described. Yet it is likely that this is the state of resources in the traditional, apparently stagnant societies which Siegel and Beals (1960) considered as showing "pervasive factionalism." Whereas they saw pervasive factionalism as the reason for the communities not combining for progressive improvement, the present analysis would suggest that causation went in the opposite direction. It is true that the existence of factionalism in the Siegel and Beals cases meant that the new resources introduced by change agents went to one faction only, and still further polarized existing splits. But a longer term view would see these newly introduced resources as just another phase in an oscillating pattern, of resources available at one moment but likely to be unpredictably few a little later. Each infusion of resources and each withdrawal over a long period created a succession of conflict situations, as to who was to benefit and who to be discriminated against. Yet the situations were not predictable or similar enough for the emergence of institutionalized relationships and rules. This (though without supporting empirical evidence) I would interpret as a common situation in traditional societies with pervasive factionalism.

This comment underlines the need to consider the resource situation as it is perceived by the local people, and not merely as viewed etically by outsiders. Change agents are seen as indicative of a new era by outsiders, but until the input of resources from a change agent has exceeded all previous inputs and until it has lasted longer than any previous increase, the change agent will be seen by local people as just another unpredictable oscillation. He will be followed, people assume, by a predictable oscillation downwards, so that everyone will strive for his own short-term gains in sharing the new inputs. The expected result would be a sharing out among the established powerful faction and a blunting of change, or, if the change agent tried to benefit the 'dissenters,' a rejection of his work by the in-group who sabotage his work.

But if this oscillating or declining pattern of change in resources has been less explicitly related to types of factionalism, there is all the more need for closer analysis of new cases, along with others of the infinite variety of potential patterns.

Internal Resource Availability

Empirically one must note that factions are always reported as involving the grouping of people with heterogeneous resources – minimally, the different resources of leadership abilities and physical strength. One might postulate that unless there is heterogeneity of resources there is no reason for a grouping to emerge, and no basis for any transaction between the participants. In practice the resources that are most commonly discussed as provided by followers are the potential for physical support in a fight, emotional support by presence at a time of strain, or electoral support through a vote; and as provided by leaders, the contacts with high-status outsiders which can lead to an inflow of benefits to the local community. In short, transactional politics emerge mainly in a context of stratification, although the stratification may involve local people versus party members or *cadres* with external contacts just as much as peasants versus landowners. Factions rely for their internal solidarity on exchangeable resources; they rely for their emergence on the existence of situations of conflict wherein a single winner can result, and wherein his success depends on the size of his support group.

Though this may be the simplest type of factional situation and one that can be seen as a model, even this model is far from a simple one. Outside contacts differ in quality as well as quantity. Even the value of individuals in a one-person-one-vote situation differs because some will advertise their vote and others will not; some will turn up, and others may be unreliable.

More complex, but theoretically more challenging is the situation where a variety of resources exist *within* a community which could potentially be grouped together to produce a sum greater than the parts – where, say, construction skills could be combined with local finance and with established contacts with outside religious bodies to build and staff local schools. In such circumstances the efficacy of a faction in a conflict situation does not depend on numbers alone, but on the effectiveness and appropriateness of selective recruitment for the particular question at issue. On the one hand this condition theoretically makes for less permanent factions, since each issue ideally demands a different factional composition; it opens matters up for greater bargaining by different individuals who see their position as more or less critical in particular conflicts, and thus should tend to produce more 'open-market' factionalism. On the other hand it tends to concentrate power in the hands of those with the scarcest but most generally relevant resource – the entrepreneurial ability to organize other people. In terms of Pareto's circulation of élites, this is a time for foxes.

The introduction of universal secret-ballot suffrage by a nation-state is one change that, as many studies show, produces a most dramatic restructuring of factional struggles which earlier were confined to an élite, or were simply dualistic. It reduces to a minimum the differences between individual supporters as resources in the struggle for the main CCG offices, at the same time as it increases the importance of external links which an office-holder develops. But then complexity (in all the cases reported) reasserts itself. Differential resources held by individuals (especially such resources as literacy, accounting skills, access to information, or organizational ability) become more significant. As suggested the composing of factions (and factional slates) to achieve a balance of different internal resources becomes a very important skill. It presages the role of the party organizer, if factions incorporate as parties. Uneven internal resource distribution, in short, is a condition for factions to exist, as well as something which factions perpetuate by their nature.

What happens if all resources are equalized in a socialist system? If our earlier analysis is correct, factions initially disappear. If previous owners of resources – middle peasants, for example – attempt to gain support from a section of the proletariat, they find this impossible in a situation where class consciousness has been fully aroused. Schryer (1974), Attwood (1974a) and Islam (1973) all give examples of initial egalitarian euphoria and freedom from factions when earlier class or ethnic privileges were abolished. But in none of these cases did a fully egalitarian system emerge. If previous differences based on private property did not reassert themselves in their previous form, the existence of a nation-state itself produced differences in access to the benefits provided by the nation-state. Factions supported brokers who promised access to these benefits, and competition between factions reemerged in practice, if unrecognized in ideology. Behavioural studies are needed of the way conflicts over the allocation of external inputs of resources into socialist communities are resolved. Do official, institutional ways always cope? Or, as Frank (1958) found when examining the way Russian managers coped with the problem of maintaining their positions (and support from their workers) in the face of irreconcilable demands and persistent shortages, are officially unsanctioned entrepreneurial techniques utilized? To complete the range of studies of variations in internal resource availability, we also need studies of perfect equality.

The Ethnography of Factions

The preceding sections have considered only two main dimensions of variation in the social and resource environment, but in them, I have tried to indicate how variations in the forms of factionalism may be seen as dependent on these variations. The same analysis has implied that a dynamic process is involved: that changes in the social and resource environment produce changes in the factions themselves as a result of differential individual reactions to those changes.

A variety of characteristics of factions have been described. Although these have been analysed as though they were dependent variables, in other frameworks of analysis, they could constitute the major foci of study or the independent variables, and a major task could have been to set up typologies of factions. Though this paper does not take that approach, its attempt to show how factionalism can take many varied forms leads one to suggest that more detailed ethnography is needed, documenting variation in factionalism as well as its common elements.

Knowledge of the number of factions involved is clearly critical to an understanding of the tactics used by factionalists. Yet it is easy to accept crude folk-models which report merely "X's group, and Y's group," but difficult to get at the reality of how people actually align themselves, and of whether (particularly in the past) there were issues which inspired other groupings to form. Both folk-models and actual behaviour need description, for both affect the decisions people make.

So too is the factional situation critically different if community members are able to ignore factional disputes and not align themselves if they do not wish to do so. What proportion of the community is involved in the factionalism? And for what reasons do they involve themselves and others abstain? Again these are data that are sometimes difficult to collect, especially when all attention is focussed on the actors who are upstage centre.

The issues of conflict are perhaps the simplest data to record as these are public – though the availability of written records to stimulate the memory of participants, who wish to remember the past as harmonious, is desirable. The details are likely to be unclear and selectively remembered by both winners and losers. Furthermore, the transactions which accompanied the conflict are, for the most part, not public (indeed, they may well be officially illegal). Even if one can find out who supported the faction leader, that is who composed factions (since this may be a matter of public record), the material goods or services flowing the other way are usually not recorded at all. Promises or expectations of goods and services, which are likely to have been the bases of recruiting support, are even less commonly recorded. Most likely they become public knowledge only when the promises are not fulfilled, or the expectations thwarted.

The degree of corporateness of a faction is critical in the present analysis. Again it is something that is hard to document, for no grouping in any context is ever fully corporate in relation to the actions of all its members all of the time. What one sees are attempts by both leaders and followers to claim lasting relationships with a wider framework (within which their transactional behaviours are embedded) and the recognition of (or refusal to recognize) these claims by other parties.

In this sense 'corporateness' is one possibility in a dimension of permanence and predictability. To speak of permanence and predictability we ideally need to know how many people remained in the same faction, and how many left it (the latter is difficult data to obtain); whether remaining or leaving was what was expected, and how often surprises happened. How do people obtain the information on which they make predictions about the behaviours of others in a factional situation?

Even this brief review of a few dimensions of ethnographic variation of factions is enough to indicate the possibilities for greater precision, and to show relationships that even the best ethnographies to date have rarely produced. One is led to wonder how the ethnographer can ever hope to do a thorough factional study, especially in a society other than his own, or one which demands that the ethnographer describe the culture as well as the factions.

Tactics and Rules

I have, deliberately, given only the briefest mention of tactics and rules in regard to factions. I have suggested that for factionalism (and not violence) to occur as a process, the circumscribing corporate group must set certain limits. It must define what is possible and what is not possible for factionalists. It may also set rules for the operation of corporate groups, which, if followed by a faction, give it claim to treatment as a corporate unit. The desirability of setting up one's political interest group or faction as a party is clear in the Canadian context, for example, for parties have parliamentary privileges which independents do not have. To academics the acquisition by a faction of a title of "Institute," "Programme," or "Centre" is the example which springs to mind of the way CCG rules relevant to corporate groups affect factional behaviour.

But it is only at these levels that I feel that the concept of rules applies to the factional process. In factions we are studying strategies of behaviour – perhaps not in pure form, for all individuals are influenced by rules obtaining in other domains where they have interests – but at least it is the strategic aspect that is the focus of study.

Strategies imply both constant reassessment of tactics and change in response to changes in the perceived situation. Perceptions of situations are conditioned in part by pre-existing structures of perception, and in part by empirical behaviour. What we can study most clearly in studying transactional politics (and particularly factions) is one way in which individuals cope, within a defined structure of perceptions, with changes in the availability of resources or in the behaviour of others, by altering their tactics, and less frequently, their strategies. Corporate groups, parties, nation states, and cultural rules provide the elements of fixity, predictability, permanence – the continuity of structures; at the point at which these emerge, we have indeed gone beyond factions. But in our study we may have clarified major issues in the analysis of where political variation ends and where political change occurs. The behavioural study of variation in factionalism has barely begun.

REFERENCES

Attwood, D. W.

1974a "Political Entrepreneurs and Economic Development: Two Villages and a Taluka in Western India." Unpublished Ph.D. Dissertation, Montreal, McGill University.

ATTWOOD, D.W.
1974b "Patrons and Mobilizers: Political Entrepreneurs in an Agrarian State." *Journal of Anthropological Research*, 30(4):225–41.
AYOUB, V. 1955 "Political Structure of a Middle East Community." Ph.D. Dissertation, Cambridge, Mass., Harvard University.
BAILEY, F. G.
1960 *Tribe, Caste, and Nation*. Manchester, Manchester University Press.
BAILEY, F. G.
1969 *Strategems and Spoils*. New York, Schocken Books.
BAILEY, F. G.
1972 "Tertius Gaudens aut Tertius Numen." Burg Wartenstein Symposium, No. 55.
BAILEY, F. G. and RALPH W. NICHOLAS
1968 "Introduction to Part Four." In M. J. Swartz (ed.), *Local Level Politics*. Chicago, Aldine.
BANFIELD, E. C.
1958 *The Moral Basis of a Backward Society*. Glencoe, Ill., The Free Press.
BETTISON, D. G., COLIN A. HUGHES and PAUL W. VAN DER VEUR (eds.)
1965 *The Papua New Guinea Elections, 1964*. Canberra, Australian National University.
BOISSEVAIN, J.
1965 *Saints and Fireworks: Religion and Politics in Rural Malta*. London, Athlone.
EVANS-PRITCHARD, E. E.
1940 "The Nuer of Southern Sudan." In M. Fortes and E. E. Evans-Pritchard (eds.), *African Political Systems*. London, Oxford University Press.
FINNEY, B. R.
1973 *Big Men and Business*. Honolulu, University of Hawaii Press.
FRANK, A. G.
1958 "Goal Ambiguity and Conflicting Standards." *Human Organization*, 17:8–13.
FRANKENBERG, R.
1957 *Village on the Border*. London, Cohen and West.
ISLAM, A. K. M. A.
1969 "Conflict and Cohesion in an East Pakistan Village." Ph.D. Dissertation, McGill University.
ISLAM, A. K. M. A.
1973 "Bangladesh in Transition: Reformation and Accommodation." *Southasian Series Occasional Paper no. 21*. Michigan University Press, Asian Studies Center.
ISLAM, A. K. M. A.
1974 *A Bangladesh Village: Conflict and Cohesion – An Anthropological Study of Politics*. Cambridge, Mass., Schenkman.
LEACH, E.
1962 *Rethinking Anthropology*. London, Athlone Press.
MAYER, A. C.
1966 "The Significance of Quasi-Groups in the Study of Complex Societies." In M. Banton (ed.), *The Social Anthropology of Complex Societies*. ASA Monograph 4, London, Tavistock.
NAGATA, SHUICHI
1970 *Modern Transformations of Moenkopi Pueblo*. University of Illinois Press.
NICHOLAS, RALPH W.
1965 "Factions: A Comparative Analysis." In M. Banton (ed.), *Political Systems and the Distribution of Power*. ASA Monograph 2, London, Tavistock.
SAHLINS, M. D.
1964 "Rich Man, Poor Man, Big Man, Chief." *Comparative Studies in Society and History*, 5:285–303.

SALISBURY, R. F.
1964 "Despotism and Australian Administration in the New Guinea Highlands." *American Anthropologist*, 4:225–39.
SALISBURY, R. F.
1968 "Formal Analysis in Anthropological Economics: The Rassel Island Case." In I. Buchler and H. G. Nutini (eds.), *Game Theory and the Behavioural Sciences*. Pittsburgh, Pittsburgh University Press.
SALISBURY, R. F.
1969 *Vunamami*. Berkeley, University of California Press.
SCHRYER, FRANS J.
1974 "Social Conflict in a Mexican Peasant Community." Unpublished Ph.D. Dissertation, Montreal, McGill University.
SIEGEL, BERNARD J. and ALAN R. BEALS
1960 "Pervasive Factionalism." *American Anthropologist*, 62:394–417.
SILVERMAN, M.
1973 "Resource Change and Village Factionalism in an East Indian Community, Guyana." Unpublished Ph.D. Dissertation, Montreal, McGill University.
SILVERMAN, S.
1968 "Agricultural Organization, Social Structure and Values in Italy." *American Anthropologist*, 70:1.
SOUTHWOLD, M.
1968 "A Games Model of African Tribal Politics." In I. Buchler and H. G. Nutini (eds.), *Game Theory and the Behavioural Sciences*. Pittsburgh, Pittsburgh University Press.
STRATHERN, A. J.
1971 *The Rope of Moka*. Cambridge, Cambridge University Press.

Patron and Patronage in Bangladesh Politics[1]

7

A. K. M. Aminul Islam

INTRODUCTION

Scholars of political science assert that political change begins at the national level, and they label the process political modernization. Earlier, I questioned this particular proposition (Islam, 1974:10) showing that the people who, in fact, bring knowledge of the political institutions of the city to the country are the brokers who are involved and committed both in urban as well as in village life. In this paper I expect to show further that these brokers, who have been referred to as individuals occupying linkage roles between patrons and clients, serve as an unmarked "midpoint" (Gluckman, 1965:191) between two end points of a continuum. The role of such individuals has been labelled as that of henchman by Fallers (1958), of patron by Salisbury (1964), and of broker by Boissevain (1964).

In recent years literature showing the interdependency of the patron-client dyad has proliferated. It is useful to see patrons as having access to primary resources and brokers as having access to secondary resources. However, among others, Silverman (1974) has demonstrated that "not only may patrons be brokers, but brokers may be patrons." The roles of brokers and patrons are thus not mutually exclusive. What I want to show is that middlemen can become either patrons or clients, patrons can become either middlemen or clients, but clients hardly ever become patrons without passing through the intermediary stage of middleman.

Bailey (1969), on the other hand, looks at the roles of brokers or middlemen from a slightly different angle. He says, "... middlemen are roles which come into existence to bridge a gap in communications ... (but) perfect communication will mean that the middleman is out of a job."

This leads us to identify two different types of middlemen. Paine (1971) and Boissevain (1974) have provided a useful distinction between "go-between," the faithful transmitter of information between arenas, and patrons and brokers, the entrepreneurs who manipulate resources. It will be shown that in the Bangladesh situation, a middleman may perform both functions simultaneously. He is both a transmitter of information and an entrepreneur who manipulates resources. Although the middleman may perform the entrepreneur's role efficiently and, as a result, promote himself to patron's rank, imperfection in communications in the second role may raise questions regarding his ability as a patron. The presence of a communication gap and a broker to fill it supports Bailey's hypothesis.

The study of the broker and/or middleman in the past has been closely associated with the study of factionalism and class conflict (Frankenberg, 1957; Geertz, 1963; Nicholas, 1965). Factions emerging out of social conflict (which is their *raison d'être*) are political groups in the sense that they organize conflict over the use of public power in certain kinds of societies and social institutions. Membership in a faction can be obtained only through a leader, although recruitment of members is based on diverse principles. Brokers, through their indirect access to resources outside the village, can become village politicians by taking control of factions. By manipulating factional disputes, they facilitate decision-making and change. The more established village politicians, the wealthy villagers (landowners) who have served as patrons for many years, are challenged by these brokers who bring their supporters not only resources from outside the village and knowledge of the political institutions of the city, but also the possibility of greater alignment of village factions with national political groupings.

Factions led by brokers continue to exist, however, only as long as the leaders have access, at least indirectly, to resources. By analysing patron-middleman-client interdependency in the context of the larger political field of peasant Bangladesh, I hope to contribute to the understanding of micro-level political arenas. Today, since the War of Independence[2] in Bangladesh, the political situation has changed drastically. The emerging leaders of the pre-war period, as a result of national economic decline and political chaos, are no longer the middlemen of the villages. New actors are appearing in the political arena, creating 'new forms' of integration.

Barth (1966) suggested that cultural integration will result progressively from repeated transactions of brokers, thus bringing the diverse elements of society into a "melting pot"; Paine (1974), on the other hand, dissatisfied with Barth's hypothesis, suggests a pluralistic approach to integration as an alternative. I would also hope to show in this paper that in Bangladesh, repeated transactions of brokers could not yet transform the country into a "melting pot," nor is Paine's pluralistic approach to integration applicable.

THE SETTING

In my previous work (Islam, 1974), I tried to show how village-level micro-politics reflected the macro-level national politics in pre-independence Bangladesh. The village of Badarpur, situated within sixteen miles of the urban center, is a typical Bengali village characterized by traditional organization, an acute rural and urban gap, and a distinct conflict between emergent and traditional leadership. In the traditional village, prior to Pakistani administration, the idea of political parties was a novel one: at that time one could easily align one's loyalties with one's *Gushthi* (kinsmen) and sect group. But between 1947 and 1971 the villager was increasingly called upon to produce a new kind of loyalty – to a political party. In order to resolve the conflict the villagers tried to blend loyalties through a well-structured system of factions.

During the pre-1971 period a challenge was presented to the traditional leadership of the village headman who had been elected to the position of local government head (Union Council Chairman) for more than thirty years as a representative of the Muslim League.[3] His patronage consisted mainly of direct economic assistance. He did not encourage much change in the traditional methods of farming, for example, or in increased government responsibility for the protection of the villagers. Emerging leaders residing in the village, on the other hand, had little power or economic assistance to offer villagers. They were dependent on regional and national political figures for providing support for the villagers, and they gained their own power through contact with these politicians. For example, one villager who became a broker gained favour with government development officers by becoming the first man in the village to use chemical fertilizers. He was also the first to adopt the Japanese method of paddy cultivation (gradually others followed suit). These new methods not only rewarded the villagers financially, but also made the innovator popular. This popularity increased when he obtained a government contract to remove the water hyacinth blocking a waterway, enabling him to provide jobs for many villagers in exchange for their loyalty. Several years later this broker was elected representative of his constituency in the local government, defeating a candidate on the Union Council Chairman's ticket.

The emerging leaders, who were village residents, and the political agents, the "outsiders," were two types of brokers to link the village with the outside world. Brokers of the second type – the political party agents, students from the city, and mass organization leaders – exerted their influence in helping villagers make decisions as to which side they should vote for. Although they were labelled "outsiders," they had the power to get the village brokers to translate the national issues and make them relevant to the villagers' way of life. Whereas forty years previously the only national issues relevant to the villagers were those concerning Muslim solidarity against Hindu landlords and the maintenance of religious purity, pre-war developments made vital to the local scene issues such as East Pakistan against West Pakistan, the Bengali language against Urdu, and guided democracy versus universal suffrage. Changes in the way political contests occurred in the village were partly due to the adoption of universal suffrage and partly to the seeking of political support by urban groups.

The students play a vital broker role in the village: by discussing issues that concern the urban population, and by relating local candidates' arguments with rural issues, they bring about an association of rural and urban issues in the minds of the rural voters. Whether the issue is national or local, the three polar types of reaction to it remain the same: the creative use of traditional techniques and values, the passive acceptance of the *status quo*, the active seeking of change and novelty.

Similar reactions to political issues at urban and rural levels, and the organization of political conflict in the village through manipulation of factions by brokers are both factors which indicate a similarity between micro- and macro-level politics. The crucial factor is the interdependency of emerging village brokers and brokers from the outside who seek village support. This interdependency of micro/macro-level relationships increases in direct relation to the access to external resources.

In 1970 East Pakistan (now Bangladesh) had its first general election since 1954. Awami League, the main political party of East Pakistan, gained 167 of a total of 169 seats in that election. Naturally, Awami League was expecting to be able to form the ministry, and when this was denied by the ruling military government of Pakistan, chaos broke out in the entire country. The ruling military government denied the Awami League its right to form the cabinet on the basis of the fact that it represented only East Pakistan and not the whole nation.[4] At one point, Awami League was also accused by the government of conspiring to secede from the country – an act called the Agartala Conspiracy. Sheikh Mujibur Rahman, the political hero of Bangladesh and president of Awami League in 1970, was accused of being the primary conspirator. Conflict between East and West Pakistan had been simmering since Pakistan won her independence in 1947.[5]

After the election in December 1970, negotiations continued between Awami League leaders and the ruling military government, which, however, finally collapsed on March 24, 1971. A country-wide strike paralyzed the government. On March 25, the government called the military in, ordering it to arrest all Awami League leaders and to subdue the strikers. At midnight, the Army came out of its barracks and indiscriminately began to kill the Bengalis.[6] Most Awami League leaders were aware of what was coming and escaped arrest except for Sheikh Rahman. With this event began a new phase in Bangladesh politics.

After the army action of March 25 frightened Bengalis began to cross the border and take shelter in India. Bengali army and police personnel tried to resist the military attack but failed totally. Many of them were killed; the survivors together with the other ten million Bengali refugees took shelter in India. Bengalis grouped together, organized a liberation army, and formed a government in exile with the patronage of the government of India. Awami League leaders took the leadership in negotiating with the government of India on behalf of the people of Bangladesh. The independence movement of Bangladesh culminated on the 16th of December when the Pakistani army surrendered to the Indian army[7] at Dacca, the capital of Bangladesh.

In the following section I intend to present three fieldwork episodes which will be the basis for my analysis in section four and discussion in section five.

FIELDWORK EPISODES

Episode I: The Chaotic Village

In January 1975, I returned to Badarpur, the village I had studied previously. One late afternoon while walking in the village with my friend, Ekram, I noticed that the acquaintances whom I passed and greeted did not respond. I wondered whether they had forgotten me in the past nine years. I commented to Ekram, "It's strange that not even one person recognizes me anymore."

"No, Islam Shahib, they did recognize you all right, but they were not sure which group you might belong to. Are you a Bangladesh supporter, (that is, an Awami Leaguer), or are you one of those who is not happy with Bangladesh and its alliance with India?"[8]

These questions were much too serious to be answered candidly. Although a Bengali by birth, and one who had participated directly in the liberation war, I was in Bengladesh this time not as a Bengali nationalist returning home, but as an American anthropologist. Having participated in the liberation war, I could not have been an anti-Bangladeshi, nor was I ever an Awami-Leaguer. Certainly, I was emotionally neutral about the Indo-Bangla alliance; I was there to find out how the villagers were reacting to the present political situation.

It was getting dark. We could hear the Muazin's call for Magrib (evening) prayer. Ekram decided to go to the mosque to say his prayers. An hour later he returned, accompanied by Siddique who, as a sixteen-year-old boy, had worked as my cook, messenger, and caretaker nine years ago. This day he happened to come to the village to see his ailing mother, and hearing that I had come back from America, accompanied Ekram from the mosque to see me. (By this time two more villagers had ignored my greetings and I was overjoyed to meet someone who welcomed me.) I asked Siddique to join us for supper and this gave me an opportunity to learn of the turn of events. "What has happened to the village and villagers? I do not hear anymore singing. I met Subhan and Azhar this evening and they did not even recognize me."

Siddique confirmed what Ekram had said earlier. The villagers did recognize me but could not be sure of my party affiliation. He added: "Islam

Shahib, it is no longer the same village you visited nine years ago. Badarpur is no longer that serene village; people are no longer happy, friendly, and hospitable. They now live in a paranoiac world, full of suspicion, jealousy, and hostility. Awami League has sold the country to the Indians."

Not wanting to comment on this, I asked about some friends we shared nine years ago (who are written about in my earlier study).

He replied, "Karim left the village with all his family members and now is a businessman in Baradi where he is minting money."

"But Karim was wealthy before; why did he leave the village which he 'ruled' for almost forty years?"

"During the war he supported the Pakistani Government. Twice the Freedom Fighters took him away to execute him. But both times he escaped, once by bribing the leader; the second time, his nephew, who was also a Freedom Fighter, rescued him."

"But that doesn't tell me why he had to leave the village."

"The villagers all supported the Freedom Fighters and they would have killed Karim if he had remained in the village. After the general amnesty, Karim came out of hiding and made some kind of arrangement with Hannan who is now taking care of Karim's property in the village."

"Didn't Hannan support the Pakistani Government? After all they are brothers."

"No, Hannan did not support the Pakistani Government, at least not publicly. Rather, he accommodated the Freedom Fighters in his home – although the gossip says that he was taking money from the Pakistani Army for supplying information at the same time. There is no doubt that both Karim and Hannan helped each other from the opposing groups: Karim from the Pakistani Army and Hannan from the Freedom Fighters."

"After the amnesty couldn't Karim return to the village?"

"Probably he could have, but he already had some business in Baradi which suddenly proliferated after liberation, and so Karim decided to live there. After all, he could never have gotten back the hold he had on the villagers."

"Does this mean that those who used to oppose Karim, such as Zaman and Pradhan, are now controlling the village?"

"No, not at all. It is a different story now. Nobody has any control on any villager, so to speak. But anyone who has some connection with the leaders in the city and who can bring some resources to the village will be important in the village until the resources are consumed."

"What sort of resources are you talking about – who can bring what from the city to the villagers?"

"Islam Shahib, this village can no longer live on its own products. None of us can earn enough cash to buy our daily necessities from the market.

The price of salt, sugar, oil, clothes – everything is exhorbitant. So we must get them through rations. And anyone who can get a permit from the city can become a distributor for these items."

"Are there no fixed dealers or fair-price shops in the village?"

"No, we do not have any such dealer or shop. The reason is that there is no regularity of supply, and so whenever there is a shipment of overseas aid, the dealership becomes available through bribery of the officials or politicians in the city. Actually, the city officials and politicians know beforehand what will be coming from where and when, and their agents in the village will grab the opportunity right away."

"How are these agents selected by the politicians?"

"As you know, previously the circle officer, or the Chairman of the Union decided who would be the right person to become a dealer. Now, many young men who fought as Freedom Fighters have connections with the politicians in the city, the latter being obligated to repay the Fighters for their allegiance to them or to their party during the war. Hence, the politicians recruit their agents from among Freedom Fighters who, in turn, recruit supporters for the politicians by distributing relief aids and goods. In this way, Freedom Fighters are a better link for the villagers than their traditional village leaders. Moreover, traditional leaders were limited in number, offering the politicians little choice in recruiting party agents. Today, on the other hand, almost all the village youth claim to have been Freedom Fighters whether or not they actually supported the Bangladesh liberation war or worked as agents of the Pakistani Army as Razakars."[9]

It was a grim picture. Nine years ago village bauls (wandering minstrels) could be heard singing their religious and mystic songs inspired by utter abandon and surrender. In the midst of total surrender and identification with the absolute, little incidents common to rural life were interwoven to establish kinship between ordinary and mystic experience. Today, that mysticism of a Bengali village is no more. People are preoccupied with daily breadwinning, and grudgingly suspicious of the fortune of others, they are heartlessly indifferent to each other's miseries. Furthermore, the structuring of village life resulting from factional affiliation was no longer present.

During the three days spent in the village I tried to meet as many people as I could. The leaders of the village had fallen back into oblivion. None of them appeared to be interested in talking about the village and village life. Some of these traditional leaders now work in the city and only occasionally visit the village to see their ailing relatives who were either too weak to accompany them or were left behind for financial reasons. I could almost hear the cries of agony and frustration all around the village. Not a single smiling face or a sight of satisfaction anywhere. Dacca's population has multiplied, as villagers migrate to the city in hopes that some of the young men related to them and who had been Freedom Fighters might be able to obtain favours from the politicians.

In Dacca well-dressed young men were visible all over the city. The war-ravaged country did not seem to have affected them much; epidemics and food shortages did not leave any trace on their faces; even the bodies abandoned in the streets, dead from hunger and disease, did not seem to concern them. Yet they were all Freedom Fighters, students who took up arms against the Pakistani Army and were now in the protective shelter of their patrons, the political bosses of the ruling party, originators of the War of Independence. Instead of the factional affiliation or groupings of old, society now seemed composed of isolated individuals linking themselves to politicians in pursuit of personal gain.

*Episode II: Major Raja's Diary**

I knew a few Bangladesh army personnel who were now in high position in the army. I decided to go and see one such officer who was just a major in 1971,[10] but is a Brigadier General now. I asked him to tell me about the war from his own perspective, and particularly about the Freedom Fighters and how they were recruited, selected, and organized. However, since he himself was not at liberty to discuss these matters with me, he suggested that Major Raja, who was forcibly retired from the army, could talk to me more freely. I quote Major Raja's diary below.

"It was a bloody war. Bengalis, not properly trained, were dying by the hundreds every day; yet the war continued. Leaders of the Awami League moved from camp to camp to recruit new personnel. Once away from Pakistani torture, humiliation and suffering, refugees forgot everything once they came under Indian shelter, and were reluctant to join the Liberation Army. Yet we managed to recruit about a hundred thousand out of whom not even one percent were Hindus; only the Muslim boys who left their parents and other relatives in Bangladesh began to join the Freedom Fighters – since they knew that they would have to go back to their country. Hindu youths, on the other hand, though not happy, were reluctant to fight as they had all moved to India and none of their relatives were left behind in Bangladesh for them to think about. They also wanted to return home but only if someone else freed the country.

There was another serious problem which hampered the organization of the liberation war. Most of the Freedom Fighters were educated youths who had always been vocal and fearless. They had dreams and most of them, after two weeks of training felt like a Che Guevera or a Mao Tse-tung! They were reluctant to accept orders from a few regular army personnel who joined the liberation war. Young students all wanted to be group leaders but no one was willing to work under another's command.

In such a chaotic situation, the Liberation Army was no better than a disorganized, agitated mass – and without a charismatic leader to guide it. Naturally, there developed only schismatic groups which split into multi-factional band organizations. Motivators of each faction began to lobby with their patrons for better resources for their followers. The Awami League, who had a better liaison with the Indian officials, could secure more resources for their followers than smaller political parties that could not contact any outside sources for aid. Awami League followers began to dominate the majority of Freedom Fighters.

*Edited.

A few political leaders, mostly Awami Leaguers, behaved irresponsibly in those days. To them, the liberation of Bangladesh was useful but the most important issue was who would take over the leadership when the country was free. They counted Sheikh Mujibur Rahman as lost and a bitter struggle for political supremacy was on, though as an undercurrent. At one stage, this struggle almost divided the ruling party. More damage was done by political rivalry within the party than by any outside interference – a fact not without repercussion on the struggle for freedom.

There was another critical problem. Screening and selection of Freedom Fighters before training was done in the youth camps by political leaders. There were complaints that suitable candidates were refused selection if found to be holding political views different from those of the politicians. Even in the training centers candidates were not free from political pressures from the politicians. For example, one Badsha of Comilla came to my sector as a recruit for training. Within a week I received a wireless message from headquarters that Badsha should immediately be made a section leader – the wish of the Foreign Minister. There were at least fifty other young men more competent than Badsha who proved their dedication and leadership during training. But I had to promote Badsha over his fellow Freedom Fighters since, according to the Commanding Officer, Badsha was from the same constituency as the Foreign Minister, was distantly related to him, and would be an asset to the Foreign Minister when they returned home after the war. Badsha's elder brother was instrumental in getting support for the Foreign Minister in the 1970 election, and it was Badsha's brother whose support was badly needed by the Foreign Minister during his election to the cabinet. Badsha's brother, though not a politician himself, could control a number of M.P.s through his multi-various business chain. Those M.P.s' support was absolutely necessary for the Foreign Minister to maintain his balance of power in party politics in his conflict with the Prime Minister."

As Major Raja continued, I could see his eyes flashing, his chin grim with anger and despair.

"This was not a solitary case. Throughout the liberation war army officers were being coerced by the politicians to have their own nominees in strategic roles. Politicians did not even hesitate to create conflicts between regular army personnel. For example, Major Zamal was the highest-ranking Bengali officer to defect from and take up arms against the Pakistani Army. He was the most natural man to obtain command of the entire Bengali Army. However, the Prime Minister-designate was very suspicious of Major Zamal's leadership and skill with the army, and feared that one day Zamal might take over control of everything and exclude the politicians. But Zamal virtually lost his entire battalion in the war and did not have much personnel left when he joined the liberation army. This led the Prime Minister to decide that Major Shafat, another major who defected from the Pakistani Army, should be made the Commander-in-Chief of the Bangladesh Army instead of Major Zamal even though, according to military personnel, the latter was much more dynamic, efficient, and deserving of the exalted position. The Prime Minister had the tacit approval of the Indian Government since Major Zamal was not happy with the Indian role during the War. According to him, "India stole the victory from the Bangladesh Freedom Fighters in the war of liberation."

I asked Major Raja if there was no officer who could speak up against all these irregularities. "Sure, there were a few. We spoke up and that is why myself, Major Jabbar, and quite a few other officers of the Bangladesh Army are out of a job, even though we fought for independence if not better, at least as well as any other officers there today."

This diary clearly shows that even during the Liberation War, inter-factional disputes were simmering among Awami League leaders. These leaders, working as middlemen between the Government of India and the Freedom Fighters, were receiving patronage from India. On the other hand, it was rather obvious that the politicians (Awami Leaguers) could visualize that after the war, these clients (Freedom Fighters) would become the middlemen or brokers between them and the average Bengalis who were almost a non-entity during the war. The following episode illustrates how the Freedom Fighters, after the war, transformed themselves into middlemen – and the Awami Leaguers became the patrons in the Bangladesh political arena.

Episode III: Bangladesh 1975/Bihari Persecution

Accused of helping the Pakistani Army during the Liberation War, most of the Biharis in the country were persecuted after the war. Bihari property was expropriated and forcibly occupied as enemy property. The following example shows how some people were harassed by the ruling party's machinery and how the middleman could negotiate with the patron for a settlement on behalf of his client.

Professor Hamid was born in Bangladesh of Bihari parents. His father died in 1961 but left a large family of five children who were subsequently looked after by Hamid and his Bengali wife in their home at Mohammadpur, Dacca, an area predominantly occupied by Bihari people who had migrated from India.

After the Liberation War in 1971, Hamid's mother and siblings were evicted from Hamid's house as they spoke the Urdu language at home and were branded as Bihari. (By that time Hamid and his wife had settled in the United States.) This act seemed highly unjust as all the children were born in Bangladesh and Hamid, himself, was educated in Bengali schools; his wife's relatives were all Bengali by birth and their children were all Bengalis who could not even speak or understand Urdu.

One of Hamid's wife's brothers, Barry, an American citizen, advised her to accompany him to Bangladesh and find out what they could do to reoccupy the house. In July of 1972 they returned to Bangladesh. Barry had been very active during the Bangladesh War, organizing the Bengalis in the United States, lobbying regularly in Washington among the American senators and congressmen, and mobilizing American public opinion in favour of Bangladesh. He also went to Mujibnagar[11] to participate in the Liberation War and work for the Ministry of Foreign Affairs. While in Mujibnagar, Barry made good contacts with high officials of the Bangladesh Government, particularly with the ruling party's leaders. In addition, the rapport he had as a student leader at Dacca University with other student leaders now stood him in good stead, as the latter were now in high positions in the ruling party's hierarchy. The Secretary General of the ruling political party (Awami League), for example, was a contemporary and friend of his.

Hamid's wife was assured by Barry that he would be able to release Hamid's home from the government without much trouble. However, unforeseen events complicated the case. After Hamid's home was expropriated, it was allotted to a Birangana (a general name given to women of Bangladesh who were raped and tortured by the Pakistani Army) who had lost her husband in the war and who was living in the house with her three orphaned children. Also, the Birangana's brother was a Thana Commander of the Liberation Army and very influential among Awami League leaders. As soon as he learned that Hamid's brother-in-law was approaching the local Awami League leaders to have his sister's house vacated, he immediately went to the Rehabilitation Minister, his friend, and reported that the house was not in Hamid's wife's name, but in the name of Hamid – a Bihari. He also added that one of Hamid's brothers, Moin, was a Razakar and was personally responsible for the death of a number of Bengali intellectuals. In the end, Hamid's wife's appeal for reoccupying the house did not merit any sympathy.

The Rehabilitation Minister politely declined to listen to Barry's arguments and advised the local police to arrest Moin as a possible murderer. As soon as the order for Moin's arrest came to Hamid's mother's notice, she became nervous and asked her children to hide; they were so frightened that even Hamid's wife's and Barry's assurances could not convince them that by hiding out they were only complicating their case.

Finally, being desperate, Barry went to the Foreign Minister in person and then to the General Secretary of the Awami League and convinced them that Hamid could not be made responsible for whatever Moin might have done, even if the accusations against Moin were all true. In the end, the Rehabilitation Minister, at the request of the General Secretary, allocated a different house to the Birangana, and ordered Hamid's house to be vacated.

In 1974, after living in Bangladesh for two more years, Hamid's family left the country and declared themselves Pakistanis. A few months later, Hamid received a letter from the Bangladesh Government stating that his house had been declared enemy property and had been taken possession of by the Government of Bangladesh.

ANALYSIS

We may begin our analysis by identifying three different types of actors who play a prominent role in the fieldwork episodes. They are the clients, the middlemen, and patrons. According to the distinctions made by Boissevain, Paine, and Silverman, it is access to resources that distinguishes a broker from a patron, and vice-versa. Clients are the recipients of patronage. Hence in the episodes cited above, we can clearly identify our clients and patrons, and attribute the middleman role to the individual or individuals who maintain the linkage roles (see chart below).

Episodes	Clients	Middlemen	Patrons	Resources
Chaotic Village	The Villagers	Freedom Fighters	Politicians/ Officials (Awami Leaguers)	Permits, Goods
Major Raja's Diary	Freedom Fighters	Awami League (Politicians/ Officials)	Government of India	Weapons & military supplies
Bihari Persecution	Biharis	Freedom Fighters	Awami League (Politicians/ Officials	Favour & various types of protection

Chart I *Classification of Fieldwork Episodes in Terms of Clients, Middlemen, Patrons, and their Resources*

From the chart above we may safely conclude that although it is convenient to conceive of patron and client as the two end points of a continuum, the middleman being somewhere in between, the mobility indicated is certainly not unidirectional. What I am trying to say is that although the roles of client, middleman, and patron remain stable, the actors performing the roles can change frequently. (The changing roles of different actors can be better understood in the chart below.)

	Roles			
Actors (Episodes)	Before War	During War	After War	Arenas
Traditional Village Headman (1)	Patron	–	Middleman	Village
Traditional Village Leaders (1)	Middleman	–	Client	Village
The Villagers (1)	Client	–	Client	Village
Freedom Fighters (1, 2, 3)	–	Client	Middleman	Nation
Biharis (3)	Patron	–	Client	City
Awami League (1, 2, 3)	Middleman	Middleman	Patron	Nation
Government of India (2)	–	Patron	–	Nation

Chart II *Changing Roles Before, During and After the War*

Patrons can fall back into oblivion as happened in the village of Badarpur where one-time village leaders now hardly play any role in decision-making in or outside the village; they are dependent on brokers, roles assumed by the village youths who became Freedom Fighters. Nine years ago these village leaders were instrumental in acquiring resources from the patrons in the city and became patrons themselves. Major Raja's diary indicates the same process wherein the Freedom Fighters took up the client role, and politicians (Awami Leaguers) became the middlemen between the Freedom Fighters, and their patron, the Government of India.

In the third episode, we find that after the war, the previous brokers (Awami Leaguers) assumed the patron roles while the Freedom Fighters, who were clients before, became the brokers.

The traditional concept of brokers occupying a position between patrons and clients allows us to understand factional politics in Bangladesh (Islam, 1974). However, Bailey's statement – "Perfect communication will mean that the middleman is out of a job" (1969) – appears to me to imply that the middleman makes an effort not to bring the communication between patron and client to "perfection." The question to consider is whether the middleman's main objective is to bridge the gap in patron-client communication and thus endanger his own job, or to leave communication a little short of perfection, thus leaving enough scope for future exploitation, thereby keeping his job in self-perpetuation. Yet, from what we have seen in the context of the larger political field, the middleman's role is not always a static one. Rather he can assume the patron's role, confirming Silverman's thesis that "not only may patrons be brokers but brokers may be patrons." It seems that even for the patron there is a saturation point after which he may fall into oblivion and later start again, either as a middleman or even as a client.

The second episode verifies a new hypothesis which states that just as patrons control clients, clientelist politics guide patrons in formulating their strategies. In this continuing interaction between clients, middlemen, and patrons, a series of pressures are built up on all three, pressures which are endemic to factional politics. In Major Raja's diary, we notice that the Government of India could direct the middleman, the Prime Minister-designate of Bangladesh, to appoint Shafat as the Commander-in-Chief, superceding Major Zamal who was assuredly more competent for the position. The clientelist politics, the politics between Majors Zamal and Shafat, guided the patron, the Government of India, to formulate its strategy: it was apparent that in post-war politics the Government could not have negotiated as easily with Major Zamal – with his negative attitude towards India – as was possible with Major Shafat.

At another level, the same hypothesis seems to have been supported in the case of Freedom Fighter Badsha and his undeserved promotion granted to him by Major Raja who was coerced directly by the Commanding Officer and indirectly by the Foreign Minister, a superior of the Commanding Officer. Through this political manoeuvring, the Foreign Minister was formulating his own future strategies. Badsha needed the support of his patron, the Foreign Minister, who again needed Badsha's brother's support to maintain his balance of power in party politics. Badsha could not have been a section leader by dint of his own merit. He badly needed the support of the Foreign Minister to pledge his case to Major Raja. Pressure on Major Raja by the Commanding Officer was all that Badsha needed to get a promotion. Similarly, the Foreign Minister felt pressure from Badsha's brother who had the M.P.s as his allies. Such a series of pressures are endemic to the art of negotiating in all political arenas of Bangladesh today.

Finally, the case of Bihari persecution indicates that despite repeated interactions and transactions of brokers, Bangladesh did not become transformed into a melting pot. Hamid's mother could not accept the Bengalis as her own people even though her grandchildren are all Bengalis. She lived there two years after the war, and together with many others like her, helped create a pluralistic structure; but no integration of the Biharis and Bengalis occurred outside of a few cases of intermarriage.

Integration implies, as I understand the term, that there is a sort of cohesiveness in a pluralistic social structure. This third study clearly indicates that the Biharis and Bengalis in Bangladesh not only failed to 'melt in the same pot,' but there was no visible interaction either, precluding pluralistic integration. Biharis were pointedly sorted out, persecuted, and harassed both by the government and by public non-Biharis. From the point of view of Biharis, even after living in the land for more than two decades, they could not yet consider the country their own. They still felt closer to Pakistan, a thousand miles away, which has no cultural similarities to Bangladesh other than a common religion. The affiliation of the Biharis to Muslim Pakistan supercedes their liking for the Bengalis of Bangladesh, although it was the Bengalis who gave them shelter and protection when they arrived as destitute refugees from Hindu India. The assimilation of the Biharis into the Bengali culture was never achieved; rather there resulted a stage of "stabilized pluralism" in what would otherwise be a homogeneous Bangladesh today. What little possibility there was in the Pakistani era (that is, between 1947–1971) for the Bengalis and Biharis of East Pakistan to be integrated, as in a "melting pot", now seems to have vanished.

Summary and Conclusion

This paper has been concerned with patrons and patronage in Bangladesh politics, showing particularly how the occupants of various roles are taking on new roles as a result of the Liberation War of 1971. One of the effects of the war has reached the remote corner of the village, bringing the city and the village into one common political platform (this does not imply that village and city politics were not linked in the past); this merging deserves closer study.

The question may be asked here as to what extent city politics directs or controls village politics, or to what extent the continuous and progressive communications between city-based patrons and village-based clients are blended into one and the same political dialogue by the intermediary middlemen who are equally mobile both within the city and the village.

This study has shown that before, during, and after the war some actors have moved from one situation to another: before, during, and after the war they have assumed, in turn, the different roles of patron, middleman, and/or client. The changing roles of the individual or group reflect the changing pattern of social dynamics of Bangladesh politics. However, not everything has changed beyond recognition; there are still some traces of pre-war interaction patterns which can be identified in post-war situations. For example, the family bond still brings people together, as we saw in Hannan and Karim's case (whereas *para* or community, occupation, and/or religion no longer create the same bond as they did nine years ago).

What we have found in this study is that client, middleman, and patron are the three concepts which allow us to comprehend politics in developing nations better than the way the political scientists do. That is, politics can be better studied by beginning at the micro-level rather than the national level. Although the responsibility for the political decision-making lies with the political leaders and bureaucrats – the patrons – it is the clients who are most affected by those decisions. Hence, there is always an attempt on the part of the clients to influence the decision-makers at the top level through intermediaries or the middlemen. This process may involve politicking among clients, and these clientelist politics, in turn, influence strategies adopted by the patrons.

The effect of clientelist politics has been shown in all three episodes. In the first, the villagers, through the Freedom Fighters, could get resources for themselves and thus were obligated to support their patrons. In episode II, the Freedom Fighters could procure more resources from the Government of India through the Awami League, and in return the Awami League could ensure the Government of India that it would not have to face a hostile Commander-in-Chief in the future. In episode III, even the Biharis could expect to have someone come to their rescue against the hostile country.

Bangladesh is not the same country it was. Factions no longer perform the function of organizing village conflict as they did before the Liberation War. Because the villagers can no longer produce enough food and other essentials to meet their needs, they are more dependent on the city and on foreign aid distributed through the city centers. As a result, faction leaders have lost their role as middlemen, and consequently, as faction leaders. In fact, factions in Badarpur are much less conspicuous than they were nine years ago, if they exist at all.

One explanation for this structural change in the village is "the failure of factional leaders to distribute resources originating outside the community to their clientele'' (Salisbury in Schryer, 1975). Most of the villagers will remain factionalists, Salisbury says, ''as long as resources obtained outside of the community and distributed to supporters exceed the cost of contributions made by supporters'' (*ibid*).

The other explanation for this prelude to structural change in the village lies in one of the great anthropological truths: function changes faster than structure. The new middlemen, the Freedom Fighters, apparently are not yet leading factions or creating new factions at this point in time, possibly because of the irregularity of their success in obtaining resources for their village relatives. They have earned their new roles as middlemen by being more successful than faction leaders in obtaining these resources because of the loyalty of the politicians to them. The resources they obtain include not only ration shop permits but also assistance in bribing the courts and police. There is much bribery and manipulation and it is ''each man for himself.''

Post-war devastation left the country in a vacuum; the Freedom Fighters, the villagers, and even the traditional village headmen and/or leaders have not yet found a way to organize new factions, not to speak of political parties. However, it can be safely assumed that from within this chaos, a pattern will emerge to blend different groups such as the Freedom Fighters and villagers into factions and probably align them to political parties when, and if ever, the situation stabilizes.

In conclusion, what this study has shown is that the increasing need for economic contacts with the world outside has opened up the possibility for a new group of people to become intermediaries between the villagers and the outside, and to communicate about national issues within the village context. It has opened up possibilities for new leadership and for structural modernization within the village, where hopefully, struggles can be resolved by more objective means than was possible in the pre-war society.

NOTES

1 I am indebted to the Wright State University Liberal Arts College Research Committee for the financial assistance provided for my field trip to Bangladesh and to all the participants of the Conference on the Anthropological Study of Factional Politics held at Orillia, Ontario (April, 1975) for their comments and suggestions on an earlier draft of this paper.

2 The war that took place between the Bangladesh Freedom Fighters and the Pakistan Army in 1971. The Freedom Fighters finally won the war with the assistance of the Indian Army.

3 The Muslim League is the political party responsible for the division of India in 1947 into India and Pakistan. After the independence of the country in 1947, the Muslim League Party dominated in Pakistan almost continuously except for a short spell between 1954–58.

4 Although Awami League had the overall majority in Pakistan, in the west it could secure only one seat out of over one hundred.

5 For details, see Islam, 1974:17–19.
6 For details of the massacre, see Payne, 1972; Chowdhury, 1972; and Rafiq, 1974.
7 All Bangladesh Army officers interviewed expressed the same feeling about the Pakistani surrender. They were disappointed that India manipulated the war and took the entire credit for the victory, depriving the Bangladesh Freedom Fighters without whose assistance India could never have won. On the other hand, the Bengali officers did not hesitate to admit that they could not have managed without India's help.
8 After the war, the Awami League leaders signed a bilateral treaty with India which many Bengali intellectuals, as well as the majority of the commoners, despise.
9 The Razakars are a militia group organized by the Pakistani Government to counteract the Freedom Fighters known as Mukti Fauz. Razakars were recruited from among idle youths who stayed inside the country during the war. Most of them were Biharis and Muslim League supporters.
10 For the sake of anonymity pseudonyms are used here.
11 The site of the Government of Bangladesh-in-exile, situated between the border of India and Bangladesh.

REFERENCES

BAILEY, F.
1969 *Strategems and Spoils*. Toronto, Copp-Clark.
BARTH, F.
1966 *Models of Social Organization*. London, Royal Anthropological Institute.
BOISSEVAIN, J.
1964 "Factions, Parties and Politics in a Maltese Village." *American Anthropologist*, 16:1275–87.
BOISSEVAIN, J.
1974 *Friends of Friends: Networks, Manipulators and Coalitions*. Oxford, Basil Blackwell.
CHOWDHURY, S.
1972 *The Genesis of Bangladesh*. Calcutta, Asia Publishing House.
FALLERS, L. A.
1958 *Bantu Bureaucracy: A Study of Integration and Conflict*. Cambridge, W. Heffer and Sons.
FRANKENBERG, R.
1957 *Village on the Border*. London, Cohen and West.
GEERTZ, C. (ed.)
1963 *Old Societies and New States*. Chicago University Committee for Comparative Study of New Nations. The Free Press of Glencoe.
GLUCKMAN, M.
1965 *Politics, Law and Ritual in Tribal Society*. Chicago, Aldine.
ISLAM, A. K. M. A.
1974 *A Bangladesh Village: Conflict and Cohesion – An Anthropological Study of Politics*. Cambridge, Mass., Schenkman.
NICHOLAS, RALPH W.
1965 "Factions: A Comparative Analysis." In M. Banton (ed.), *Political Systems and the Distribution of Power*. ASA Monographs No. 2. London, Tavistock.
PAINE, ROBERT
1971 "A Theory of Patronage and Brokerage." In Robert Paine (ed.), *Patrons and Brokers in the East Arctic*. St. John's, Institute of Social and Economic Research, Memorial University of Newfoundland.

PAINE, ROBERT
1974 *Second Thoughts about Barth's Models*. Occasional Paper of the Royal Anthropological Institute No. 32. London, Royal Anthropological Institute.
PAYNE, R.
1972 *Massacre: The Tragedy at Bangladesh and the Phenomenon of Mass Slaughter throughout History*. New York, The Macmillan Company.
RAFIQ, M.
1974 *A Tale of Millions*. Dacca, Bangladesh, Adeylebros & Company.
SALISBURY, R. F.
1964 "Despotism and Australian Administration in the New Guinea Highlands." *American Anthropologist*, 4:225–39.
SCHRYER, FRANS J.
1975 "Village Factionalism and Class Conflict in Peasant Communities." *Canadian Review of Sociology and Anthropology*, 12(3):290–302.
SILVERMAN, M.
1974 "Encapsulation, Resources and Middlemen." Paper presented at the American Anthropological Association 73rd Annual Meeting, Mexico City.

Opposition and Freedom in Moenkopi Factionalism[1]

8

Shuichi Nagata

Introduction

Among the contemporary reservation communities of the American Indians, tribal councils can be regarded as the most basic formal political organization. They were created by the Indian Reorganization Act of 1934 by means of which the Government of the United States hoped to establish in the reservations the principle of self-determination based on the model of constitutional democracy. Numerous evaluations of this attempt at political modernization among the native peoples of America were subsequently written, but they tended to over-emphasize the administrative and judicial aspects of the tribal councils (for example, Shepardson, 1963) whereas analyses of processes in council politics have been infrequent. Significantly, much of the concern with the basic civil rights of Indians on reservations (Schusky, 1965; Brophy and Aberle, 1966) derives from considerations, not of political, but of legal procedures within the reservation government.

To determine to what extent American democratic parties are incorporated in tribal councils, one might subject a sample of tribal councils to a detailed analysis based on the presence or absence of such practices. One such practice is the role of the opposition. In the following, I propose to describe certain characteristics of the political processes in the Hopi community of Moenkopi and to compare them with democratic opposition as characterized by some political scientists. Unfortunately my data for this exercise are subject to one serious limitation which I present below.

The Hopi tribal council and its branch, Upper Moenkopi Village Council, in contrast to numerous other tribal or village councils, lack effective authority over the entire Hopi tribal or village populations on the reservation. About half of both the tribal and the village populations do not regard the decisions of these bodies as authoritative and binding. At the time the tribal constitution was framed, it was expected that everybody would belong to these organizations, but this did not happen. Consequently there is a situation that approximates what Siegel and Beals called "schismatic factionalism" (1960) between those who follow the council's decisions and those who do not. The model of schismatic factionalism is quite appropriate, I think, when applied to Hopiland proper. There are eleven Hopi villages on the reservation, each of which is either a council or a non-council village, depending upon the participation of the village leaders in the tribal council, or lack thereof. In Hopiland proper, therefore, factions have territorial bases. In Moenkopi, a neat territorial division between the village council and the faction that goes against it is not as obvious. I shall discuss this aspect in greater detail later. At any rate, because of this imperfect territorial division between the village council and its opponents, I was more interested in the political interaction between these two sides and particularly, their opposition behaviours. The comparability of these behaviours with democratic opposition can be maintained only if we assume that the council and its opponents form a single political community. This assumption does not hold in Moenkopi. The role of opposition which I shall discuss, therefore, is not that which obtains within one and the same political community but between two 'segments,' each of which has been trying to be a political community of its own. In this sense, the opposition is somewhat like the one observed in a segmentary political system. I shall return to this point shortly.

To the extent that the original constitution envisaged the formation of a political community out of Moenkopi as a component unit in the Hopi Tribal Council (Art. 3, Sec. 4 and Art. 4, Sec. 5), the attempt at political modernization in this village was as much a failure as the attempt to create a single tribal council to which all the Hopi villages were expected to adhere. But there is another and, in my opinion, not sufficiently appreciated aspect to these failures. In spite of, and perhaps, because of the cleavage and the opposition behaviours confirming it, the people appear to be 'liberated' from the moral constraints that used to bind them to, what looked to many outside observers, a tightly-knit pueblo community (Titiev, 1944:65). In short, if the democratic theory maintains that the principle of legitimate opposition is one mechanism to ensure individual freedom, something similar can be said of the politics of Moenkopi, although in the latter case, the opposition is not viewed by the people as legitimate. This is my thesis.

Factionalism in Moenkopi

Moenkopi is a Hopi community on the Navajo Reservation in northeastern Arizona. Moenkopi is the most strategically located of all the Hopi villages with respect to the opportunity for wage work in Tuba City, the site of the Western Navajo Subagency, about two miles from the village. A Hopi can commute there on foot and spend his leisure hours at home in the general surroundings of a Hopi pueblo. Neither an urban ghetto nor an isolated reservation settlement, Moenkopi offers a happy combination of both the Indian and white worlds. This attraction, together with the origin of the village as a farming colony of Oraibi in the midst of Navajo Indian territory, has contributed to the mobility and instability of the population.

In 1962–63, there were about 600 residents divided into 106 households or dwelling units (Nagata, 1970) and evenly distributed between two residential segments of Upper and Lower Moenkopi. Since the establishment of the Hopi Tribal Council in 1936, this division has been officially recognized as an administrative one in the tribal constitution, with one council representative allocated to each district. For various reasons, however, only Upper Moenkopi has been taking part in the council and Lower Moenkopi has consistently refused to do so, remaining instead under the general leadership of a hereditary chief. On the other hand, the leadership of Upper Moenkopi has been collective and is assumed by a small number of people who, since 1959, formed a closed elite by occupying, in rotation, most of the available official positions in the Upper Moenkopi Village Council.

In the following discussion, I use the term 'faction' to refer to the two groups under the leadership of the Upper Moenkopi Council and the Lower Moenkopi chief, respectively. As I pointed out previously, the usage of 'faction' may be objected to on the grounds that the members of the two groups, along with a small number of others, do not form a single political community within which factions form (Boissevain, 1964:1275–6). Considering the generally schismatic nature of Hopi factionalism (Siegel and Beals, 1960) and that of Moenkopi in particular, the objection is quite reasonable. On the other hand, there are numerous aspects in which it still makes sense to speak of Moenkopi as a community. First of all, surrounded by the Navajo Indians, the people consider themselves as residents of a small Hopi village. Kinship and occupational ties closely bind them in a network of daily prestations irrespective of their affiliations to a particular leadership. Although the people have never cooperated for common activities for more than thirty years, there is a strong feeling of identity as Hopi and as residents of Moenkopi pueblo. On this basis, one may characterize the political process that has been going on in Moenkopi as that of two political communities within a single society, in the same way as Mair talks of the Nuer (1962:46–7). I also strongly suspect that had the same process occurred half a century ago, the fission of Moenkopi into Lower and Upper divisions would have been completed by now, as was the case with Oraibi in 1906 (*vide infra*). As it happened – perhaps unfortunately for the people of Moenkopi – this course of fission was slowed down, if not totally arrested, and the people were more or less forced to go through a rather messy sorting-out process. In my judgement of the history of schismatic factionalism in Moenkopi, the events of 1962–63 to be described later appear to belong to the penultimate phase of this fission, and it is what happened in this phase that deserves some analysis for the larger question of political modernization among the Indians.

Finally, and more importantly for my argument, is the manner in which the people of Moenkopi view these groupings. This view is by no means neutral or indifferent but strongly tinged with moral connotations – something that should not have been. Leaving aside the details of this until later, it is because of such a moral vector in the people's view of these groupings that my use of 'faction' is best expressed in the sense used by Madison: "By a faction, I understand a number of citizens, whether amounting to a majority or minority of the whole, who are united and actuated by some common impulse of passion, or of interest, adverse to the rights of other citizens, or to the permanent and aggregate interests of the community" (1948:42).[2] In other words, a faction is a political grouping regarded as illegitimate by those in the community that do not belong to it. The Hopi do not possess a word that corresponds in meaning to a faction (cf. Voegelin and Voegelin, 1957:49), but say *kansul* for the people who go along with the Upper Moenkopi Council or, slightly derogatorily, *kansulhoyam* ("little council people"); and for those going along with the Lower Moenkopi chief, *aiyave* ("non-conformist"), a term that was never used for self-designation until recently. Otherwise I was given expressions like *hisat sinom* ("ancient people"), or *hopivitsukami* ("those who observe the Hopi way") for those against the Upper Moenkopi or tribal council in general. More interesting are the terms for the people with the Upper Moenkopi Council: *pahanvinaguti* ("those who live white man's way"), *tsotsivalhoyam* ("those who meet," obviously referring to their frequent meetings), and *pensilhoyam* ("little pencil people," referring to their predilection for keeping written records) (Nagata, 1970:93). The fact that there are no generic words to refer to 'faction' induces me to think that these groupings are considered illegitimate.

The sphere of influence of each group of leaders does not coincide with the residential division of Upper and Lower Moenkopi. Because Moenkopi territory is not precisely defined either in the Hopi custom or in the reservation regulations of the Bureau of Indian Affairs, each area does not take on the character of a territory the residents of which are controlled by its respective leaders. Consequently, about one third of the component households in one of the two residential segments claim to follow the leadership of the other. Numerically all the households are broken down as shown in Table 1.

This table indicates several aspects of factionalism in Moenkopi. First a household is a unit of participation in factionalism; as a factional arena, it is unstable and reorganizes itself either through the divorce of a married couple or the withdrawal from participation in one or the other faction. However, faction affiliation tends to be homogeneous within a household. Secondly, the criteria of membership in factions are diverse; they may consist of participation in the *kachina* ceremonies as in Upper Moenkopi, or in the use or non-use of electricity in the households as in Lower Moenkopi – not to mention kinship, occupational ties, and patronage of a more economic nature (renting homes or farming land, lending cash, and

TABLE 1

Faction Affiliations of Moenkopi Households

Factions	Upper Moenkopi	Lower Moenkopi	Total
Upper Moenkopi Council	28	16	44
Lower Moenkopi Chief	15	30	45
Hotevilla Leaders	4	0	4
Neutral	8	5	13
Total	55	51	106

the like). Generally, because of the multiplex role structure of Moenkopi, these criteria cannot be segregated into single and exclusive categories, but they frequently overlap (see Nicholas, 1965:42). Finally, there are "neutral" households (cf. Pocock, 1957:300; Bailey, 1957:225; Epstein, 1962:132, 135–6; Nicholas, 1965:23) that were described by my informants as "neutral," "inactive," or sometimes "nothing." Some of them are the households of widows and divorcees and can be regarded as politically disenfranchised. The remainder of the "neutrals" consists of young households recently established from elsewhere and whose economic basis lies entirely outside the village; they are potential recruits to either faction but have not been so yet. The group following the Hotevilla leadership are original inhabitants of Moenkopi and once played an important role in the council. Through a series of incidents during the 1940s and '50s, however, they repudiated their council membership and became followers of the Hotevilla leaders. Their opposition to the council often brings them into coalition with the Lower Moenkopi chief and his faction. The existence of neutral households within the village indicates the weakness of the Moenkopi leaders.

No apparent correlation exists between factional affiliation and the degree of household acculturation or types of occupation. The use of electricity in Lower Moenkopi is an exception as the chief refuses to permit it on his land allotment which covers half the Lower Moenkopi site. However, this cannot be taken for a correlation since his supporters in Upper Moenkopi are equipped with electricity. At least one of the chief's close followers, his lieutenant in Lower Moenkopi, installed a gasoline generator for electricity. (Although Lower Moenkopi households do not possess electricity, they are not necessarily deprived of its benefit; one young member uses his pair of electric hair clippers at the home of his maternal uncle in Upper Moenkopi who has electricity but no hair clippers.) In terms of automobiles, gas refrigerators, and cooking ranges, no recognizable difference exists between the council homes and those of the chief's followers. Several council homes, including that of a council secretary, still depend on firewood for cooking and heating. Because of the crowded pattern of settlement, the homes of Lower Moenkopi may present a more depressing sight than those of Upper Moenkopi, and the council faction frequently exploits this image *vis-à-vis* outsiders. However, it does not appear to reflect the reality of culture change between the two factions. The chief's followers are just as eager to assert their modernity on the one hand and the backwardness of the council people on the other. This is one of the reasons that the dichotomy of 'progressive' and 'conservative' is inadequate in describing Moenkopi factionalism.

A similar situation prevails in types of employment. Occupational specialization is still limited to a handful of young householders who earn their living solely from skilled trades. Otherwise an attempt is made by the members of each household to engage in all three major occupations of farming, grazing, and wage work. Land allotments that formed the basis of farming in Moenkopi half a century ago are concentrated among the followers of the Lower Moenkopi chief, but subsequently many plots of land were granted the council people outside the allotment area. Cattle raising, on the other hand, has been dominated by the council followers. Yet their dominance has never been complete: of the present six herding outfits, one is composed of the chief's followers, another of individuals following Hotevilla, while the third is of mixed composition.

As a result of the drastic decline in farming and grazing, more than 75 percent of the households in each segment are now engaged in wage work in Tuba City most of which is provided by two governmental agencies, the Bureau of Indian Affairs and the Public Health Service. In addition to the increased volume of employed since the implementation of the Navajo-Hopi Rehabilitation Act of 1950, numerous private business enterprises have been lured to Tuba City and offer further opportunities for wage work. All these establishments compete for labour of Moenkopi Indians as they are a fairly stable reservoir and of higher quality than the Navajo.

In this general abundance of job opportunities, factional differences are of little relevance. A number of informational posts in the local Bureau office are held by council people, but this is due largely to the possession of certain skills and not to factional affiliation as such. One woman whose household supports the Lower Moenkopi chief occupies a job of a similar nature there. It is true that in the past the council charged that those following the chief could not accept government employment since they were against the government as represented by the Bureau of Indian Affairs. The chief himself, consistent with the ideology of the anti-council faction of the Hopi as a whole, has never taken a government job. These charges, however, have never deterred the chief's followers from assuming wage-earning jobs. The chief, as a leader, recognizes the need of his followers for cash and accepts the importance of government employment for them. As for himself, he belongs to a construction labourers' union and earns wages from irregular labour.

To conclude, there appears to be no significant difference between the people of the opposing factions in their lifestyles or productive activities; both factions are heavily committed to a cash economy in wage work and a consumer market in nearby towns. If these aspects of life in Moenkopi are not relevant to factions, what role do they play?

Function of the Opposition

Two major factions are in control of *kachina* ceremonies, residential sites, and reservoir water for irrigation. One must obtain permission from the leaders of the respective factions to join a *kachina* dance, to reside in either segment of Moenkopi, or to irrigate a field with the reservoir water. To avail oneself of these resources, however, what seems crucial is to belong to one or another faction, irrespective of the particular ideological commitments of the leaders. The use of reservoir water for irrigation illustrates this point.

Unique among Hopi farming villages, Moenkopi depends chiefly on two systems of irrigation: Hopi reservoirs and Moenkopi Wash. Only the former are controlled by the factions. The reservoirs were originally constructed by the Mormon pioneers in the late nineteenth century. Their maintenance is now equally entrusted to the council and the chief, both of which possess keys to the reservoir gates. In order to draw irrigation water to a farm, one must in theory obtain permission from the respective leaders. Having irrigated the plots, one is expected to close the gates and return the keys. However, the people who farm a tract of contiguous fields usually arrange to leave the gates open until all the fields are irrigated. These people often belong to opposing factions. The leaders do not punish such a default and as one informant put it, they cannot: for a defaulter, when refused by one leader, can always go to another.[3] The leaders are responsible for the maintenance of the reservoirs and irrigation ditch for which they depend on assistance from their followers, and so they can ill afford to deny them their requests. Recruitment for this labour is not an easy task since a considerable number of Hopi do not depend on reservoir irrigation for farming, and farming itself is a declining industry.

The more important use of factions in the contemporary context of Moenkopi is the provision of political opposition which, while preventing the leaders from creating a single political authority over their respective areas, ensures the opportunity for each individual household to pursue economic activities in and outside the community. An incident I encountered during field work may suffice as illustration.

In the winter of 1963, damage in the nearby sewer lagoons of the Navajo Tribe created a danger of contamination in the Moenkopi spring and fields.

Immediately the Upper Moenkopi Council collected signatures from the villagers for a petition to remove the lagoons from the present location. The petition was addressed to the Navajo tribe and other related governmental agencies and the signatures were collected on the occasion of a mass innoculation programme by the United States Public Health Service from Tuba City. Although the petition was managed by an official of the council, a considerable number of the Lower Moenkopi chief's followers also signed the petition, presumably on the understanding that the signature was required by the government and not by the council, and that it was to indicate the receipt of the injection. Soon after this, however, a rumour spread that all who had signed the petition now joined the council in political activity against the government and Navajo Tribal Council and that, therefore, they could be fired from government employment. This rumour exploits the idea, prevalent among many Moenkopi residents, that as federal government employees, they should refrain from participation in politics. The origin of the rumour remained ambiguous and it is not clear to me why it was thought possible that the council, an instrument of the U.S. Government, could undertake an action that would oppose the government. My argument to this effect had failed to convince the agitated followers of the chief, among whom the general consensus was simply that the rumour was engineered by the Upper Moenkopi Council. Consequently some followers of the chief urged him to make a counter-petition to the Hopi Indian Agency at Keams Canyon, indicating that the signers in the chief's petition were withdrawing their names from the council petition and that they preferred a direct negotiation with the Navajo tribe to a legal suit, an action recommended in the council petition. In the end nothing substantial came out of these manœuverings, and although the Navajo tribe repaired the damage to the Hopi fields, the lagoons remained in the same location.

This incident may be interpreted along the lines suggested by Firth (1957:293) and Nicholas (1965:57); that is, in default of agreed-upon rules of decision-making for the entire village, Moenkopi factions present the only means of political participation by making alternative leaders available and mobilizing support. More important, however, is the role of factions in providing a check, in the form of opposition, against the possibility of monolithic control by either faction which may restrict access to external economic opportunities. To illustrate further, when the council, with the tacit understanding of the Tuba City Agency, attempted to charge cash for irrigation water, the chief was once again summoned by his people to block the measure.

The chance of such unilateral domination is more apparent in the council, an instrument of reservation development for the federal government that tends to become the sole agent of innovation in the village. The villagers are well aware of this and often characterize the rule of the council as "dictatorship." However, the same danger is perceived regarding the leadership of the chief and criticisms about his arbitrariness are not entirely absent. For the interests of individual residents, therefore, factionalism in Moenkopi is a guarantee of an open society.

Distribution of Power

A number of conditions also disperse the power of the community and restrict the effectiveness of the faction leaders. Although gossip and rumours are exchanged perhaps as frequently as in the past, their force of subtle sanction appears to be on the decline. In one case, a middle-aged lady, when hearing of a rumour about her adulterous behaviour, caused a nocturnal clamour when she went to a house and confronted the lady who was allegedly the source of the rumour. The sewer lagoon incident also shows that not only did the rumour fail to intimidate the people, but it led them to a political counteraction (see Cox, 1970). In addition, with better medical services provided by the government and increased economic opportunities, another traditional means of social control, witchcraft accusation, is becoming less effective; the medicine men in the village appear to thrive mostly on Navajo patients. There is a tendency, it seems, that as life in the village becomes occupationally more diverse, the web of the mystical nexus between misfortune and the moral code gets somewhat loosened: misfortune tends to receive 'natural' explanations, whereas a breach in the moral code, insofar as it impinges upon interpersonal relationships, tends to be rationalized in 'political' terms. Neither does public ridicule of the clowns in *kachina* ceremonies seem to provide sanctions against deviance; on one occasion, an old lady, whose son's misdemeanour was being acted out by a group of clowns, rushed out of her audience seat and began unashamedly beating a clown on the head. In fact, in Upper Moenkopi, the trend is for the council to rely increasingly on 'external control' by the Hopi Tribal Police. Once again, however, the effectiveness of the Hopi Police is limited because of its identification with the council and the ambiguity in jurisdiction between itself and the Navajo Police.

The administrative ambiguity of Moenkopi is of a greater significance to the distribution of power between Moenkopi factions. Since participation in the wage economy in Moenkopi requires not only working in Tuba City but also residing in the village, the residential site emerges as the most important resource at present. Yet the site secure to the Hopi is found only in Lower Moenkopi, where it stands on two Hopi allotments, and the Upper Moenkopi site is in theory on the Navajo Reservation.

In the Upper Moenkopi constitution of 1959, its boundary is only vaguely specified. Although this vagueness in the territorial boundary of Upper Moenkopi weakens the council's position, nevertheless the Lower Moenkopi chief cannot secure control over the site. For not only does one of the allotments belong to a follower of the council, but also, because of the rule of inheritance of allotment lands enforced by the Bureau of Indian Affairs, the title to the chief's allotment is divided between a number of his relatives – his 'legal' share being only a fraction of it.[4]

Cash-earning opportunities outside the community can, under certain conditions, be made the basis of factional power. (The example of Kluckhohn and Leighton's Agency Indians [1948:106] points to this possibility when a limited number of acculturated Indians came to monopolize the mediation between an Indian agency and its charge) (see Mayer, 1967). This appears especially true when the demand for cash is increasing among the Indians at the same time as the employment opportunities are becoming limited, as was observed in an isolated Navajo community of Shonto (Adams, 1963:101).

These conditions do not exist in Moenkopi (cf. Hopi Hearings, 1955:296): first, because the two largest employment agencies in Tuba City are responsible mainly for the Navajo Indians, and secondly, because no official administrative linkage exists between them and the Upper Moenkopi Council,[5] which has no privileged access to these agencies but conducts such transactions with similar agencies in Keams Canyon. Consequently factionalism in Moenkopi, a serious concern of the Hopi Agency in Keams Canyon eighty miles away, bears little importance to the Tuba City Agency whose main interest is to fill the available jobs to carry out the programs for the Navajo. The absence of discrimination, *de jure* or *de facto*, by the government agencies regarding Hopi factionalism appears to attract to Tuba City those Hopi from elsewhere in Hopiland who would otherwise refuse to accept government services on account of their factional commitment. Thus a chief of Shongopavi, a second Mesa village, who had never been in the hospital in Keams Canyon was persuaded to come to the Tuba City Public Health Service Hospital through his anti-council follower in the village who had a close friend, a Hotevilla follower, in Moenkopi; the latter in turn maintained a fairly close friendship with the hospital staff through a Navajo nurse and her relatives employed there. (For other such examples, see Nagata, 1970:230.) Finally the volume of employment is large enough to eliminate possible domination by either faction but not the factions themselves (cf. Siegel and Beals, 1966:138).[6]

The involvement of the people in a wage economy outside the village has a restrictive effect on the power of the leaders. Since economic opportunity within the village is extremely limited, the people are generally indifferent to village affairs as shown in the difficulty the leaders have in recruiting cooperative labour. This cannot be construed as sheer political apathy, however, for in Lower Moenkopi it is frequently the people rather than the chief who call the faction into action in times of crises.

Finally the leaders of Moenkopi possess no other resource, supernatural or otherwise, that might make the villagers dependent on them. The advantages the council may cull from their mediatory role for the Keams Canyon Agency are limited in number and immediacy. Only the Lower Moenkopi chief extends emergency cash loans to his close followers, but the value of this act of patronage is again restricted against the expanding economic frontier of the village.

The diffuse pattern of distribution of power in Moenkopi provides a balance in factional opposition. Three conditions seem important in creating a balance in conflict: first, providing the source of conflict or things to fight about; secondly eliminating the possibility of coalition; and finally avoiding the possibility of unilateral domination by force or coercion; in other words, to make sure there will be no fission, coalition, or conquest. Difficulties in calling the factional competition a draw by fission exist, I think, first in the overlap of jurisdiction by the two factions over the same resources. The Moenkopi reservoir complex is such an example. The village plaza in the Lower Moenkopi site had been shared by the Upper Moenkopi Council until recently (*infra*). The Moenkopi spring is still claimed by both the council and the chief. Secondly, the faction members are distributed across the *de facto* boundaries of the two residential sites, thereby making it almost impossible to draw a clear line of territorial separation between them.[7] Interestingly the leaders seem aware of this difficulty. The Lower Moenkopi chief once startled me by saying that if only the government respected who his follower was and who was not, he would not mind accepting the government projects. I do not know if a rather neat numerical balance in factional membership in Moenkopi is a diarchic tendency unique to the Hopi as a whole or a characteristic of a certain type of factionalism. For the Hopi as a whole, the breakdown of the constitutionally allocated Tribal Council representatives between those that take part in the council deliberations and those that refuse to do so is 9/8 and a similar division in terms of 'recognized villages' and two Moenkopi 'districts' is 5/5 (E. A. Kennard, personal communication).

Coalition appears even a more difficult feat than fission. In the past the villagers once closed their ranks to expell a Mennonite missionary. At the time of Moenkopi's beginnings as a stable colony of Oraibi, the threat of the Navajo alerted the villagers to the necessity of having a common leader. Since the U.S. Government took over, however, the external relationships of Moenkopi have become much more complex and the outside world assumed an equivocal character to the interests of the people. Finally, because of the colonial status of Moenkopi in the Third Mesa social system (see Connelly, 1956; Eggan, 1964), the factionalism in Moenkopi is articulated with that in other villages in the system and to Hopi factionalism as a whole; since there seems to be no solution in store for Hopi factionalism, coalition in the local context of Moenkopi alone is made more difficult.

Forceful domination by one faction over the other is also a remote possibility. This is implicit in the distribution of power resources already described. Furthermore the tribal articulation of Moenkopi factionalism results in a tendency for any conflict within the village to become a tribal issue. Trouble in Moenkopi does not remain in the village but spreads to other villages of Hopiland proper, and the leaders, instead of fighting out an issue with each other, seek mediators outside the village to do the work of negotiation or bargaining. This avoidance of direct confrontation by the leaders or "politics without confrontation" referred to elsewhere (Nagata, 1970:82ff., 1968:28–9; see also Spiro, 1968:416–7) appears to work in such a way as to protect the leaders from coming to a showdown at the same time as it perpetuates their factions.

More important in this and other regards is, of course, the role of the U.S. Government. While insisting that the present tribal council is the only legitimate representative of the entire Hopi, it has so far refused to bar those against the council from deriving benefits from government assistance; nor does it overtly encourage the council to force its policies upon the anti-council village communities.[8] This applies with greater truth to Moenkopi where the jurisdictional separation between the Hopi and Navajo Agencies is ambiguous.

Opposition and Freedom

In a recent article, Bujra spells out several conditions which promote the institutionalization of factionalism (1973:145ff.). Some of these conditions such as the duration of factionalism, "without either side winning an effective victory," and the articulation of the factions into the wider political system and ideological appeals are present in Moenkopi factionalism. Although the details of the stratification system of traditional Hopi society are hardly known to us, the origin of Moenkopi factionalism, as that of the classical schism in Oraibi (Titiev, 1944), appears to be related to the cleavage between the ceremony-owning clans (*pavansinom*, "powerful people") and the clans without ceremonial prerogatives (*shikyabunsinom*, "ordinary people") (Nagata, 1970:44). The present leaders of the Upper Moenkopi Council emerged from the latter and are now ironically called *pavansinom*. Applying Bujra's argument still further, Moenkopi factions, as they operate now, approximate more stable political organizations such as "local councils," although, as she also points out, the support of the faction leaders cuts across the community "diagonally" rather than "horizontally" or "vertically" and, along with the diffusion of power in the community, results in the leaders' having a weak sanctioning power and a brittleness in the relationship between the leaders and their followers.

The stability of the relationship between a leader and his followers is no doubt dependent upon a number of circumstances but, in general, Bailey's remark is applicable here; namely, that the proportion of the investment a follower makes in the political stock of his leader, relative to the total investable resources available to the former, determines the degree of compliance the leader can expect from the follower (1969:75–6). In contemporary Moenkopi, apart from the small leadership core of each faction, the amount of investment, either moral or economic, which an average follower makes to the faction leader, is extremely limited. The expected return from such an investment is small in comparison to alternative opportunities for investment available outside Moenkopi. One also suspects that it is simply not strategic to commit oneself exclusively to one faction over and against the other, insofar as the resources outside the community remain accessible through a division in the leadership. On the other hand, to have 'friends' outside the village is an important means to ensure accessibility to these resources, and hence, it should not be surprising to see many Moenkopi Hopi have, what they call, *pahan kwachi* ("white friends") whom they invite to *kachina* ceremonies and life passage rituals.

Consequently, the support committed to the faction leaders by the grass-roots followers tends to be shallow and of a tentative nature and switching sides between the two factions does not appear to incur a heavy cost. In fact, the grass-roots strategy consists of presenting the appearance of being yet-to-be-recruited so that individuals could price their support dearly in the event that the leader of either faction came soliciting it. Given this strategy and given further the rather bullish council leadership bent on accomplishing various government projects, and the relatively self-sufficient, bearish Lower Moenkopi chief, what frequently happens is a sequence of movements in which the council leaders, in order to achieve a specific aim, try to mobilize the grass-roots. Some of the latter, fearful of council domination, then turn to the Lower Moenkopi chief who is only too willing to oblige them for the opportunity to publicly legitimate his otherwise inert leadership by taking an opposite stand. There is yet another implication of this brittle relationship.

For a small number of households in Upper Moenkopi, the current pattern of factional opposition appears to be a condition of social freedom (Oppenheim, 1961:110ff.) as was illustrated in the domestic water-sewage project completed in 1964. The present condition of Moenkopi factionalism is temporary and, I suspect, primarily applicable only to the last three decades. A serious change is now taking place in the area as the Hopi of Moenkopi begin negotiating with the Navajo for a more equitable distribution of land rights (Brugge, 1968). The political implication of the Moenkopi water-sewage project must also be sought in this trend of political change. As was shown in the previous discussion, the only feasible stabilization of politics in Moenkopi would be to bring about the creation of two political communities, or fission. One of the difficulties of this solution, however, is the ambiguity of jurisdiction over a number of the community resources. The water-sewage project may, therefore, be interpreted as an attempt to clarify this situation by creating a new basis of power for the council.

The project was initiated in 1960 by the Upper Moenkopi Council under the sponsorship of the U.S. Public Health Service (pursuant to the Indian Sanitation Facilities Act) on the traditionally defined site of Upper Moenkopi; it was meant to centralize the distribution of domestic water and sewage disposal. The Public Health Service helped to install toilet facilities in individual households at reduced cost, and the villagers were to pay maintenance fees to the council each month. The implication of the project soon became apparent. Immediately after the system came into operation, the council called in a Hopi policeman from Keams Canyon and, in his presence, suspended water service to several households who were followers of the chief and Hotevilla and who failed to pay the first dues (*Navajo Times*, July 22, 1965; Nagata, 1970:77).

This attempt by the council to create a corporate political unit was met by two counteractions. First, the Lower Moenkopi chief, on the strength of his claim to land allotment, denied the council further use of the plaza and *kivas* on the Lower Moenkopi site. The council met this action by building its own *kiva* and holding dances on the Upper Moenkopi site. The net result of this series of actions was to increase the fissionary trend.[9] The second and more important counteraction came from a few of the households whose water was shut off for about two months. During this time they obtained water from the outside faucets of neighbouring households, or reverted to the custom of carrying water by hand from the village spring. They then decided to have a private drilling outfit from an off-reservation town dig wells on their house lots. One woman mentioned to me that they had confirmed the legality of such an action from the Keams Canyon Agency through the intermediary of Mr. Barry Goldwater, then Senator of Arizona. To accomplish this her household had to make a much greater financial outlay than it would have cost to subscribe to the Upper Moenkopi system. However, her home became equipped not only with its own water supply, but also with its own sewage tank and all other internal plumbing.[10] Throughout this course of action, the council could neither prevent these households from digging their own wells, nor could it punish them for it.

It may be objected that the council had control in this interaction since it almost forced the dissenting households to do as they did (see Oppenheim, 1961:55). I do not think this objection holds, however, since the council's cutting off the water supply was intended to force the people to become part of the system of water distribution. Secondly the action of the dissenting households was entirely unexpected by the council. Finally the dissenters did have the following alternatives: creating their own system of water distribution, joining forces with the Lower Moenkopi people for another system, or setting up a water delivery service. In short, the consequences of the council action were unpredictable and resulted in a demonstration of the council's lack of control.

Condition of Freedom in Moenkopi Factionalism

Social scientists as well as practicing politicians have long been interested in the function of social cleavages that provide the bases for articulation of political interests. James Madison saw the importance of cross-cutting cleavages as a check against the tyranny of the majority (1948:47, 267). Simmel (1950), Kroeber (1917), Gluckman (1955), and Dahrendorf (1959) noted the same as a condition for political stability. Ellis (1951) and Murphy (1957) discussed a consequence of such cross-cutting ties in the projection of aggression to the outside – as in aggressive warfare. Sociological discussion on political opposition appears to follow this line of reasoning. Both Coser (1956) and Blau (1964) see the function of opposition within a society as a safety-valve mechanism. They regard a line of cleavage as absorbing social discontent and legitimating it in the form of an opposition ideology. Firth suspected the same when he stated that factions "let off steam" (1957:294).

In Moenkopi, the emotional involvement in factional disputes is quite intense, particularly among women, whereas men, including the leadership core, assume a more pragmatic attitude when faced with specific issues. But these emotions are deceptive at best. Naive fieldworker that I was and taken in by the hostility of emotion, my attempt at some practical solutions to what appeared to be realistic issues was, upon reflection, a sheer error of interpretation: a touch of *doladoli* perhaps (Bailey, 1969), but my experience confirmed the lesson given me earlier by more experienced Hopi researchers that one should not take gossip too seriously. Yet in contrast to *doladoli*, emotions and hostilities are not expressed in public confrontations but as gossip, within each faction, or as happens frequently, to outsiders such as myself. Thirdly, although the people do restrain their emotions and hostile attitudes from interfering with their inescapable daily interactions across factional lines (hence the more pragmatic attitude among the men who have to work together on various jobs), they reduce the frequency of interaction in the village by simple avoidance. Thus a woman used to send her small adopted daughter to do minor, nightly shopping at a village store run by a family of the opposite faction.

Beals and Siegel criticized Firth's view as a biased interpretation "in favour of functionalism" (1966:159). Although I do not entirely share their criticism, I must insist that psychological opposition alone is not sufficient to explain the significance of factional opposition in Moenkopi. The fundamental issue of factionalism both in Moenkopi and in Hopiland as a whole revolves around the form of government: whereas the council advocates a government based on the current tribal constitution, its opponents assert the supremacy of hereditary chieftainship. Because of this disagreement, the factional opposition in Moenkopi can be regarded as neither loyal opposition nor as "political competition," but rather as "opposition in principle" (Kirchheimer, 1966:237). It is important, however, to note that this opposition, in principle, is radically different from what is ordinarily conceived of as opposition in democratic theory. The crucial difference is the absence in factional opposition of what Kirchheimer called "an eternal paradox: the principle that impediments to political action may be wholesome and are therefore to be protected" (1957:127).

It is obvious that the people of Moenkopi do not subscribe to this principle in forming factions. Both factions regard the other as politically and morally unacceptable, that is, illegitimate, and refuse to accept decisions by the opposite faction as authoritative and binding. In this sense Moenkopi does not form a single political community (Easton, 1959:229). The existence of opposition in Moenkopi, therefore, is not due to the popular consensus regarding the freedom of dissent, but to the external power which is responsible for the present factionalism to begin with, and which so far has refrained from helping either faction to impose itself upon the other. This power is the U.S. Government. Tolerance of opposition in Moenkopi is a result of *Pax Americana*.[11]

The principle of legitimate opposition, a landmark of liberal democracy (Ionescu and Madriaga, 1968), is usually considered as an expression of individual freedom in a democratic system. The democratic theory appears to maintain that some social constraints are inevitable to ensure this freedom (Malinowski, 1944; Lee, 1959, 1963); hence the idea of "freedom under law" (Parsons, 1964:296). Weber warned against an excessive promotion of this idea as he saw its association grow with increasing bureaucratization (Gerth and Mills, 1958:70ff). Leach objected to it by indicating the existence of inherent inequality in legal systems in general and the relativity of freedom within a particular society (1963). Because of this the democratic theory usually adds a rider that the constraints are internalized and "we love them" (Homans, 1950:329, 332–3), and that the freedom is of a negative variety (*freedom from*) in contrast to a positive one (*freedom to*) pursued by totalitarianism (Berlin, 1958). This does not alter the fact, however, that political opposition is taken to operate as a dual principle: one is free to oppose so long as a particular issue is not decided, but 'unfree' (Oppenheim, 1961:68ff.) to do so once it is. It consists of an interplay of "freedom of political action" and "freedom of political obligation" (Dahl, 1966:389). Opting out of the system is not within the purview of democratic freedom and polity is coextensive with society.

That there are viable societies which allow opting out of the system has been shown by Weber (Gerth and Mills, 1958:323ff.) and Dumont (1960) with reference to Hindu and Buddhist renouncers of the world, and by Pospisil on the voluntary banishment of the Kapauku Papuans (Leach, 1963:85). Likewise the social freedom in Moenkopi factionalism is not of the democratic variety, but rather a consequence of the opposition between the factions, each of which claims an incomplete sovereignty and is unable to control its constituents. An individual remains free to choose between them, and the availability of alternatives permits him to pursue his own interests in and outside the *society* of Moenkopi.[12] Radcliffe-Brown already suggested the importance of a type of political system based on balanced opposition and warned against a restrictive definition of political systems by "sovereign, territorial states" alone (1940:xx). The subsequent work on segmentary lineages demonstrates the value of his remark and it is significant to note that Evans-Pritchard described the Nuer as being "deeply democratic" (1940:294). Finally I must quote from Durkheim who stated "... the two parties, face to face, turn from the conflict realising that it solves nothing and content themselves with the retention of their former situations. They tolerate each other, not being able to conquer" (1964 ⟨1933⟩:98).

The image of a Hopi community in the past has been one of peace and harmony, where every individual conformed to all the community norms through rigorous religious concentration and ceremonial performances (Aitken, 1930; Eggan, 1943). Even in such an integrated society, there were persons who resisted community pressure and deviated from community norms. These individuals were often accused of being witches (*poaka*), called dangerous (*nukpana*), and stigmatized as non-conformists (*aiyave*). When the community could not slough them off with its "second line of defense" (cf. Aberle, 1951:124; Connelly, 1956; Eggan, 1964), it finally went through the process of fission (see Cushing, *et al.*, 1922:283; Aitken, 1930:383ff.; Parsons, 1939:14; Eggan, 1950:17; Spicer, 1962:500). The split of Oraibi is the last such case (Titiev, 1944:69ff.; Siegel and Beals, 1960:394). The process of political change in Moenkopi may be regarded as the same, but in slow motion. Yet the confinement of the Hopi to a reservation appears to have made this type of conflict resolution extremely difficult. At the same time, the Hopi tribe itself is now dichotomized between the two large factions, and the term, *aiyave*, is often used to describe those against the Tribal Council. As the *aiyave* became more numerous, however, the term ceased to convey a sense of opprobrium and acquired a degree of respectability. Individual Hopi also appear to have become less afraid and increasingly emancipated from the narrow bounds of the village community.

As I previously indicated, this state of affairs in Moenkopi is, in the last analysis, dependent on the policy of the U.S. Government. To the advocates of liberal democracy and Indian self-determination, this state may seem disappointing (see Dobyns, 1968:182). In matters of administration, it deprives the government of "majority affiliation" (Barnett, 1953:327) and makes it almost impossible to obtain cooperation for community-wide projects. To many Indians of Moenkopi, however, the present state of factionalism allows them to pursue the dictates of self-interest.

The political problem of Moenkopi, further, should not be taken as unique or deplorable. Many newly independent countries suffer from a similar lack of political stability and, from the democratic viewpoint as well as that of central administration, it may be said of Moenkopi that "what is needed is not an opposition but a majority" (Aron as quoted by Emerson, 1960:6). On the other hand, the Hopi distrust of American democracy and government-in-law is in keeping with de Tocqueville's commentary on American dealings with the Indians: "It is impossible to destroy men with more respect to the laws of humanity" (1968:1). The freedom of the Hopi is the refusal of the Socratic hemlock (see Mill, 1912:32).[13]

There is one final angle from which to appreciate the Hopi pursuit of freedom, and that is to relate it to the range of choice available to Hopi individuals who are liberated from the constraints of the community. The job opportunities available to them outside the community are exclusively blue-collar, mainly of an unskilled nature. At the same time, the chances of accumulating wealth and moving up the social scale of prestige recognized by the larger American society are extremely limited. In this respect, the Hopi Indians are not different from the majority of the American Indians, uneducated and poor. If the village community no longer fulfills their needs, the society outside the village is accessible only by way of low-paid, unskilled labour. To be sure, their participation in wage-work in the environs of Tuba City has been extensive, but this could be interpreted as a direct result of the decline in the Moenkopi economy, itself, because of the penetration of the cash economy and over-population. Yet the income from this work is not enough to lure them out of the village, and thus the majority continue to live there, maintaining two fields of activity.

In other words, one of the consequences of political modernization, as it was imposed by the American government, was to weaken the basis of community solidarity. The moral ties binding individuals together were loosened and released them from the grip of the pueblo, so that the 'free' individuals could serve the larger economy in the capacity of proletarians and yet, it is important to add, without contributing to the formation of the proletarian class.

Conclusion

Having looked at the situation in Moenkopi, one may ask if a similar situation exists in other villages of Hopiland. This question is difficult to answer mainly because of the manner in which the council and traditional village structures interlock with each other upon their respective *mesas*. To wit, eleven Hopi villages in Hopiland proper are grouped into three clusters upon the First, Second, and Third *Mesas*, respectively. The villages on each *mesa* share a basic cultural homogeneity *vis-à-vis* those on other mesas with respect to ritual performance, dialect, and to a certain extent, craft specialization. In contrast to this arrangement, there are council and traditional villages in one *mesa*, each of which is reasonably well demarcated from the others territorially and administratively so as not to have the untidy problems seen in Moenkopi. In short, each village possesses a unitary 'government' which is less subject to manipulation by the people (than in Moenkopi). Consequently factional oppositions in each village are not as saliently organized as in Moenkopi. This by no means implies that a village in Hopiland proper is all peace and harmony; on the contrary, disputes and conflicts there are quite common, but they tend to consist of disconnected, interpersonal bickerings and quarrels. When a dispute becomes prolonged, involving an increasing number of people, a violent encounter ensues, as happened in Hotevilla regarding the introduction of electricity in 1964. The chance for such violence depends, as is to be expected, upon the nature of external pressure, and increases when a village is confronted by a government project that affects it as a whole and that is supported by large resources. Because of the monolithic control by either the village council or a small group of traditional leaders including a village chief, individuals, dissatisfied with village leadership and unable to form an effective opposition, are left with the alternative of migrating out of their villages to other communities such as Moenkopi or to off-reservation towns. There are, of course, numerous other reasons for Hopi to leave the reservation of which the economic factor may be as important as the political one. Yet, as Dozier pointed out for Santa Clara Pueblo (1966), factionalism also contributes to the encouragement of migration among the Hopi. In fact, Moenkopi appeared to have played a role in absorbing the dissidents from Oraibi, its mother village. At the time of my field work, I was told by a number of people in Hotevilla that if people in that traditional village wished to live "the white man's way," they should move to Moenkopi where such a style of life was more or less tolerated.

That Moenkopi is viewed by the Third Mesa Hopi in just such a manner points to, what appears to me to be, a built-in strategy with which the Hopi protect their tradition against powerful outside cultural influences. It consists, in short, of differentiating a number of village communities according to the degree to which external influences are permitted to infiltrate. Thus, on each mesa, there is a council village (that is, a village whose loyalties lie with the council) which assumes a 'contact position' between the traditional village and the 'larger' society and acts as buffer to external pressures. Dozier's description of First Mesa clearly indicates this articulation pattern (1954). Shipaulovi on Second Mesa and New Oraibi on Third Mesa also play the contact role to Shongopavi and Oraibi/Hotevilla respectively. On a smaller scale, Moenkopi is, I suspect, undergoing a similar process of differentiation. On these mesas in Hopiland proper, therefore, inter-community rivalry tends to be more pronounced than intra-community conflict, the former further heightened by inter-mesa competition.

There is an indication that this tendency for internal differentiation as a mode of adapting to the environment represents a structural aspect of Hopi culture, as shown by Connelly (1956) and Eggan (1964), at the level of Hopi lineage organization. From this perspective, I am inclined to regard the pattern of Moenkopi factionalism as another case of *plus ça change, plus c'est la même chose.*

NOTES

1 Data for this paper were collected between 1962 and 1965 while I was a research associate in Hopiland of the late Julian H. Steward.

2 For Madison's definition of "faction," see Bailey's essay (this vol.). Dahl points out the difficulty with this definition: a lack of agreement about the specific content of "the rights of other citizens" and "the permanent and aggregate interests of the community" (1963:25–7). The absence of such an agreement is often characteristic of factionalism among American Indians. It is no exaggeration that for almost any overt exercise of power and influence, there are some Hopi who regard it as "adverse to the community" and hence illegitimate and factional. Such well-known Hopi politicians as Lomahongyoma and Yokioma were suspected of being witches (Titiev, 1943:553, 1944:79–80, 106). See also French, 1962:241.

3 In fact I did not hear of any refusals during my field work. What seems to be important in this informant's statement, however, is the belief among the people that they will not be refused and this is apparently sufficient to forestall possible refusals by the key holders.

4 This is the basis on which the Upper Moenkopi Council challenged his authority as a representative of Lower Moenkopi in a meeting with the Navajo Tribal Council.

5 The Upper Moenkopi Council made three attempts in the past to participate in the administration of local affairs by sending its members to the local organizations of the Navajo Tribal Council, including the police, in the late '40s and early '50s. However, as the incorporation of the Navajo tribal administration proceeded and the Navajo members of these organizations were placed on the tribal payroll, the Hopi members were inevitably refused further participation; the Hopi policeman of the Navajo Tuba City police left about the same time for a different – factional – reason (Nagata, 1970:59).

6 Alexis de Tocqueville would have agreed with Beals and Siegel: "Love of wealth therefore takes the place of ambition, and prosperity quenches the fires of faction" (1968:1, 378). The people of Moenkopi surely love wealth but are not, in their estimation, prosperous yet.

7 This is an empirical approximation to the difficulty Dahl hypothesized in establishing a majority rule in Wysteria (1963:53).

8 This statement needs qualification. The Hopi Agency has forcefully attempted to execute some of its policies in the face of active resistance in the past: for example, enforcement of school education in the early 20th century, the regulation of recent oil exploration permits, and the jailing of Hopi draft dodgers during WWII.

9 When the council project was nearing completion, the chief and his followers started a

similar project. Though nothing materialized, it shows another aspect of factional competition that bears no correlation to the desire to accept foreign innovations. It may be argued that indirect factional competition encourages cultural change (Nagata, 1968; Schwartz, 1969).
10 Barth reports a similar political situation in which Pathan chiefs installed wells and electric pumps for irrigation water "in spite of the considerably greater cost" (1965:117).
11 In a remarkable analysis of non-conformity among the Hopi, Aitken stated: "The *sect of one* probably never survived until the era of American protection" (1930:382; original emphasis).
12 Schattschneider states that "The conflicts of church and state and of the king and barons are closely related to the origins of liberty, because the little people profited by the divisions among the powerful" (1960:126).
13 It has been observed that a Hopi "cannot do away with himself without ... losing his reputation as a brave man" (Colton as quoted by Eggan, 1967:48), and hence the Hopi "suicide pact" (Brandt, 1954:194, 346; Eggan, 1967:48).

REFERENCES

ABERLE, DAVID F.
1951 "The Psychological Analysis of a Hopi Life History." *Comparative Psychology Monographs*, 21:1–133.
ADAMS, WILLIAM Y.
1963 *Shonto: A Study of the Role of the Trader in a Modern Navajo Community*. Bureau of American Ethnology, Bulletin 188. Washington, D.C., Smithsonian Institute.
AITKEN, BARBARA
1930 "Temperament in Native American Religion." *Journal of the Royal Anthropological Institute*, 60:363–87.
BAILEY, F. G.
1957 *Caste and the Economic Frontier*. Manchester, Manchester University Press.
BAILEY, F. G.
1969 *Strategems and Spoils*. Toronto, Copp-Clark.
BARNETT, HOMER G.
1953 *Innovation*. New York, McGraw-Hill.
BARTH, F.
1965 *Political Leadership among Swat Pathans*. London School of Economics, Monographs on Social Anthropology, No. 19. London, Athlone.
BERLIN, ISIAH
1958 *Two Concepts of Liberty*. Oxford, Clarendon.
BLAU, PETER M.
1964 *Exchange and Power in Social Life*. New York, Wiley.
BOISSEVAIN, J.
1964 "Factions, Parties and Politics in a Maltese Village." *American Anthropologist*, 66:1275–87.
BRANDT, RICHARD B.
1954 *Hopi Ethics*. Chicago, University of Chicago Press.
BROPHY, WM. A. and SOPHIE D. ABERLE
1966 *The Indian: America's Unfinished Business*. Norman, University of Oklahoma Press.
BRUGGE, DAVID M.
1968 "Recent Negotiations with the Hopis." *Navajo Times*, Window Rock, Arizona.

BUJRA, JANET
1973 "The Dynamics of Political Action: A New Look at Factionalism." *American Anthropologist*, 75(1):132–52.
CONNELLY, JOHN C.
1956 "Clan-lineage Relations in a Pueblo Village Phratry." Unpublished M.A. Thesis, University of Chicago.
COSER, LEWIS
1956 *The Functions of Social Conflict*. New York, Free Press.
COX, BRUCE A.
1970 "What is Hopi Gossip About? Information Management and Hopi Factions." *Man*, 5:88–98.
CUSHING, FRANK H., J. WALTER FEWKES and ELSIE C. PARSONS
1922 "Contributions to Hopi History." *American Anthropologist*, 24:253–98.
DAHL, ROBERT A.
1963 *A Preface to Democratic Theory*. Chicago, Chicago University Press (Phoenix Paperback).
DAHL, ROBERT A.
1966 "Epilogue." In R. A. Dahl (ed.), *Political Opposition in Western Democracies*. New Haven, Yale University Press.
DAHRENDORF, RALF
1959 *Class and Class Conflict in Industrial Society*. Stanford, Stanford University Press.
DE TOCQUEVILLE, ALEXIS
1968 *Democracy in America*. London, Collins (Fontana Library Paperback).
DOBYNS, HENRY F.
1968 "Therapeutic Experience of Responsible Democracy." In S. Levine and N. O. Lurie (ed.), *The American Indian Today*. Florida, Everett and Edwards.
DOZIER, EDWARD P.
1954 "The Hopi-Tewa of Arizona." *University of California Publications in American Archaeology and Ethnology*, 44:259–376.
DOZIER, EDWARD P.
1966 "Factionalism at Santa Clara Pueblo." *Ethnology*, 5:172–85.
DUMONT, LOUIS
1960 "World Renunciation in Indian Religions." *Contributions to Indian Sociology*, No. 4.
DURKHEIM, EMILE
1964(1933) *The Division of Labor in Society*. New York, Glencoe Free Press.
EASTON, DAVID
1959 "Political Anthropology." In B. J. Siegel (ed.), *Biennial Review of Anthropology*. Stanford, Stanford University Press.
EGGAN, DOROTHY
1943 "The General Problem of Hopi Adjustment." *American Anthropologist*, 43:357–73.
EGGAN, FRED
1950 *Social Organizations of the Western Pueblos*. Chicago, University of Chicago Press.
EGGAN, FRED
1964 "Alliance and Descent in Western Pueblo Society." In R. A. Manners (ed.), *Process and Pattern in Culture*. Chicago, Aldine.
EGGAN, FRED
1967 "From History to Myth: A Hopi Example." In D. H. Hymes and W. E. Bittle (eds.), *Studies in Southwestern Ethnolinguistics*. The Hague, Mouton.
ELLIS, FLORENCE H.
1951 "Patterns of Aggression and the War Cult in Southwestern Pueblos." *Southwestern Journal of Anthropology*, 7:177–201.

EMERSON, RUPERT
1960 "The Erosion of Democracy." *Journal of Asian Studies*, 20:1–8.

EPSTEIN, T. S.
1962 *Economic Development and Social Change in South India*. Manchester, Manchester University Press.

EVANS-PRITCHARD, E. E.
1940 "The Nuer of Southern Sudan." In M. Fortes and E. E. Evans-Pritchard (eds.), *African Political Systems*. London, Oxford University Press.

FIRTH, R.
1957 "Introduction: Factions in Indian and Overseas Indian Societies." *British Journal of Sociology*, 8:291–95.

FRENCH, DAVID H.
1962 "Ambiguity and Irrelevancy in Factional Conflict." In M. Sherif (ed.), *Intergroup Relations and Leadership*. New York, Wiley.

GERTH, H. H. and C. W. MILLS
1958 *From Max Weber*. New York, Oxford University Press. (Galaxy Paperback).

GLUCKMAN, M.
1955 *Custom and Conflict in Africa*. Oxford, Blackwells.

HOMANS, GEORGE C.
1950 *The Human Group*. New York, Harcourt, Brace.

HOPI HEARINGS
1955 *Hopi Hearings*, conducted by a team appointed by Commissioner of Indian Affairs. Phoenix, Arizona.

IONESCU, CHITA and I. DE MADRIAGA
1968 *Opposition*. London, C.A. Watts.

KIRCHHEIMER, OTTO
1957 "The Waning of Opposition in Parliamentary Regimes." *Social Research*, 24:127–56.

KIRCHHEIMER, OTTO
1966 "Germany: The Vanishing Opposition." In R. A. Dahl (ed.), *Political Oppositions in Western Democracies*. New Haven, Yale University Press.

KLUCKHOHN, CLYDE and DOROTHY LEIGHTON
1948 *The Navajo*. Cambridge, Mass., Harvard University Press.

KROEBER, ALFRED L.
1917 "Kuni Kin and Clans." American Museum of Natural History, *Anthropological Papers*, 18(II):39–205.

LEACH, E. R.
1963 "Law as a Condition of Freedom." In D. Bidney (ed.), *The Concept of Freedom in Anthropology*. The Hague, Mouton.

LEE, DOROTHY
1959 *Freedom and Culture*. New York, Prentice-Hall (Spectrum Paperback).

LEE, DOROTHY
1963 "Freedom and Social Constraint." In D. Bidney (ed.), *The Concept of Freedom in Anthropology*. The Hague, Mouton.

MADISON, JAMES
1948 *The Federalist* (with Alexander Hamilton and John Jay). Oxford, Basil Blackwell.

MAIR, LUCY
1962 *Primitive Government*. Harmondsworth, Penguin Books.

MALINOWSKI, BRONISLAW
1944 *Freedom and Civilization*. New York, Roy Publishers.

MAYER, A. C.
1967 "Patrons and Brokers: Rural Leadership in Four Overseas Indian Communities." In M. Freedman (ed.), *Social Organization*. London, Cass.
MILL, JOHN STUART
1912 *On Liberty, Representative Government, the Subjection of Women*. London, Oxford. University Press (the World's Classics).
MURPHY, ROBERT F.
1957 "Intergroup Hostility and Social Cohesion." *American Anthropologist*, 59:1018–35.
NAGATA, SHUICHI
1968 "Political Socialization of the Hopi 'Traditional' Faction." Unpublished paper read at the 1968 meeting of the Northeastern Anthropological Association.
NAGATA, SHUICHI
1970 *Modern Transformations of Moenkopi Pueblo*. Illinois, University of Illinois Press.
NAVAJO TIMES
1965 *Navajo Times*, July 22. Window Rock, Arizona.
NICHOLAS, RALPH W.
1965 "Factions: A Comparative Analysis." In M. Banton (ed.), *Political Systems and the Distribution of Power*. Association of Social Anthropologists, Monograph 2. London, Tavistock.
OPPENHEIM, FELIX E.
1961 *Dimensions of Freedom*. New York, St. Martin's Press.
PARSONS, ELSIE C.
1939 *Pueblo Indian Religion*. Chicago, University of Chicago Press.
PARSONS, T.
1964 *The Social System*. New York, Free Press.
POCOCK, DAVID F.
1957 "The Bases of Faction in Gujerat." *British Journal of Sociology*, 8:295–306.
RADCLIFFE-BROWN, ALFRED R.
1940 "Preface." In M. Fortes and E. E. Evans-Pritchard (eds.), *African Political Systems*. London, Oxford University Press.
SCHATTSCHNEIDER, E. E.
1960 *The Semisovereign People: A Realist's View of Democracy in America*. New York, Holt, Rinehart and Winston.
SCHUSKY, EARNEST L.
1965 *The Right to be Indian*. South Dakota, Institute of Indian Studies.
SCHWARTZ, NORMAN B.
1969 "Goal Attainment through Factionalism: A Guatemalan Case Study." *American Anthropologist*, 71(6):1088–1108.
SHEPARDSON, MARY
1963 *Navajo Ways in Government*. Memoirs of the American Anthropological Association, No. 96. Menasha, Wisconsin.
SIEGEL, BERNARD J. and ALAN R. BEALS
1960 "Pervasive Factionalism." *American Anthropologist*, 62:394–417.
SIEGEL, BERNARD J. and ALAN R. BEALS
1966 *Divisiveness and Social Conflict: An Anthropological Approach*. Stanford, Stanford University Press.
SIMMEL, GEORG
1950 *The Sociology of Georg Simmel*. New York, Free Press.
SPICER, EDWARD H.
1962 *Cycles of Conquest*. Tucson, University of Arizona Press.

Spiro, Melford E.
1968 "Factionalism and Politics in Village Burma." In M. J. Swartz (ed.), *Local Level Politics*. Chicago, Aldine.

Titiev, Mischa
1943 "Notes on Hopi Witchcraft." *Papers of the Michigan Academy of Science, Arts and Letters*, 28:549–57.

Titiev, Mischa
1944 "Old Oraibi." *Papers of the Peabody Museum of American Archaeology and Anthropology*, 22:1–277.

Voegelin, Carl E. and Florence M. Voegelin
1957 *Hopi Domains*. Memoirs of the International Journal of American Linguistics, No. 14.

Factions and Class Conflict in Rural Western India[1]

9

D. W. Attwood

INTRODUCTION

Factional conflicts have been given a variety of descriptive labels: "pervasive," "segmentary," "schismatic," "asymmetrical," and so on. What factors govern the occurrence of one type or another? Rather than approach this as a typological question, we may ask instead whether several different kinds of conflict can occur as phases of a single overall process. If we seek to link the growth and transformation of factions to such long-term processes, we may also discover connections between local conflicts and regional patterns of social change. The study of local factions is not always linked to the study of change; yet as Cohen (1974:244) points out: "There is a crucial relationship between conflict, its resolution, and social change. The constellation of power relations subsequent to the resolution of conflict is the essential evidence not only of social change itself but of the factors underlying that change and its direction." In this respect, Cohen is reviving a perspective used earlier by Bailey (1960:253).

According to Bujra (1973:141ff) factions may evolve in one of three directions: towards schism, reunification, or institutionalized competition. Surely there are possibilities for change along other dimensions? The focus of this paper will be on changes in the direction of cleavage between conflict groups, or more precisely, on changes in the recruitment patterns of such groups. We will discover that, in relation to the long-term processes discussed below, factionalism may even lead to class conflict (and vice versa). In order to portray and analyse such transformations, I have devised a model called a "conflict cycle." The essence of the cycle is that factionalism may alternate with class conflict in a given arena, and that these alternations depend on a process of mutual feedback whereby one type of conflict tends to stimulate the other.

Before we can explore the interactions between factionalism and class conflict, it will be necessary to give them provisional definitions. "Faction – like patronage – is a concept that is frequently used in differing senses by anthropologists and political scientists" (Sandbrook 1972:110), an inconsistency which should be avoided in a study of local/regional interaction. As Miller (1965:18) points out, factions are often seen by anthropologists as processes of conflict and adjustment *within* a 'community' – processes involving the circulation of limited resources in an enclosed arena, as in a zero-sum game (see, for example, Nicholas, 1966:58; Bailey, 1968:281–4).

Consequently village factions are sometimes described as "nonadaptive" forms of conflict (Siegel and Beals, 1960a:107).

Political scientists, on the other hand, usually discuss factions in the context of political parties which may be successful and durable organizations, acting to circulate all manner of resources and demands between local interests and state governments (Sandbrook, 1972:111). The apparent inconsistency between these two points of view can be avoided if we do not think of factions as sub-units or parts of something else such as a community or a party organization. Factions are better thought of as patronage networks (*ibid*) which are likely to cut across the boundaries of institutions and arenas and which are, therefore, often successful at exploiting new resources and opportunities in situations of change. In other words, factions are often built on the connections which run from competing village leaders to competing party politicians and others at the state level. At the local level, factions are usually recruited across class boundaries, with the leaders or patrons at a higher level than many of their supporters or clients (see Fig. 1). Since factions are built on inter-class alliances, and since they foster conflict between clients who belong to the same class, it is often assumed that factionalism invariably inhibits the growth of lower-class consciousness and mobilization. This paper is written in order to challenge that assumption.

In comparing factional with class conflict, we should note that in the former there is no question of who is or is not allowed to participate in the decision-making process within a given arena; it is rather a question of which leader's influence will prevail and of whether it would be more expedient for other leaders to comply with or oppose him.

In the case of class conflict, the real issue is precisely whether an "out-group" can force its way into the decision-making process within the arena, against the wishes of the "in-group." (This seems to be the general meaning which Dahrendorf attaches to the notion of "class conflict" [1959:204].) Thus, by "class conflict" I simply mean open conflict between the political elite which has power over a given arena and the non-elites who are usually obliged to follow the decisions of the elite (see Fig. 2).

There is, of course, considerable debate over the general relationship between *economic* classes and *political* classes (defined in terms of access to institutionalized power positions). Space does not permit a lengthy discussion of this issue; my position is simply that the relations between wealth and power are flexible and non-deterministic. Property is an important source of political power, but not the only one. In my research locality, elites and political aspirants depended for access to political power variously on education, business skills, ethnic loyalties, family contacts, administrative positions, inherited prestige, publicly and privately financed

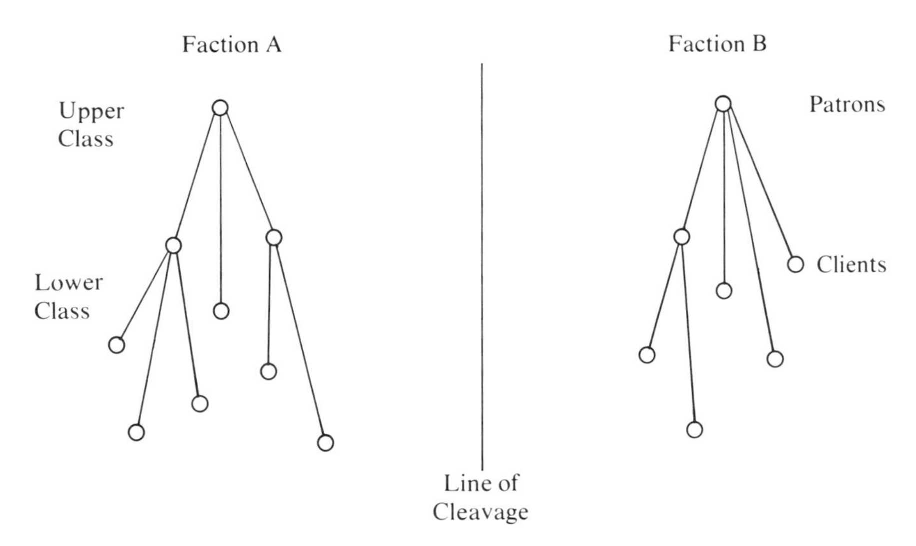

Figure 1 *Factional Conflict Between Patron-Client Networks*

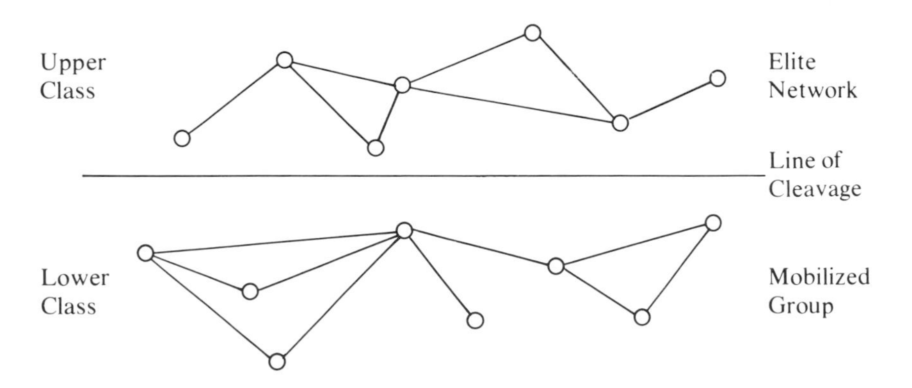

Figure 2 *Class Conflict Between Elite Network & Mobilized Group*

development projects, popular support, and many other kinds of resources.

In other words, I agree with Lenski (1966:75–79) that stratification systems (or "distributive systems," as he calls them) are multidimensional, particularly in complex societies. Thus, one society and its distributive system may encompass several "class systems" based, respectively, on political power, property, occupation, and ethnic status (*ibid*. p. 80). For present purposes, I would simplify this to say that in India we can distinguish three important class systems or dimensions of stratification based on (1) political power; (2) wealth, occupation, and education; and (3) ritual status (or in other words, caste). The dimensions of caste, economic class, and political power overlap; but they must be kept analytically distinct, especially because they tend to become less correlated as social change and modernization increase (Lenski, 1966:76; Beteille, 1965).

In the background to the case study which follows, I will sketch in the points at which these dimensions overlap. We shall see that, though analytically distinct, the economic class system and the caste system have important influences on the political struggles which are described. (Some would argue that either one or the other has a determining influence, but I remain skeptical of such simple, all-encompassing explanations.) It should be kept in mind that the focus of this paper is on struggles for control of institutionalized power positions. Consequently, when I mention "class conflict" without qualification, I am referring to conflict between classes defined in terms of their access to political power positions.

Some consideration has been given previously to the relationship between village factionalism and class (or caste) conflict in India. Nicholas (1968) presents a survey of conflicts in nineteen Indian villages. The cleavages in these villages tend to be "vertical" (between factions) or "horizontal" (between castes or classes) (see Figs. 1 and 2). Nicholas finds that the direction of cleavage depends to some extent on the distribution of the village population across two variables: caste membership and land ownership. Actually, "In most villages there is a combination of horizontal and vertical forms of political cleavage at work at the same time" (Nicholas, 1968:280). It is the dynamics of this combination which I plan to discuss below, moving outside the limits of Nicholas's study along two dimensions: spatial and temporal. I intend (1) to analyse local conflict not as a closed, segmentary system (based on the distribution of resources within a single village), but as part of the total interaction between local and regional politics; and (2) to consider how this interaction has developed over time.

In a recent paper I discussed political entrepreneurs and the alternative uses which they can make of different forms of alliance (Attwood, 1974b). I have suggested that in stratified societies, there are at least two elementary forms of political alliance which can be labeled "patronage" and "group mobilization." Patronage involves a vertical alliance between one actor who is superordinate in power and another who is subordinate. Group mobilization involves a horizontal alliance between actors who are more or less equal in power and who seek to challenge others possessing greater power. These are highly formalistic and arbitrary assumptions; they become more interesting when the alternative geometric patterns are redefined as entrepreneurial processes operating within a local class system involving elite networks, client networks, and mobilized groups. They become still more interesting when it is realized that the processes of patronage and mobilization constantly interact with, and stimulate each other.

Turning from alliances back to cleavages, it seems that patronage alliances are normally associated with conflicts between factions. On the other hand, opposition between a mobilized group and an established elite or elite segment represents a form of class conflict. Consequently, if there is a dynamic pattern of interaction between the patronage and group mobilization processes, we may also expect to find a pattern of mutual stimulation between factional and class conflicts. This is the pattern embodied in the conflict cycle.

In the following section I discuss the shifting political cleavages within one local arena in western India over a period of fifteen years. In the third section I outline the conflict-cycle model, and in the final section I discuss how this model can be used to relate local events to socio-political trends of large scope and duration.

CONFLICT IN A COOPERATIVE SUGAR FACTORY

The arena which I have selected for analysis is the Olegao cooperative sugar factory established in eastern Poona district (Maharashtra state) in 1955.[2] This factory was the most important focus for political competition in thirteen surrounding villages (cf. Baviskar, 1968, 1969; Rosenthal, 1973). Its establishment and growth were linked to a number of historical changes in the agrarian society of western India. A large irrigation canal was constructed near Olegao village in 1885. The farmers in this area committed more resources, as time went on, to the costly and profitable cultivation of sugar cane. As a result, the new economic problem facing the large- and medium-scale was the periodic fluctuation in sugar prices, a problem which became a disaster during the world depression of the 1930s. In 1950, after Indian independence, a cooperative sugar factory was started in nearby Ahmednagar district (Gadgil, 1952). This experiment was based on local initiative among the cane farmers, aided by advice from a distinguished economist and financial assistance from the state government (Inamdar, 1965:2–8). It was hoped that the cooperative factory would, among other things, provide a stable market at reasonable prices for the members' cane. The success of this experiment prompted the government to plan the licensing and financing of several more cooperative sugar factories; and local organizers in several districts began collecting share capital from their neighbours. The Olegao cooperative sugar factory was registered in 1955 and commenced production in 1957.

As of 1969, this factory had expanded its original crushing capacity by 50 percent, and further expansion was under way. The factory had entirely repaid the original government loans and nearly all the subsequent loans for expansion. Its technical efficiency, expressed in the rate of sugar recovery, was about as good as that of the nearby private factories.

The Olegao factory has about 2700 village cane farmers as shareholders. Each share corresponds to one-half acre of sugar cane, which must be supplied to the factory every year. Every member thus has shares more or less in proportion to his irrigated landholding. However, in the factory elections, each shareholder has only one vote. The shareholders include most of the landowning cultivators who live in the thirteen canal-irrigated villages within a radius of five miles from the factory.

Castes and Classes

It is necessary, at this point, to say something about the distribution of castes and economic classes in the area, and how they are represented in the factory. Table 1 summarizes data collected in Olegao village, one of the largest villages in the factory area. Marathas constitute the most numerous caste in every agricultural class, and they form the absolute majority among all the landholders. It is also significant that those Brahman and merchant-caste families which appear among the agricultural classes do so mainly as large- and medium-scale farmers, whereas the distribution of the service castes is almost exactly complementary. This general pattern is probably typical of the whole area around Olegao, except that a few villages are dominated by peasant castes other than the Marathas (see, for example, Orenstein, 1965).

In most cases, the Maratha landowners have always been the 'dominant caste' at the village level. Due to their general lack of education, however, the Marathas were formerly quite vulnerable when it came to dealing with the outside worlds of business and government (worlds which were largely controlled by merchant castes and Brahmans). The expansion of trade and the new British legal system increased this vulnerability during the 19th century, resulting in violent attacks by peasants against their moneylenders (the ''Deccan Riots'' of 1875). The concept of 'dominant caste' is therefore too simplistic to deal with this situational relativity of power relations; and it glosses over those historical changes which have enabled the Maratha farmers to become more effective in their dealings with the regional systems of government and business (see section IV, below). Since 1885, in the canal villages at least, the peasant-caste farmers have become steadily more prosperous, better educated, and more politically aware. The service castes have also become better educated, and some have become highly politicized; but their small or non-existent landholdings prevent them from acquiring greater wealth or power within rural society.

The relations of production in this canal-irrigated region are fairly simple. Nearly all the farms are owner-operated. (Tenancies and semi-feudal

TABLE 1

Agricultural Classes of Olegao Village: Distribution of Families in Selected Castes.[3]

Castes	Agricultural Labourers		Small Farmers[d]		Medium Farmers[e]		Large Farmers[f]		Total	
	No.	%	No.	%	No.	%	No.	%	No.	%
Brahman	0		2	1.0	13	6.4	9	9.6	24	1.8
Lingayat Wani[a]	0		0		9	4.4	3	3.2	12	0.9
Maratha	329	38.7	116	56.6	120	58.8	64	68.1	629	46.5
Other Peasants[b]	268	31.5	38	18.5	29	14.2	18	19.2	353	26.1
Service Castes[c]	253	29.8	49	23.9	33	16.2	0		335	24.8
Total	850	100	205	100	204	100	94	100	1353	100

[a]Merchant caste.
[b]Hatkar Dhangar, Shegar Dhangar (Sagar Rajput), and Mali.
[c]Ramoshi, Muslim, Chambhar, Mahar, and Mang.
[d]Families owning less than 0.7 standard irrigated acres per consumption unit.
[e]Families owning between 0.7 and 2.4 standard irrigated acres per consumption unit.
[f]Families owning more than 2.4 standard irrigated acres per consumption unit.

holdings were of minor importance before the 1950's and were virtually eliminated thereafter.) The small-scale farmers (owning less than about three acres per family) provide most of their own labour requirements; and they, with their wives, also work as hired labourers on the farms of others. The medium-scale farmers (owning from about three to eleven acres) are more self-sufficient, their holdings being large enough to absorb all the labour which their families can provide. During some seasons, the medium-scale farmers also rely on hired labourers to cope with the demands of the cane crop. Small- and medium-scale farmers each account for about 41 percent of the landowning population, large-scale farmers for the remaining 18 percent. The latter provide less of their own manual labour, but they are quite active in the management of their complex, commercial enterprises. Only large-scale farmers can afford to grow grapes – a new and expensive crop which requires intensive management. There are presently few, if any, absentee landlords.

As in past centuries, there is a pool of landless or nearly landless labourers available from the lower service castes attached to each village. In addition, there was a large influx of labourers during and after the construction of the canal in the late 19th century. The canal, of course, provided insurance against drought; but it also made possible a more intensive use of the land, which, in turn, required correspondingly larger inputs of labour. Droughts occurred somewhere in the state nearly every year, causing many villagers (including peasant-caste landowners) to leave the dry areas and migrate to the canal villages in search of employment. Some migrated seasonally and some settled permanently in the canal villages.

Eighty-two percent of the factory shareholders own just one or two shares, corresponding to one-half or one acre of cane supplied each year. Another 15.5 percent hold shares representing 1.5 to 5 acres of cane per year. (In most cases, the farmer's total irrigated holding must be at least three times the area of the sugar crop pledged to the factory.) In other words, the overwhelming majority of shareholders are small- or medium-scale farmers (mostly Marathas and other peasants), who have all benefited to some degree from the solvency, efficiency and steady expansion of the factory operation. In nearly every case, the directors of the factory have been large farmers.

All the active and secondary political leaders in Olegao village are large- or medium-scale farmers. The active leaders (including a few present and former factory directors) are all large-scale farmers. However, within this economic class an individual's power is not necessarily proportional to the scale of his farming operation. Some of the biggest farmers prefer to keep their attention on business, not on politics; and some who do campaign for public office find that they are not as successful as their less-wealthy competitors. (Such discrepancies between relative wealth and power are due to various factors: skills, motivation, caste status, social connections, and others).

The factory's board of management consists of eleven elected directors (all of them cultivators and shareholders), plus three representatives from the government financing agencies. At present, each board is elected for a three-year term by a vote of the general membership; the chairman is then elected by the board members from among themselves. The chairmanship is vested with great power, being the most important elected office standing between the thirteen villages and the district and state politicians who represent them at higher levels.

Except for a special representative of the village cooperative credit societies (whom we can ignore for the moment), the elected members of the board presently consist of those ten candidates who draw the most votes. Although nearly all of the candidates are grouped together in slates, they are each voted on individually, and the top ten often consist of any mixture of candidates from two or more slates. (This tends to make the election of the chairman an unpredictable affair, causing the rapid breakup and realignment of previous coalitions.) The ordinary voter has several alternatives. He can vote for one whole slate, or he can vote for all the candidates who belong to his own lineage, village, or caste, regardless of their slates; or else he can vote for just one or two leaders who are his personal patrons. There is ample evidence that the latter two alternatives were the ones which voters preferred from 1962 to 1970.

Origins of Conflict

In 1955 a board of directors was nominated by the cooperative department of the state government from among the local farmers who were the most active in selling shares and promoting the new venture. The chief promoter and first chairman was a wealthy and progressive farmer of the Brahman caste who resided in the market town located a few miles from the factory site. He was one of the original pioneers of large-scale sugarcane farming in the area, and also the first to succeed with grapes. The remainder of the nominated board consisted of another town-dwelling Brahman (a lawyer and landowner), plus nine peasant-caste leaders (six Marathas, two Dhangars, and one Mali) who formed a roughly representative sample of the local landowning population. The board was made broadly representative in order to inspire confidence among the shareholders. For that reason, it included four "Freedom Fighters" from the recent independence movement.

During the first few years of operation, the sugar factory was controlled by the Brahman chairman whose influence derived not only from his expertise as a business manager, but also from his network of connections in the state administration and the commercial-industrial circles of Poona and Bombay cities. Managerial competence was crucial to the factory in its early stages, not only for the sake of technical efficiency, but also in order to build confidence and loyalty among the shareholders.[4] Consequently, although the peasant-caste representatives were in a majority on the nominated board, they were slow to assert their power as a group, since it was clear that the fate of the enterprise rested on the efficiency of the decisions made by the chairman. But once the factory had become established, the peasant-caste leaders felt more inclined to assert the importance of political over technical decision-making criteria.

The crucial source of conflict was employment policy. Each of the peasant-caste board members was under pressure from his relatives and neighbours to provide jobs and other favours. The Brahman chairman, on the other hand, preferred to hire on merit alone. Hiring on the basis of merit tended to favour educated Brahmans or non-natives of the local area, thus inhibiting the patronal influence of the peasant-caste leaders. The question of whom to hire for various jobs was, therefore, a source of simmering factional dispute among the factory leaders. Cases tended to arise and be resolved through a shifting pattern of alliances, since the momentary advantages for each director would vary from case to case. It was, after all, a matter of bargaining for personal (not class) advantages.

However, something happened to change all this, an event which caused the Maratha-caste majority of board members to unite and to call on their village brethren for support. This event was the first board election, to be held (in 1960) when the government-nominated board was due to retire. (Elected leadership was, of course, a policy goal of the state government in financing and supervising the cooperatives.) The board members foresaw that their ability to dispense employment would have a strong effect on their chances of retaining their seats in the election. They also realised that the most populous peasant-caste lineages would carry the greatest weight in the balloting. In other words, the board of management was faced with a change of rules (from nomination to election) which would be more favourable to the tactics of machine-style politics (the bargaining of votes for favours) than to the maintenance of a closed elite council. This presented the Maratha leaders with an opportunity to expand the scope of conflict over hiring policy and settle the issue through sheer strength of numbers. The high-caste leaders and their allies, on the other hand, were alert to this threat; and they initiated a classic flanking manoeuvre.

Other groups were feeling threatened by the Marathas at about the same time. These were the minority peasant castes: the Dhangars, comprising three endogamous "sub-castes" or *jatis*, and the Malis. As a result, the high-caste leaders set up an alliance with the minority peasant castes. The product of this alliance was a carefully balanced slate of minority-caste representatives, a slate which swept nine out of eleven seats on the board.

The nine winners consisted of one Brahman, one Lingayat Wani, two Hatkar Dhangars, two Shegar Dhangars (Sagar Rajputs), one Khatik Dhangar, and only two Marathas (who were included to help split the Maratha vote).

The contest, in other words, was one in which the Marathas were attempting to curtail the influence of the urban, high-caste minority in favour of their own village-based majority, while the high-caste leaders were organizing a successful revolt by the minority peasant castes against the Marathas. Unfortunately, the strength of the minority coalition was based on the Maratha threat. Having subdued that threat for the time being, the new directors were unable to agree on a strong chairman. The question was, of course, which minority should have precedence over the others. Having been roused to a defense of their collective interests, the peasant castes were now disinclined to allow a Brahman or Lingayat to take the chair; and the latter, for their part, regarded most of the minority peasant castes as even more 'bumpkinish' than the Marathas. As so often happens under such circumstances, they compromised on a chairman who was neither very objectionable nor very attractive to any party: the new chairman was a Maratha! He was, however, a person of high status and personal qualifications, who was not attached to a large peasant lineage, and who would consequently not be pressured to employ large numbers of relatives at the expense of other groups.

With their new allies, the high-caste leaders had won the immediate battle, but in the long run they lost more than they gained. In order to win, they were compelled to widen the scope of the conflict even further than their opponents – to use weapons of mass participation which would alter the whole system of power they were seeking to retain (cf. Schattschneider, 1960:15–16).

New Conflicts and New Leaders

The Marathas came back in force in the next election, and the minority coalition, without a strong center, collapsed. There followed, from 1962 to 1970, a period of nearly complete factional anarchy in which election slates did not endure in any form from one term to the next: indeed, they usually broke up and re-grouped between the election of each board and the election of its chairman. In this period, no slate won a decisive majority, which was the main reason that the election of the chairman always involved defections and realignments. From the perceptions of the actors and the patternless results, I conclude that few of the shareholders voted for any slate as such. Instead, they cast their ballots either in favour of individual patrons or else for the closest members of their own lineage, caste, or village, regardless of slate. The main strategy was to try to seat a friend on the board, somebody who might give you or your brother a job.

This was an era of patronage politics and "factions as usual" with a vengeance. There was no semblance of steady group conflict during this interim period; and yet, at the end of the decade, quite different group interests were being served by the political process than at the beginning. This can be illustrated by the elections of 1967 and 1970.

The 1967 election was at first typical of what had occurred before. There were three slates initially, two of which were half-elected to the board. These two elected segments were each composed of two smaller segments, each managed by a relatively autonomous leader. Any two of these four little groups could block a quorum, and so the winning chairmanship strategy demanded a coalition of three. A stable three-way coalition might have been impossible, except that a young Congress party leader had just been elected MLA (Member of the Legislative Assembly) in this constituency. It happened that three of the four leaders on the board had supported the MLA in his campaign, and he, in turn, brought these three together in an extraordinary compromise whereby they would rotate the chairmanship and vice-chairmanship each year during the three-year term.

This young MLA became more influential in the following years, so that by 1970 he had even stronger control of his supporters in the factory election. This election was in some ways similar to the 1960 election and therefore different from all those which occurred in between. From among his supporters, the MLA selected a carefully balanced slate, giving proportional representation to the Marathas and the minority peasant-castes, to the old, successful leaders and the young novices, and likewise to the different villages according to their populations. As in 1960, this carefully balanced slate was voted in as a slate: it won ten seats out of eleven. The only difference between the two situations was that in 1960, the balanced slate was a rearguard action fought by an old elite caving in under democratic pressures, whereas in 1970 the decisions were made by a master of the new machine-style politics who came from an ordinary peasant-caste background.[5]

Leaving aside the intervening years of political confusion, these two elections at either end of the decade represent a decisive shift of power away from an older, urbanized, managerial, high-status elite to a younger, peasant-based coalition of competitive machine politicians. This shift is partly obscured by the almost continuous presence of a Maratha majority on the board of management. It is important to realize, however, that the factory was not a closed arena and competition within it was not a "zero-sum game". One factor in gaining decisive control of the board was the nature of a leader's external contacts. During the '50s administrative and commercial contacts were still crucial in setting up a local enterprise, and these contacts were best managed by the Brahman chairman and his allies. It was only during the '60s that a local party politician (the MLA) became the all-purpose broker, settling disputes and obtaining resources through external contacts. Indeed, the period of factional anarchy in the factory was undoubtedly prolonged by the complete absence, before 1967, of a strong MLA in the local constituency. The local growth of machine-style politics proceeded by fits and starts. In 1960, the new voting strength of various groups became a source of unbridled competition and confusion; in 1970, it was made into a source of organized party support.

In the beginning, the peasant-caste representatives and their followers formed a "quasi-group," or a set of quasi-groups (Dahrendorf, 1959:180). As conflicts over hiring developed, the peasant-caste leaders began to recognize their common interests; a Maratha "interest group" emerged, followed shortly by the minority peasant castes as another set of interest groups. This involved not merely new coalitions among the leaders, but an expansion of the scope of conflict, the active seeking of support from those who had the greatest number of votes. The formation of these interest groups brought the minority peasant castes, in 1960, into a position of unusual power. This abated somewhat during the rest of the decade, but the intense factional competition of that period helped to confirm the minority peasant castes as an influential set of vote blocs which could make or break a coalition. Consequently, these castes were carefully integrated into the balanced slate of 1970, and the wisdom of this process was confirmed by the result: three among the top four vote-getters in that election were members of the minority peasant castes. Thus, for many villagers, access to political power was decidedly more open and competitive in 1970 than in 1955 – this access depending to a considerable degree on the strength of numbers.

The MLA contributed much to bringing this competitive process of expanded participation under control. But his power to intervene should not be regarded as a purely exogenous factor. One of the main sources of the MLA's increasing influence grew out of the local need to resolve internal conflicts in the factory; and he needed a stable base of support as much as the factory leaders needed a strong patron. Change was brought about by means of a bargain from which both sides benefitted and to which both sides contributed.

THE CONFLICT-CYCLE MODEL

We have been suspending specific consideration of the factional anarchy which engulfed the board of management during most of the 1960s. What relationship, if any, does this episode have with the long-term shift in elites and their bases of power? My argument is that this period represents an important and perhaps inevitable phase in the shifting balance of power (though I would certainly not suggest that this phase must last for a decade). At this point it will be helpful to present a simple model[6] (see Fig. 3).

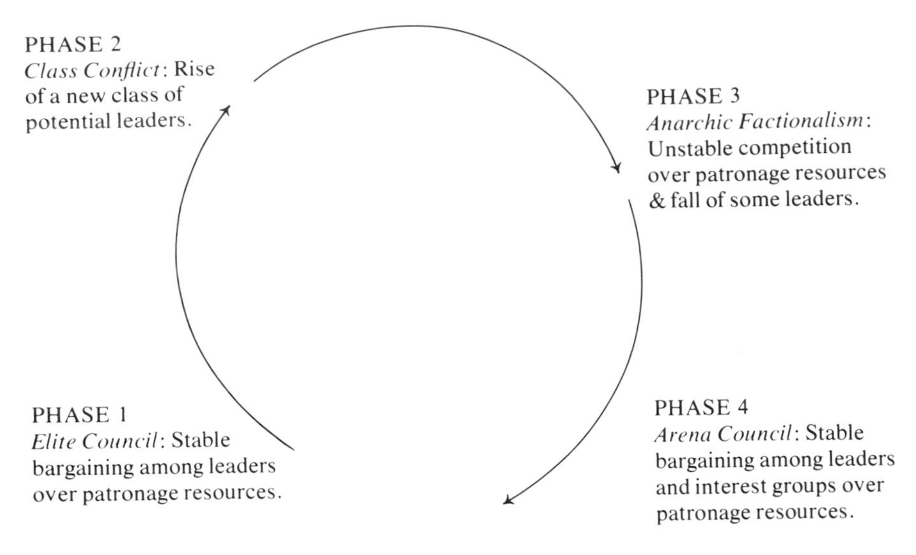

Figure 3 *Conflict Cycle*

The Conflict Cycle

Phase One. The balance of power in a particular arena rests in the hands of an established elite. Factional competition and bargaining for resources within this elite group is carefully shielded from the public behind a façade of 'consensus.' This is what Bailey calls an "elite council" (1965:10). The elite group may derive much of its power from connections with a regional elite network outside the arena boundaries.

Phase Two. Another group struggles either to enter the elite council or to take over more influence in the decision-making process. This may lead to open group confrontations between the 'ins' and the 'outs.' In other words, this is the phase of group mobilization and class conflict. Political action is organized around group interests.

Phase Three. If and when the new contenders achieve a share of the decision-making power through confrontation, class conflict evaporates because it is no longer necessary for the realization of individual ambitions. With the entry of a whole new set of decision-makers into the arena, it is now necessary to determine, on a competitive basis, who has the ability to re-organize and control the decision-making process. Consequently, there follows a period of experimentation in which alliances shift very rapidly, with no regard to the former distinctions between 'ins' and 'outs.' Individuals appear to rise and fall in chaotic fashion – though in fact, there may be a definite, selective pattern beneath the turmoil. This is the period of "factions as usual", a period which is governed by opportunistic patronage and competition, and a complete lack of class loyalties. Such a condition has been labeled "pervasive factionalism" by Siegel and Beals (1960b).

The pattern which may be hidden beneath the surface turmoil is one in which many of the old ruling group are gradually driven out, one by one as *individual* losers in the competition – simply because their bases of support were rendered partly obsolete by the successes of Phase Two. In a few cases, individuals from the old ruling group are able to adapt to the new selective pressures and establish new bases of support, as we shall see below. This phase of conflict is in many ways the most interesting, precisely because it is so difficult to interpret in relation to a systematic, long-term process.

Phase Four. A new, stable ruling group is eventually formed by those who cope most successfully with the challenges of Phase Three. We have now returned full circle to the situation in Phase One, with the emergence of a new elite council. But the new situation is different in that it is more like an "arena council" in which the demands of various groups of constituents (those activated in Phase Two) have a stronger effect on the decisions taken by the ruling group (Bailey, 1965:10–11). As in Phase One, the power to form the new ruling group often depends on external connections.

This cycle is obviously a model for the circulation of elites as well as for a sequence of conflicts. I would like to postpone discussion of elite circulation until later when I shall consider the ways in which the cycle relates to social change.

Anarchy and Survival

In section II above, I outlined the beginning and end points of the conflict cycle in the sugar factory in order to demonstrate the basic power shift which took place over the course of fifteen years – a shift stemming from the process of group mobilization in Phase Two. Now it is appropriate to inquire into the peculiarities of Phase Three: to see whether there is indeed a pattern, hidden within the anarchic competition, of natural selection acting on many individual careers. The career pattern of each leader in the factory is unique, and a full outline of these patterns would take many pages. However, the general trends can be roughly summarized under the headings of "town-dwelling" and "village-dwelling" leaders.

Town-dwelling leaders. The Brahman founder and chairman died during the board's first term and was replaced by his son. The son and a Brahman lawyer, who was also on the nominated board, both retired from the forefront of factory politics in 1960. In the election that year they were replaced by another progressive Brahman farmer and a Lingayat Wani, with a law degree and considerable experience in the business world, who were the chief organizers of the successful minority coalition. The Lingayat retired after one term on the board, to become the managing director of the factory. The new Brahman, on the other hand, proved phenomenally successful in factory politics during the 1960s. He was the only factory leader to hold onto a seat continuously from 1960 to 1970, and he even managed to become chairman in 1968–69. He was the proverbial exception that proved the rule, for his success was due to a wide base of personal contacts, diligently cultivated, in all the factory villages – a base which was broader, in fact, than that of most peasant-caste leaders. This was possible because a Brahman was not attached by birth to any peasant lineage, and thus was not a threat to any other. It is likely that the dissident minorities in every village gave him their votes, as a hedge against the stronger lineages or factions around them. In two board elections, this Brahman polled the highest number of votes among all the candidates. His activities demonstrate that individual members of the old elite may adapt successfully to the new conditions of competition by generating wider bases of support. (The Lingayat, on the other hand, adapted by stepping outside the electoral process.) The remaining town-dwelling directors after 1960 were all members of the peasant castes.

Village-dwelling leaders. It is simplest to refer here to the examples provided by one village, Olegao, where the factory is located, and where I did much of my research. This is one of the largest and most influential villages in the factory's area of operation. All the factory leaders from this village have been of peasant-caste origin; but there has been a definite shift in their social backgrounds and methods of generating support.

The leader who fit best into the old elite pattern was Ramsingh, a high-status Maratha whose ancestors were *jagirdars*, the virtual rulers of Olegao village until 1952. Ramsingh was college-educated; he understood sound management principles, was not connected to a peasant lineage, and was opposed to patronage in the factory. He became the chairman in 1960 and again in 1962; but after losing that position in 1964 he dropped out of local politics. He was considered too high-status and aloof to be an effective competitor in the new machine-style politics.

Next to Ramsingh, Balasaheb was the richest landowner in the village. His family belonged to the large Jagtap lineage (or Maratha caste) which included most of the village landowners. Balasaheb and two of his college-educated nephews (who were all members of a joint family) held seats on the factory board from 1955 to 1964, and again from 1967 to 1970. However, like Ramsingh, they were too aloof to build up a personal following in the village, and their position was gradually undermined by the rise of ambitious young leaders from a variety of other lineage and peasant caste backgrounds. There were clear signs of this weakening after 1967, and in 1970–71, Balasaheb's family lost their seat on the factory board as well as their hold on the chairmanship of the village council, which they had monopolized for about thirty years.

Mugutrao Jagtap was an old political ally of Balasaheb's, and another member of the powerful Jagtap lineage. He was on the factory board from 1955 to 1960, and again from 1964 to 1973. Mugutrao managed to increase his power while Balasaheb's waned – primarily because Mugutrao was adept at compromising with, and coopting, the rising younger leaders.

The most outstanding among the latter was Namdev who belonged to an upwardly mobile family of recent immigrants within the small Dhangar minority in the village. Namdev had at first opposed Mugutrao in an effort to get the Dhangars accepted into the ruling group of the village cooperative credit society and the sugar factory. (This was around 1960, when the minority peasant castes were challenging the Marathas across a broad front.) Later, Namdev and Mugutrao became close allies, uniting Mugutrao's status and sagacity as a political arbiter with Namdev's oratorical skill and his unsurpassed knowledge of both his local constituents and the intricate details of district- and state-level party politics. They were elected to the factory board on the same slate in 1967, and again in 1970 when Mugutrao became chairman for a full three-year term.

Thus village leadership has shifted perceptibly away from those men with old-elite qualifications to those who are more competitive, upwardly mobile, and sometimes lacking in family status, but making up for this by much more active and extensive contacts with their supporters. (Mugutrao, however, is an example of the old-style leader who adapted successfully to the new competitive pressures.)

To summarize our findings on the enigmas of Phase Three: there are no confrontations between interest groups of any sort during this phase. Yet the rise and fall of individual careers under the selective pressure of expanded competition reveals a significant shift in the patterns of leadership recruitment and their bases of support.

THE CONFLICT CYCLE AND SOCIAL CHANGE

What makes the conflict cycle revolve? The answer to this question is also, in part, the answer to another: what connection does the cycle have with social change?

Internal Forces

Dahrendorf has noted that some political situations encourage individual competition and mobility within a pluralistic framework of cross-cutting interest groups, whereas other situations tend to generate class conflict

(1967:18–22). The question is, of course, what determines the type of situation in a given arena? Both types are generators of social change: the competitive-pluralist situation can generate a selective shift from one pattern of leadership to another, and the class-conflict situation can lead to a more dramatic turnover. In the conflict cycle, individual competition is the driving force in one phase, group mobilization in another. Successful group mobilization opens up expanded opportunities for individual advancement, while the blocking and damming up of personal ambitions may cause the rise of an interest group and its mobilization. One process stimulates the other: the conflict cycle may repeat itself many times, as we shall see.

But what controls the sequence of phases in the cycle? There are both internal and external forces which set them in motion. One internal driving mechanism is the tendency for an elite segment, in competition with other segments, to try to recruit new allies among the non-elites (cf. Carter, 1974:178). Bujra (1973:148) has alluded to this tendency, though in terms which are characteristically geometric rather than dynamic: "Although the [faction] leaders recruited support from all sections of the community, using various social linkages, their main appeal was to a particular category of people – a category to whom a general ideological appeal could be made in terms of their common interests. These 'factions' then, rather than dividing the community either 'vertically' or 'horizontally,' divided it 'diagonally.'"

The same point has been made by Boissevain (1974:215–233), in arguing that opposing factions are often "asymmetrical" with reference to their class composition and political resources. I would simply add that the degree of asymmetry may tend to vary in a cyclical fashion. Elite-council factions tend to be nearly equivalent, or symmetrical (see Fig. 1). If these factions begin to grow asymmetrically, we may be observing a transition from Phase One to Phase Two. 'Pure' class conflict, if there is such a thing, is completely asymmetrical in terms of the class composition and resources of the opposing groups. Underlying the transition toward greater asymmetry is a consistent process in which various segments of the elite try to get the upper hand by bringing in new categories of non-elite supporters. This process is most likely to begin when an old elite council is threatened by unavoidable changes. Schattschneider (1960:16) argues that the losing side is always prone to widen the scope of a conflict, in order to reverse its fortunes. "Competitiveness is the mechanism for the expansion of the scope of conflict. It is the loser who calls in outside help." Obviously, a one-sided expansion of the scope of conflict is often countered by an equivalent move from the other side. Thus the town-dwelling, high-caste leaders took the minority peasant castes under their wing in 1960 as a counter-attack against the Maratha peasant leaders. This process continued, in a less organized fashion, throughout the 1960's, with the minority peasant vote-blocs being wooed by various individuals and coalitions.

The terms on which dissident or defensive elites may unite with new groups of non-elites admit of endless variation – from pure co-optation (as a mechanism of patronal manipulation) to capitulation in the face of organized group pressure from below. This means that a purely geometric study of cleavages and alliances neglects a crucial set of variables: the terms on which different conflict groups, or different leaders and followers, are able to negotiate with each other. For example, the period around 1960 in the sugar factory witnessed various peasant-caste leaders struggling for recognition of their nascent interest groups. By 1970 these groups were established vote-blocs; most of the negotiation and competition in this later period was concerned with who would be their representatives.

External Forces

It is also plain that much of the driving force behind the cycle in the sugar factory derived from external factors such as: (1) the change in political rules (from appointment to election) required by the state government; (2) the rapid expansion of state resources channelled into agriculture through the cooperatives; and (3) a regional political culture which was concerned with the relative resources and interests of Brahmans, Marathas, and other castes. All these external factors, taken together, determined that there would be class conflict in the Olegao factory, and that the old elite council would not endure.

Moreover, the conflict cycle in the sugar factory tied in with a long series of other cycles in the same local area. This series reveals a trend which has been highly significant at the level of state and national politics: a gradual shift of political power, over the last fifty years, away from urban, educated, high-caste leaders, (employed mainly in business and the professions) towards rural, less-educated, peasant-caste leaders (employed in agriculture). The non-Brahman movements in western and southern India, from roughly 1900 to 1935, stimulated this shift through open conflict while the rise of Congress party support from the rural areas during the 1930's added further impetus. After independence (1947) and the beginning of universal franchise, this trend culminated in a decisive shift of electoral power toward the rural majority. By the 1960's, representatives from the rural areas were becoming numerically dominant in the national parliament and the state legislatures (Rosenthal, 1970:182).

In the canal villages, this rise of a new political élite was facilitated by the long-term economic changes alluded to earlier: the commercial prosperity of the villages, the rise of medium- and large-scale agricultural entrepreneurs, the increased involvement with government agencies seeking to control and stimulate production, and the spread of education. The results of all these changes included a rapid rise in political awareness and participation.

Linkages between Arenas

In responding politically to these trends, the leaders of the Olegao sugar factory were affected not merely by the spread of political consciousness among formerly apolitical sections of the population, but also by certain institutional conditions: namely, that the sugar factory was interlinked with a host of other political arenas of various shapes and sizes. The rural cooperatives were organized so as to produce a set of interlocking directorates between institutions of different scopes and functions (that is, between village credit societies, sugar factories, lift irrigation societies, marketing societies, district central banks, land development banks, and so on). In addition, the *panchayat* system (consisting of village, block, and district councils) had its own interlocking arenas which overlapped in various ways not only with those of the cooperatives, but also with the local, district, and state committees of the Congress party and the constituencies of the state legislature. The process of group mobilization and class conflict moved at different rates and involved different interest groups in these diverse arenas. This meant, for example, that a particular arena might be dominated by an old elite, while all around it a new group was coming to power. Sometimes there was a visible domino effect, in which the capture of another seat in one directorate had immediate repercussions on the balance of forces in others. All this means that it is inherently deceptive to focus on a single arena as though the internal conflicts in it were equivalent to a zero-sum game.

There were several earlier conflict cycles, in the area around Olegao village, which contributed to the long-term rise of the new peasant leadership. For example, there was a cycle during the late 1940s in a cooperative marketing society in the town near Olegao. The local Freedom Fighters, riding on the crest of the independence movement, were able to force their way onto the board of management of the marketing society. This board had been a true elite council managed by consensus among the local aristocrats, the big commercial farmers, and the administrative staff (Phase One). The Freedom Fighters (who were generally of middle- or low-status origins) brought in open, competitive elections and pressures for popular representation (Phase Two). Having accomplished this much, they also generated about five years of intense factional competition during which the old leaders gradually dropped out, and the new competitors shifted alliances through every conceivable combination (Phase Three). The anarchic period was brought to a close by the rise of a machine-style 'boss', an expert at patronage and competition, who put all the other challengers out of business (Phase Four). This new boss was a descendent of one of the old, elite-council members, but he worked with new methods and new interest groups.

During the 1950's, this same local boss moved up into the District Central Cooperative Bank. One of his henchmen was the bank's first chairman elected from a rural, peasant-caste background. (The management had been largely urban and Brahman up to that point.) This chairman substituted Marathi for English as the official language of the board of directors, and he began a policy of hiring non-Brahman employees. Strong factional conflict later developed among the emergent rural leaders.

In other words, we find the regional trend reflected in a series of local conflict cycles, moving from one arena to another as the opportunity arises. Each local arena passes through a succession of phases in which it is dominated by different elites, just as a patch of cleared forest passes through a succession of phases dominated by different plant species. In those arenas which were closely linked to the Olegao sugar factory, the crucial phases of succession can be dated as follows: (1) The Freedom Fighters fought for control of the marketing cooperative in the middle '40's. (2) The new boss of the marketing cooperative took control of the District Central Bank in the middle '50's. (3) The minority peasant castes fought the Marathas for a share of power in the Olegao village credit society around 1960. (4) A new district council system was taken over by rural, cooperative-based politicians soon after it was set up in 1962 (see Carras, 1972:80–103; Rosenthal, 1972:1742–5). (5) The MLA seat was won in 1967 by a young, Maratha politician with strong connections in the national party leadership. (Previously, the local MLA's were weak and more or less under the control of the District Congress Committee; they were not able to represent local interests and demands effectively.) These conflicts were not all fought between the same castes or classes, but they all involved a shift of power away from centralized administrative and party structures (which were usually, in the past, controlled by high-status, urban minorities) to local, village-based, peasant-caste leaders.

Social Change

These examples illustrate how local, small-scale cycles can grow out of, and contribute to, a regional and national trend toward social change. The actual linkages between local cycles and regional trends are activated by the political middlemen who operate between different arenas. Examples mentioned here include the MLA, the Brahman founder of the sugar factory, the Freedom Fighters, the boss of the marketing cooperative, and others. As middlemen, their influence within local institutions is dependent on the nature of their contacts in regional networks and arenas. The converse is also true.

A local series of conflict cycles does not involve a mere repetition of phases. Cohen (1974:243–4) has criticized "processual-phase analysis" for not taking account of the relations between local conflict and social change. Repetitive cycles without change correspond to what Bailey calls "maintenance" (1969:13) and the Wilsons call "social circulation" (1945:58–61). In contrast, the cycle in the sugar factory had an evolutionary trajectory because it was linked to regional processes of political mobilization, enfranchisement, and the rise of a peasant class. These linkages generated a Phase Four which was at least more of an arena council than Phase One.

If this cycle generates social change, and not merely circulation, what does it tell us about the circulation of elites? The conflict cycle is not a model of social equilibrium maintained through the circulation of individuals into and out of the elite (cf. Pareto 1935:1423–31; Bottomore 1964:52–3, 59). Instead, the cycle shows how new political forces are transmitted between state systems and local arenas. These forces include the rise of a new regional class (the large- and medium-scale, peasant-caste, commercial farmers), with a new set of political leaders and new methods of transmitting political demands, resources, and support. The success of this class was made possible by a growth and decentralization of resources in the state political system: by the expansion of the franchise and the powers of locally elected councils, on the one hand, and by the expansion of state support for rural development projects, on the other. This meant that there were more political favours to be distributed in exchange for more votes, a situation which inevitably led to the appearance of a much larger set of local political middlemen, rooted in their newly-activated constituencies.

If the conflict cycle does not conform to Pareto's theory of circulation, it is equally obvious that this model is not based on the notion that change and conflict derive simply from economic class interests. Class conflict is essential to the cycle, but such conflicts need not be based on interests defined in terms of property or occupation. In Phase Two (in the sugar factory) the opposing sides were partly self-defined in terms of ethnic (caste) categories – though they also differed in the average size of landholding and amount of education, business, administrative contacts, and other respects. In any case, the objectives of the group mobilization process had little, if anything, to do with the relative caste status or wealth of the parties concerned: they were directed toward political control over institutionalized power positions. The succeeding Phase Three, with its lack of stable group or class alignments of any sort, demonstrates this point conclusively.

The most significant modality of social change within the conflict cycle is one pointed out by Lenski (1966:81): "... the struggle for power and privilege involves not only struggles between individuals and classes, it also involves *struggles between class systems, and thus between different principles of distribution.*" (Italics in original.) In the sugar factory this involved a shift from an elite which governed by virtue of its education, managerial expertise, administrative contacts, and high status, to one which governed by virtue of contacts within the peasant lineages, mobilization of voting blocs, and connections with the Congress Party. The conflict cycle did not simply realign individual competitive positions, it manifested evolution in the local and regional systems of stratification.

Comparison and Conclusion

Do all local conflicts follow the same sequence of phases? Obviously, the answer is no; and it becomes necessary to define the conditions which govern the emergence of the conflict cycle. In the literature on local conflicts in rural India there are several instances of cycles similar to the one I have outlined here – particularly where such conflicts have been re-studied after a decade or so (for example, Epstein, 1962:129–140; 1973:180–4; Seigel and Beals, 1960b; Beals, 1974:169–170). There are also cases of conflict comprising different phase sequences. Frequently, for example, a mobilizing group does not have enough resources to change the local distribution of power (for example, Cohn, 1955), and the cycle reverts to Phase One or to something else. To put this another way, stratification systems which are changed by the conflict cycle also set important constraints on the processes which occur.

If conflict cycles are studied in a broad range of contexts, we can expect to find many variations in sequence. The pattern I have outlined here is just one possibility out of many. (As several readers have pointed out, it is likely that a contraction of resources, for example, might lead to a completely different cycle.) It is already apparent that the timing of phases in one arena depends on the changes occurring in others with which it is connected – both through the formal interlocking of institutions and the informal transactions of political middlemen.

In the conflict cycle, each phase has a specific pattern of competition and cleavage which sets it apart from the others. The first phase is one of elite domination in which there is competition among more or less equivalent or "segmentary" factions within the elite, and in which the followers are relatively passive. Out of the dual pressures of competition among elites and discontent among non-elites, "asymmetrical" or class conflict develops; and this leads later on to a period of anarchic or "pervasive" factionalism, followed at the end by the rise of a new dominating elite. All this implies that factionalism is not in itself a thing or process, a unified topic for discussion. Rather, the term embraces a heterogeneous assortment of conflict situations arising out of more fundamental processes such as elite domination, class conflict, and the rise of new elites. In any event, it is clear that some attention to long-term phase sequences is necessary in order to make sense of the many kinds of momentary conflict situations which have been observed.

NOTES

1 The research for this paper was supported by The Canada Council, the Shastri Indo-Canadian Institute, and the Centre for Developing Area Studies (McGill University). I am grateful to Satish Saberwal, B. S. Baviskar, D. P. Apte, and V. M. Dandekar for their invaluable suggestions at various stages of the research, and especially to Richard Salisbury for his guidance throughout the research and analysis. I am also grateful to Philip Salzman, Rhoda Attwood, and the members of the conference for their helpful comments on an earlier draft of this paper.

2 The period of research extended from October 1969 to September 1971. Statements made in the present tense refer to conditions in 1970–71. All names of persons and localities are fictitious. Fuller details concerning the events mentioned here may be found in Attwood, 1974a:156–222.

3 This table includes only those castes which have some landowning members in the village; it does not include families which are fully dependent on non-agricultural occupations. The size categories among landowning families are measured in terms of standard irrigated acres per consumption unit, following Epstein, 1962; see Attwood 1974a:39–48 for details. The agricultural labourers in this table do not include the migrant contract teams of bullock-cart owners who harvest and transport sugar cane to the factory during the winter. Most of these are small Maratha farmers from the dry villages.

4 A critical problem in the sugar industry is the steady supply of cane to the factory. If the shareholders want to, they can violate their contracts and not deliver the cane (although they might have to pay a penalty). When the price of raw sugar increased more than that of refined sugar (in 1966–67), some of the Olegao shareholders did not deliver their full quota of cane to the factory. The factory usually ensures the loyalty of its members, however, by paying the maximum cane prices feasible under the government price controls (which vary from year to year).

5 The MLA's grandfather was a landless Maratha immigrant to the area, a manual worker. In other words, this family did not have great status, wealth, or kinship support in the peasant lineages. Nevertheless, the MLA's father became an official in the local cooperatives, and the MLA himself acquired a college education. These were rather unusual attainments, in their day, for local members of the Maratha caste.

6 This cyclical model was partly stimulated by Fox (1971) and Leach (1954).

REFERENCES

Attwood, D. W.
1974a "Political Entrepreneurs and Economic Development: Two Villages and a Taluka in Western India." Unpublished Ph.D. Dissertation, Montreal, McGill University.

Attwood, D. W.
1974b "Patrons and Mobilizers: Political Entrepreneurs in an Agrarian State." *Journal of Anthropological Research*, 30(4):225–41.

Bailey, F. G.
1960 *Tribe, Caste, and Nation*. Manchester, Manchester University Press.

BAILEY, F. G.
1965 "Decisions by Consensus in Councils and Committees: With Special Reference to Village and Local Government in India." In M. Banton (ed.), *Political Systems and the Distribution of Power*. New York, Praeger (ASA Monograph 2, London, Tavistock).
BAILEY, F. G.
1968 "Parapolitical Systems." In M. J. Swartz (ed.), *Local Level Politics*. Chicago, Aldine.
BAILEY, F. G.
1969 *Strategems and Spoils*. New York, Schocken Books.
BAVISKAR, B. S.
1968 "Cooperatives and Politics." *Economic and Political Weekly*, 3:490–95.
BAVISKAR, B. S.
1969 "Cooperatives and Caste in Maharashtra: a Case Study." *Sociological Bulletin*, 18:148–66.
BEALS, ALAN R.
1974 *Village Life in South India*. Chicago, Aldine.
BÉTEILLE, ANDRÉ
1965 *Caste, Class and Power: Changing Patterns of Stratification in a Tanjore Village*. Berkeley, University of California Press.
BOISSEVAIN, J.
1974 *Friends of Friends: Networks, Manipulators and Coalitions*. Oxford, Basil Blackwell.
BOTTOMORE, T. B.
1964 *Elites and Society*. Harmondsworth, Penguin Books.
BUJRA, JANET
1973 "The Dynamics of Political Action: A New Look at Factionalism." *American Anthropologist*, 75(1):132–52.
CARRAS, MARY C.
1972 *The Dynamics of Indian Political Factions: A Study of District Councils in the State of Maharashtra*. Cambridge, Cambridge University Press.
CARTER, ANTHONY T.
1974 *Elite Politics in Rural India: Political Stratification and Political Alliances in Western Maharashtra*. Cambridge, Cambridge University Press.
COHEN, EUGENE N.
1974 "Political Conflict and Social Change in an Italian Commune." *American Ethnologist*, 1:243–53.
COHN, BERNARD S.
1955 "The Changing Status of a Depressed Caste." In McKim Marriott (ed.), *Village India*. Chicago, University of Chicago Press.
DAHRENDORF, RALF
1959 *Class and Class Conflict in Industrial Society*. Stanford, Stanford University Press.
DAHRENDORF, RALF
1967 *Conflict after Class: New Perspectives on the Theory of Social and Political Conflict*. (University of Essex, Noel Buxton Lecture.) London, Longmans, Green.
EPSTEIN, T. S.
1962 *Economic Development and Social Change in South India*. Manchester, Manchester University Press.
EPSTEIN, T. S.
1973 *South India: Yesterday, Today and Tomorrow: Mysore Villages Revisited*. New York, Holmes and Meier (London, MacMillan).
FOX, RICHARD G.
1971 *Kin, Clan, Raja and Rule: State Hinterland Relations in Preindustrial India*. Berkeley, University of California Press.

GADGIL, D. R.
1952 *Economic Policy and Development*. Poona, Gokhale, Institute of Politics and Economics.
INAMDAR, N. R.
1965 *Government and Co-operative Sugar Factories*. Bombay, Popular Prakashan.
LEACH, E. R.
1954 *Political Systems of Highland Burma*. Boston, Beacon Press.
LENSKI, GERHARD E.
1966 *Power and Privilege: A Theory of Social Stratification*. New York, McGraw-Hill.
MILLER, D. F.
1965 "Factions in Indian Village Politics." *Pacific Affairs*, 38:17–31.
NICHOLAS, RALPH W.
1966 "Segmentary Factional Political Systems." In M. J. Swartz, V. W. Turner and A. Tuden (eds.), *Political Anthropology*. Chicago, Aldine.
NICHOLAS, RALPH W.
1968 "Structures of Politics in the Village of Southern Asia." In M. Singer and B. S. Cohn (eds.), *Structure and Change in Indian Society*.
ORENSTEIN, HENRY
1965 *Gaon: Conflict and Cohesion in an Indian Village*. Princeton, Princeton University Press.
PARETO, VILFREDO
1935 *The Mind and Society* (4 volumes). New York, Harcour, Brace.
ROSENTHAL, DONALD B.
1970 "Deurbanization, Elite Displacement and Political Change in India." *Comparative Politics*, 2:169–201.
ROSENTHAL, DONALD B.
1972 "Sources of District Congress Factionalism in Maharashtra." *Economic and Political Weekly*, 7:1725–46.
ROSENTHAL, DONALD B.
1973 "From Reformist Princes to 'Co-operative Kings.'" *Economic and Political Weekly*, 8:903–10, 951–56, 995–1000.
SANDBROOK, RICHARD
1972 "Patrons, Clients, and Factions: New Dimensions of Conflict Analysis in Africa." *Canadian Journal of Political Science*, 5:104–19.
SCHATTSCHNEIDER, E. E.
1960 *The Semisovereign People: A Realist's View of Democracy in America*. New York, Holt, Rinehart and Winston.
SIEGEL, BERNARD J. and ALAN R. BEALS
1960a "Conflict and Factional Dispute." *Journal of the Royal Anthropological Institute*, 90:107–17.
SIEGEL, BERNARD J. and ALAN R. BEALS
1960b "Pervasive Factionalism." *American Anthropologist*, 62:394–417.
WILSON, GODFREY and MONICA WILSON
1945 *The Analysis of Social Change: Based on Observations in Central Africa*. Cambridge, Cambridge University Press.

Village Factionalism and Patronage in a Rural Municipio of Mexico

10

Franz Jozef Schryer

INTRODUCTION

The political life of contemporary peasant communities in poor, underdeveloped countries is commonly associated with a pattern of political behaviour which emphasizes patronage, clientelism, and particularly factional disputes. These factional disputes occur primarily among members of the local upper class (landowners, merchants, or rich peasants) who tend to compete for access to office and its rewards by forming rival political groupings cutting across class boundaries. This pattern, which is based on purely pragmatic, individualistic transactions, can be partly accounted for by the nature of the agrarian structure of the area where it is found.

I have previously argued that village factionalism, as the predominant form of political activity on the local level, is most evident in agrarian regions, characterized by a specific class structure and mode of production: the absence of large-scale *latifundism*, combined with a large percentage of destitute, landless wage labourers and many separate and autonomous units of production (Schryer, 1975). In such regions overt class conflict is generally absent or weakly developed. Moreover, such areas belong to the especially underdeveloped sectors of the third world, and frequently suffer from economic stagnation or decline. Political activity on the local level, then, is often a very important means for reinforcing or obtaining economic power as well as gaining access to external resources (jobs, promotions, and public projects) available in the wider political arena. One of the tasks of the political anthropologist is to determine how the type of political system, operating on the national level, as well as variations in local class structures jointly determine the form of village factionalism in specific peasant communities.

This paper focuses on a rural *municipio* in Mexico where such factional struggles take place in the context of a one-party system. The area in question (located in a mountainous, semi-tropical region of northern Hidalgo) has experienced both economic decline and a series of bitter, and sometimes bloody, struggles between rival politicians. Most of these conflicts occurred within the official government party. My case study is intended to throw light on the interaction between national and village-level politics in the context of the Mexican political system and to provide a greater understanding of the impact of larger economic forces on the local structure of power. I will trace the network of personal contacts between local, regional, and national politicians and examine in detail the nature of the alliances and pay-offs in the local arena. I will also deal with the role of land reform as a cooptative mechanism and a form of patronage in the factional politics of rural Mexico.

The Mexican countryside is firmly controlled by the PRI (Institutionalized Revolutionary Party). This party and its predecessors which have held a virtual monopoly on power in Mexico since 1929 carried out land reform on several occasions. Various political scientists (see Hansen, 1971) have noted that this monopoly of power is responsible for the long period of stability that Mexico has so far enjoyed. This apparent stability is a major factor in the exceptional growth of the Gross National Product (Hansen, 1971:42; Singer, 1969:45), since the early 1950s. However, this economic growth has taken place at the expense of an increasingly unequal distribution of wealth and shocking regional disparity (see Hansen, 1971:182; Aguilar, 1967:161; Singer, 1969:149). Herein lies the paradox of the ''Mexican Miracle'': the PRI, which has been able to remain in power despite a stagnant or decreasing standard of living of the lower half of the population (Hansen, 1971:76), combines socialist rhetoric with policies basically geared to the interests of private investors.

It will be shown that such a reform, consisting of the piece-meal distribution of land to the peasants, is not necessarily incompatible with the interests of the rural elite who dominate local political life. In fact, many 'agrarian' politicians within the PRI are themselves owners of small or medium-sized plots of land, or businessmen who employ wage labourers at extremely low wages. The actions of such political leaders in Mexico illustrate the attempt to control or even to foment agrarian conflict in order to consolidate their own power and support in the factional struggle for influence and public office on the local and regional levels. This strategy is politically advantageous in the context of a state government officially committed to land reform.

The realignment of political factions over this issue in the area under study was based to a much greater extent on personal connections to higher government officials and regional strongmen (*caciques*) than to any stable ideological commitments. Members of the local upper class gave verbal support to an agrarian ideology, or else vehemently opposed land reform as a matter of simple political expediency. For example, many local agrarian leaders who supported local land reform in the 1930s later switched their support to a conservative *cacique*. But in 1965 these same upper class politicians returned to agrarianism and supervised the distribution of one landed estate among the local peasants. In order to understand such dramatic switches of allegiance and the constant realignment of factions on the village level, one must look carefully at the personal motivations of these politicians and the 'pay-offs' they received within the context of the larger regional and national political arena. We shall therefore examine the impact on local political life of such policies as the acceleration of land reform under Cardenas in the 1930s, the conservative consolidation of Aleman after 1945, and the return to land reform by Lopez Mateos in 1958. My main conclusion is that the PRI has exercised a monopoly of power, at least in this region, not so much by ensuring the loyalty of the majority of peasants through land reform, but by manipulating and controlling intra-class conflicts among members of the rural upper class, who are forced to compete for office and influence within the framework of a single party.

A brief account of the historical background and the class structure of the *municipio* under investigation is first presented. This is to be followed by an outline and an analysis of the major political events, with special reference to the interplay between factionalism and the opposition of class interests. Most of these events which occurred over a fifty-year period consisted of horizontal disputes between rival factions led by upper class leaders. They continually flared up prior to local or national electoral campaigns, and took the form of personal confrontations. The high level of intra-class factional conflict in this region was directly linked to the lack of political participation of the majority of peasants (the day-labourers). It also appears that the severity of these disputes, shown by a high rate of political homicide and the unusually rapid realignment of loyalties, can be related to the economic decline experienced by the region. The subsequent downward mobility of the majority of landowners and merchants made it that much more important for them to gain access to resources available in the external political system in order to protect their social and economic position.

Not all peasants remained passive to the economic pressures. The radical behaviour of one particular type of peasant, the small landless tenant producers (whom I shall refer to as middle peasants), was especially evident in their concern for the distribution of land and the right to form an independent political organization. They were extremely militant, in contrast to the day labourers, because a certain degree of economic independence and security enabled them to engage in politics. Nevertheless, they were also coopted and manipulated by upper class leaders. The numerical weakness of these small self-employed peasants and the uncoordinated and often individualistic nature of their struggle meant that these disputes did not present an effective challenge either to the hegemony of the landowning class or to the factional pattern of politics it dominated.

THE MUNICIPIO OF CONCHINTLAN[1]

Conchintlan (pop. 10,000) is located in a geographically inaccessible and poverty-stricken region of Mexico. Like so many other mountainous areas which have been bypassed by asphalt highways, Conchintlan has experienced increasing impoverishment and out-migration over the past fifty years. The founding of Conchintlan dates back to the early 19th century when the absentee landowner of an extensive cattle estate established his residence in the valley where the administrative centre of the county (pop. 1,000; also known as Conchintlan) is located today. The region was sparsely inhabited and was subsequently settled by migrants from other parts of Mexico who came to set up small businesses and farms. The main town of Conchintlan, which later became the municipal centre (*cabecera*), developed into a small, prosperous commercial centre which served as an *entrepôt* between one of the highland regions of Mexico and the low-lying Huasteca region on the Atlantic coast. Today there are over forty villages or hamlets ranging in size from half a dozen to over a hundred families within the *municipio*.

The dominant pattern of land tenure which emerged at the end of the nineteenth century was that of small *haciendas* or *ranchos*. Unlike other parts of Mexico, the degree of concentrated ownership of land and landlord absenteeism remained relatively low and plenty of unused land (municipal land or tracts not worked by the landowners) was available to the day labourers who worked and lived on these estates.[2] Over time, some hard-working or loyal peasants were able to improve their economic position by engaging in petty production on these lands rented out by the municipal government or by the local landowners; they thereby constituted a class of small tenant farmers. Although small haciendas (50 to 900 hectares) with resident landowners did not represent a large percentage of the surface area of rural Mexico around the turn of the century (see Hansen, 1971:27–8; Stavenhagen, 1968:93), this pattern of land tenure and its accompanying class structure were nevertheless found in many densely populated mountainous regions. Such regions probably included (and still include) a significant proportion of the rural population.

The agrarian turmoil and the revolution that swept Mexico between 1910 and 1917 did little to alter this land tenure pattern or the relationship between landowner and peasant in Conchintlan. By the 1930s, however, the new highway which bypassed Conchintlan was virtually deserted. Since then the agriculture of the region has also declined and both profits (of the majority of landowning farmers) and real wages have fallen.[3] A short-lived coffee boom in the 1940s did not prevent further economic deterioration. Some of the largest landowners and most successful merchants left the area to establish themselves in towns along the new highway. Most of the remaining landowning farmers have since cut back on their operations and are finding it increasingly difficult to survive.

The main commercial crops grown in Conchintlan today are sugar cane (locally processed into *piloncillo* or sugar loaf) and coffee. The landowning farmers who employ wage labourers on a seasonal basis generally also raise cattle and engage in speculative commercial activities. In order to keep their land cleared, these landowners (who represent less than 20 percent of the population) rent out their pastures to the peasants for corn cultivation. But only twenty of them own nearly half of the arable land in the *municipio* and use more than one worker year round. These larger landowners (the top 4 percent) are now converting their cropland into permanent pastures, hence reducing the amount available to landless peasants for subsistence or small-scale cash cultivation.

As mentioned, the middle peasants generally do not own their own land. This class (which represents about 19 percent of the population) consists of self-employed cash-crop cultivators who may occasionally resort to the use of hired hands for specific labour-intensive tasks. In the mountainous zone of the *municipio*, the middle peasant cultivates anywhere from 800 to 4000 coffee trees, and generally processes a part of his own harvest. In the valley of Conchintlan (the warmer zone) a number of middle peasants cultivate sugar cane and rent the *trapiche*[4] and the mules used for pressing the cane stocks for making sugar loaf. Several small producers also specialize in growing corn with the use of oxen and plough (rented), harvesting just enough to sell a small amount or fatten some pigs. There are even a few middle peasants who own a donkey or a cow or two which graze in the pastures of other farmers, and some of them also sell soft drinks or cigarettes in their own houses from time to time. Although slightly better off than the day labourers from whose ranks most of them rose, this economic class finds itself in a precarious position. They are now faced with increasing competition and fear losing access to the lands they work. It is not unusual for them to supplement their income from time to time by migrant labour.

The rest of the peasants who represent the majority of the population primarily depend on local wage employment. However, most of them also cultivate small plots of corn or beans for subsistence, using slash-and-burn methods. These poor peasants constitute a rural semi-proletariat who, in the past, were tied to their employers by paternalistic bonds by being provided with loans, parcels of land, and even aid in times of sickness. This was part of a wider strategy used by the local upper class in order to ensure the permanent presence of a cheap labour force, used only at certain times of the year. In the last two decades, however, most landowners have reduced both their seasonal and permanent labour force and are no longer willing to "help the poor" (an expression used by many older peasants). Today the majority of these wage-earning peasants work on several farms scattered throughout the county on a seasonal basis, and become migrant workers in other areas during the slack season. Apart from the three main social classes described (the day labourers, the middle peasants, and the commercial, landowning farmers), there are also merchants, self-employed artisans, and a few rich tenant farmers. But these latter social categories do not represent an important segment of the population in numerical terms (less than 6 percent of the population).

THE POLITICAL LIFE OF CONCHINTLAN (1922–1973)

By the middle of the nineteenth century Conchintlan had become a small town with an influential middle class of artisans, independent mule-driver merchants, and small commercial landowners. Most of these men supported the liberal cause on the national level (represented by Benito Juarez), which stood for the repartition of corporate landed estates (owned by the Church or native communities) and the abolition of internal tariffs. During the ensuing period of dictatorship led by Porfirio Diaz (1884–1911), a local landowner and sugar cane distiller emerged as the local *cacique* or strongman. His economic and political power was subsequently reinforced by personal links with the powerful Cravioto family who wielded power in the state of Hidalgo during most of this period. In the two decades prior to the Mexican revolution, considerable friction developed between this *cacique* and other landowners and merchants of the area who included the descendents of the original founder of Conchintlan. However, there is no evidence of violent class conflict – in contrast to a much older neighbouring *municipio* where several Indian peasant uprisings took place in the nineteenth century.

During the revolution (1911–1917) a member of a family of landowning farmers and artisans who had long been opponents of the *cacique* of Conchintlan became a revolutionary general under Carranza. In 1914, he brought a troop of soldiers into the area and burned down an entire block of houses and a still belonging to the local *cacique* who had declared his support for the counter-revolutionary general, Victoriano Huerta. The *cacique* was later executed by the Carrancista forces and the same fate befell another landowner in the *municipio* who supported one of the many rival factions, on the national level, opposed to Carranza. Both of their estates were expropriated by the revolutionary forces and were later sold to an outside politician as a reward for military services. These properties eventually became one of the main sources of contention in local politics.

Politics Between 1923 and 1940

During the decade after the revolution armed confrontation occurred between two rival strongmen or revolutionary *caciques* who lived in different towns. In the *municipio* of Conchintlan, contending political factions were allied to each of these strongmen and they dominated the political life of the area for the next thirty years. The leading contenders were general Gregorio Marquez who lived in Acitlan (the district administrative centre) and general Emiliano Rubio. These men had been allies during the revolution, but became adversaries in the early twenties.[5] Emiliano Rubio lived in Agua Zarca where he bought extensive properties and settled down to a life of farming. General Marquez turned his attention to state politics.

In the wider political arena, Marquez supported the agrarian cause and was strongly anti-clerical, whereas Rubio was a conservative who sought the support of the landowners of the region. Like other generals who became small landowners, Rubio organized a para-military force of hired gunmen who patrolled the region under his control. The ensuing conflict between these two politicians (both loyal to the new government) was typical of the struggles between rival strongmen who controlled large parts of Mexico in the first two decades after the armed revolution. In addition, like so many other *caciques* in rural Mexico (see Pare, 1972), they formed part of a hierarchy of power which extended to the state or national level.

Between 1920 and 1930, the *municipio* of Conchintlan was dominated largely by Rubio, but in the '30s several politicians from Acitlan infiltrated Conchintlan and gained the support of the leading townsmen who then formed an armed defense against Rubio's soldiers. The principal leader of this opposition (a small landowner) and his closest associates were members of a local elite of merchants and agricultural entrepreneurs. They switched their support from Rubio to Marquez because the latter had recently gained considerable influence in the state of Hidalgo to which the *municipio* belongs. He was able to exert influence himself in the appointments of local leaders to such posts as tax-collector and municipal president. The new political clique in Conchintlan initiated an agrarian petition for the partition of the *hacienda* that had been expropriated during the revolution and sold by the state governor to an outsider. These upper class 'agrarian' leaders then recruited a number of landless peasants in the *cabecera* and in other hamlets of the *municipio* with the promise of land. Their most active supporters were, for the most part, small tenant producers (middle peasants) who had once been day-labourers. Most of the poor wage-earning peasants either supported their employer's faction or tried to stay out of this dispute.

The owner of the *hacienda* under attack was a state deputy and a former friend of general Marquez, but he had fallen into disfavour with Marquez because he ran against him in a federal election for member of state congress. When the agrarian petition made possible an invasion of his property, this landowner sought the protection from the conservative Rubio. He also sold several sections of this estate to local conservative supporters who opposed the agrarian cause. Several landowners who had shifted their support to Marquez also now re-allied themselves with Rubio because they were afraid that the agrarian ideology of the political leaders of the *cabecera* might lead to excesses. A series of armed clashes involving ambushes, assassinations, and intrigues ensued. Several agrarian leaders were killed and the defense committee of the *cabecera* later led punitive expeditions against local landowners who were henchmen of Rubio. However, despite these violent encounters and the good connections of local upper class agrarian leaders to a regional strongman (Marquez), the *hacienda* was not divided among the peasants of Conchintlan.

In order to understand this failure of local land reform during a period when land reform was sweeping other parts of Mexico, the network of personal connections between local and national politicians must be more closely examined. In 1933, when the fight between the agrarian politicians and their conservative opponents had just begun, a national electoral campaign was in full swing. That year, Lazaro Cardenas, the future president of Mexico, who would implement the largest redistribution of land since the revolution, actually came to the village of Conchintlan. Because of past personal contacts, his strongest supporter and only personal friend in the region around Conchintlan was the conservative Rubio.[6] Thus, although he became an agrarian president, he was linked to the strongest anti-agrarian politician in the Conchintlan area at the same time.

Conchintlan was, of course, not typical of those areas where large landed estates (*latifundios*) were expropriated during this period. In 1920, it comprised mainly relatively small *haciendas* which were not eligible for partition. The few estates that did surpass the legal limits were soon subdivided or sold by the owners themselves. In fact, we have seen that the only large landed properties expropriated by the new government were expropriated because of the political stance of their owners, and not because of their large size; they were even sold *en bloque* to an outside politician (the deputy) who had been a revolutionary leader himself.

When Cardenas assumed power in 1934, many other local politicians also became open supporters of land reform. For only as agrarians could they hope to advance their careers in a reform-oriented government party. For example, the deputy mentioned above, who had already sold part of the *hacienda* under dispute to several of Rubio's conservative supporters, suddenly decided to donate these lands to the Department of Agrarian Affairs for distribution to the peasants of Conchintlan. In 1935, he wrote a letter to the head of the department in question in which he gave the following reasons for this sudden change of heart: "I consider that in this manner the rural and urban proletariat will finally achieve its liberation. ... I am therefore fully in accord with the ideology upheld by the peasant and workers' federation of the state of Hidalgo to which I belong."[7] The deptuy made this modest sacrifice in order to boost his sagging image in the government party. However, in spite of the fact that this document later became the legal basis for the creation of an *ejido*[8] in Conchintlan, the

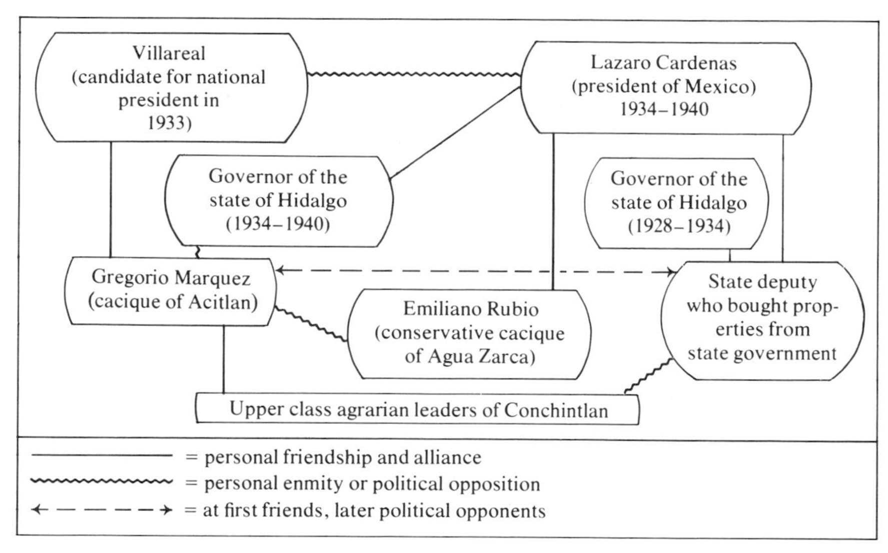

Chart 1 *Linkages between political leaders on the local, state and national levels*

government authorities responsible for implementing the distribution of land did not immediately carry out the wishes of the deputy.

The agrarians of Conchintlan did not obtain the land in question because the deputy was assassinated in the district capital by political opponents, in 1937, and his two common-law wives (really mistresses) decided to claim the property he had already donated to Conchintlan with their written approval. These two women had good political connections in the state capital. Moreover, many prominent officials did not like the agrarian clique in Conchintlan because of the fact that they were allied to general Marquez, and general Marquez had also fallen into disfavour with the new state governor appointed by Cardenas. (All of these men were 'agrarians.') Since Conchintlan did not suffer from an acute shortage of land or face a dangerous situation of militant class conflict requiring appeasement, the matter was conveniently forgotten.

The failure to implement land reform in the *municipio* of Conchintlan was thus, in part, the result of unfortunate coincidences: the wrong set of political connections, two influential women with a personal grievance, and a sudden change in the balance of power on the regional level. It so happened that the attempt of certain local political leaders from the upper class to use land reform as a "reward" for some of their clients did not work. Because of the unnecessary loss of lives, as well as the fact that the land of a local *hacienda* was not distributed to the peasants, many people still regard this period as a time of "dirty politics" (*la politica cochina*): a time when the so-called agrarian leaders tried to use the agrarian movement for their own political advantage and not for the benefit of the majority of peasants. The resulting bitterness and suspicion towards local authorities were well summed up by a peasant I interviewed, who had fought on the side of the armed defense of Conchintlan against Agua Zarca: "Our struggle was a matter of pure politicking ... the agrarian question was a matter of personal interest, like a business venture, because the very leaders of the agrarian movement already owned land which they did not even work. They were without shame!"

Politics Between 1940 and 1945

In 1940, the national electoral campaign gave rise to another upsurge of factional politics in Conchintlan. It was the only campaign in which an official candidate of the government party (Avila Camacho) was effectively challenged by an opponent (Almazan). Almazan started off as a possible candidate for the PRM (the predecessor of the PRI) but soon formed his own "Revolutionary Party of National Unification" (PRUN), when Camacho was nominated. Almazan's party represented diverse interests such as disgruntled revolutionaries now out of power, business interests in northern Mexico, to a certain extent the Catholic Church, and civil rights for women. Although he represented a more conservative tendency, the platform and ideology of the two major opponents was basically similar.

The agrarian leaders of Conchintlan supported Camacho whereas the majority of the inhabitants of the mountain villages were supporters of Almazan. Many people in the main town also favoured the latter candidate.* Emilano Rubio, the conservative *cacique*, did not take an active part in this campaign (his connections to Cardenas obliged him to support Camacho), but he was personally connected to many local members of the party of Almazan.

The pro-Camacho authorities in Conchintlan did everything in their power to weaken the Almazan faction. They even tried to bribe the local campaign leader for the opposition by promising to give him and his closest associates public positions if they withdrew from the campaign. The possibility of violence loomed in the background when the core of Camacho supporters appeared at the municipal offices carrying Mauser rifles. A large group of townswomen then gathered in front of the municipal palace to throw stones and hurl insults at the pro-Camacho authorities. On the actual election day, however, many Almazan supporters fled town and went to vote in other villages or to hide out for a few days. On the national level, the support of the entire political apparatus, including the armed forces, was thrown behind Camacho, the official candidate of the government party.

* Ironically, Almazan was also supported by Diego Rivera, the muralist-painter, a member of the radical left, whereas the communist party favoured Camacho (Michaels, 1971).

Despite overwhelming support in many regions, Almazan lost the election. In Conchintlan the power of the agrarian clique that had supported Camacho was reinforced and their opponents were humiliated. Some of those who had supported Almazan then left town permanently and became open supporters of Emiliano Rubio in the regional political arena.[9]

The 1940 electoral campaign illustrates the manner in which the powerful government party that came to power as a result of the Mexican revolution forces all local and regional politicians to operate within a single hierarchical structure. By suppressing all forms of formal opposition, local opponents have no other recourse but to seek allies and patrons among public officials at a higher level in the bureaucracy, or to attach themselves to regional strongmen associated with another wing or faction of the official government party. In this manner, the PRI can control and institutionalize local level conflict as well as provide a channel for upward mobility and patronage to those with political ambitions, including agrarians and non-agrarians alike.

After the election of 1940, the political opposition between Conchintlan and Agua Zarca continued. There were more armed clashes between the armed defense of Conchintlan and the soldiers of Rubio, while the agrarian committees of various hamlets sent further petitions to the department of agrarian affairs. By their continued agrarian activities, the political leaders of Conchintlan hoped to maintain the loyalty and support of the local peasant population as well as gain recognition from influential officials within the goverment party. However, it soon became apparent to most politicians of Conchintlan that using agrarian politics, so prevalent during the 1930s, would no longer work to their advantage. Not a single piece of land had been divided among the peasants; thus an important source of popular support was undermined. Moreover, with the advent of Camacho's more conservative government on the national level, identification with land reform was no longer a necessary prerequisite for gaining access to political patronage on a higher level.

In 1944, a dramatic event marked a major realignment of loyalties in Conchintlan: the main agrarian leader of Conchintlan (a small landowning farmer), who was also the strongest supporter of General Marquez in Acitlan, was ambushed and shot on his way to a fiesta in another village. This assassination, carried out by Rubio's henchmen, took place with the prior knowledge and collaboration of some of the members of the agrarian faction of Conchintlan. They turned against their own informal leader and hoped that by forming an alliance with Rubio, peace and stability would be restored and a conflict that had already caused so much bloodshed and destruction would be brought to an end.

The region had also suffered economic hardship during this period because of the construction of a highway that bypassed the *municipio*.

What little commerce continued was hindered by Conchintlan's reputation for violence. Moreover, at the time of this switch of allegiance, not a single politician of any stature in the state of Hidalgo was favourably disposed to General Marquez. This minimized the chances for his local clients to gain promotion or other rewards.

Later in the year a meeting of reconciliation was arranged in Agua Zarca, thus bringing to an end more than a decade of armed conflict and the influence of General Marquez in the political life of the *municipio*. Many former supporters of Rubio were able to return to Conchintlan. The *hacienda* under dispute remained the property of the two surviving (absentee) "widows" of the ex-deputy, and the agrarian committee of the *cabecera* was disbanded. Although the struggle for land was pursued by small groups of militant middle peasants in several outlying hamlets, their petitions went unheard. Several peasant leaders from these hamlets were even assassinated by local henchmen who had once declared their support for local land reform.

Politics Between 1945 and 1950

Between 1945 and 1950, a complex series of realignments again took place among local politicians. In spite of the fact that the former supporters of General Marquez and their local conservative opponents were now reunited, personal enmities and competing political ambitions were not easily resolved. First, the old supporters of Rubio's conservative *cacique*, most of whom had also joined the Almazan party in 1940, used their connections with a new state official to oust the ex-agrarian leaders of Conchintlan who had betrayed General Marquez.[10] A tinsmith and farmer (the main Almazan organizer in the *cabecera* of 1940) emerged as the informal leader of this new faction in Conchintlan. Despite his formal opposition to the ruling party and to Camacho in 1940, he pledged his allegiance to the PRI and became a good friend of the new state governor of the state of Hidalgo.

In 1946, the leader of this new conservative faction decided to reactivate the agrarian committee of Conchintlan and thus to seek the support of those peasants who no longer had any confidence in their old leaders. In this manner he hoped to reinforce his own local political influence and to dissociate himself from the *cacique* of Agua Zarca, without having, at the same time, to ally himself with General Marquez. This political move was possible only because he had established close personal ties with the new governor of Hidalgo who was somewhat sympathetic to piece-meal land reform. He also decided to support a small group of peasants in one of the mountain hamlets in their struggle for a piece of municipal land that had been illegally usurped by a local landowner. Public opinion seemed to be turning in his favour as a result of these manoeuvres, and many former

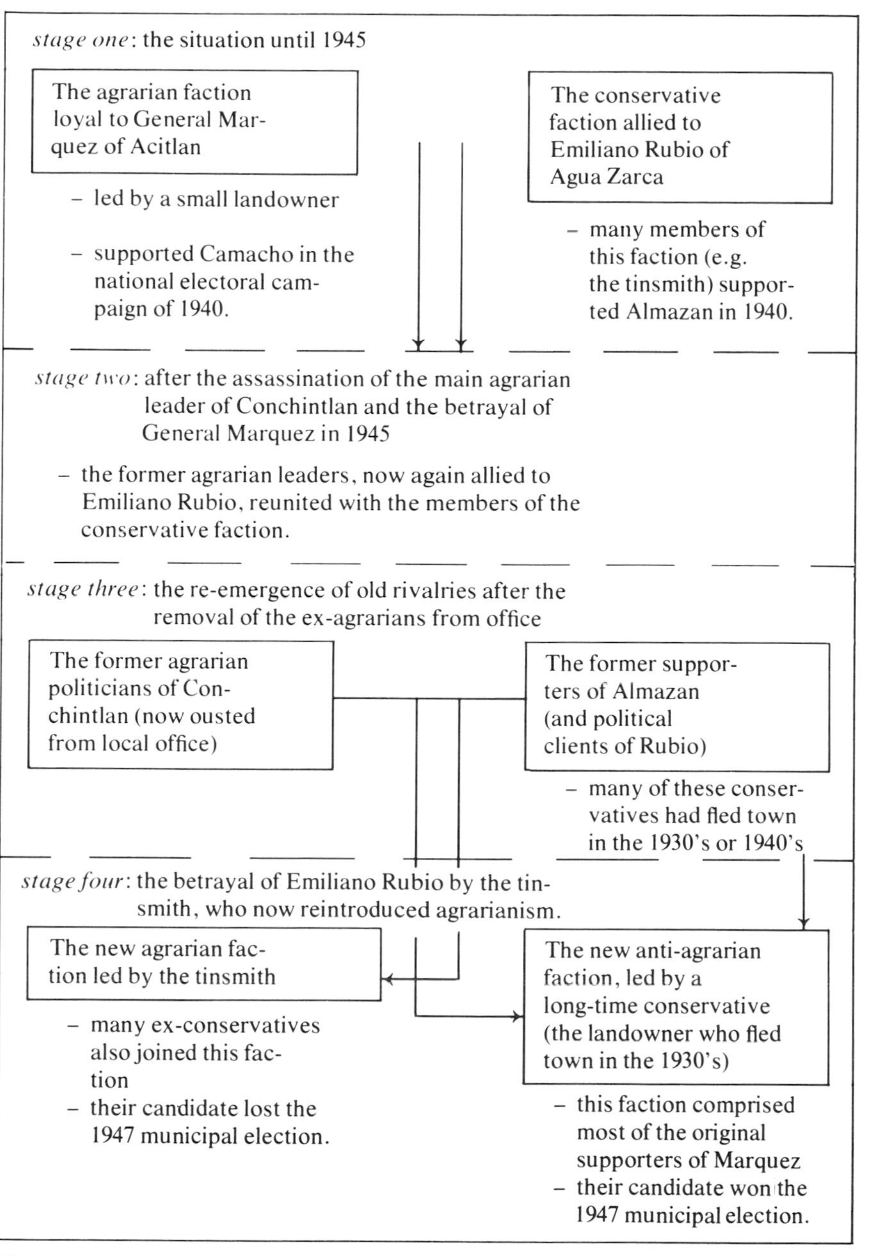

Chart II *Lines of cleavage and changing composition of factions in Conchintlan (1940 to 1947)*

members of the anti-agrarian faction in Conchintlan suddenly espoused the ideals of local land reform.

However, one of the ex-Almazan supporters and conservatives (a landowner who had fled to Agua Zarca in the 1930s), opposed this tactic and remained loyal to Rubio. This man allied himself with the ex-agrarian leaders (previously associated with General Marquez) who had just been ousted from power in the *municipio*. The new anti-agrarian faction then managed to win control over the local government by getting a candidate of their choice elected to the post of municipal president in 1947. Several members of the new agrarian faction led by the tinsmith received only minor posts in the local municipal administration, although the tinsmith himself was appointed chief tax-collector (see Chart II). The outcome of this election, held in 1947, was largely determined by the good political connections on the part of the leader of the new anti-agrarian faction with a regional opponent of General Marquez, called Perez, who now enjoyed the strongest position within the PRI in northern Hidalgo. Although Perez was officially an agrarian (and also a former ally of Marquez), he had allied himself with Rubio in order to extend his influence in Conchintlan. This political connection outweighed the personal friendship between the leader of the new agrarian faction and the state governor.

The municipal election of 1947 shows that the informal structure of power often assumes greater importance than control over formal political office on the municipal level. In fact, the election or appointment of public officials is often the result of prior consultation with regional *caciques*. Most of the elections that took place in Conchintlan, as well as numerous case studies on local-level politics in other parts of Mexico (see Pare, 1972; Simpson, 1937) illustrate this principle well. The role of the state authorities, especially the governor, as mediator in local factional disputes also became apparent in this dispute. Whenever opposing slates of candidates for the PRI are presented to the government (this happened in 1947), members of both factions are often appointed to the municipal council. The choice of municipal president, which is the most important position of power on the local level, however, is ultimately determined by the strength of political contacts and patronage on both the regional and state levels.

Shortly after this local election, the informal leader of the new anti-agrarian faction (which now held the dominant position of power in Conchintlan) was shot. Rubio held the tinsmith personally responsible and ordered his henchmen to assassinate the new agrarian leader. This tinsmith now found himself in an impossible situation. Despite his personal connections to the state governor, both Rubio and the new regional strongmen in northern Hidalgo (Perez) were his opponents. He therefore decided to seek the aid and protection of an old enemy, General Marquez of Acitlan. The subsequent meeting with Marquez was described to me as follows: "I had

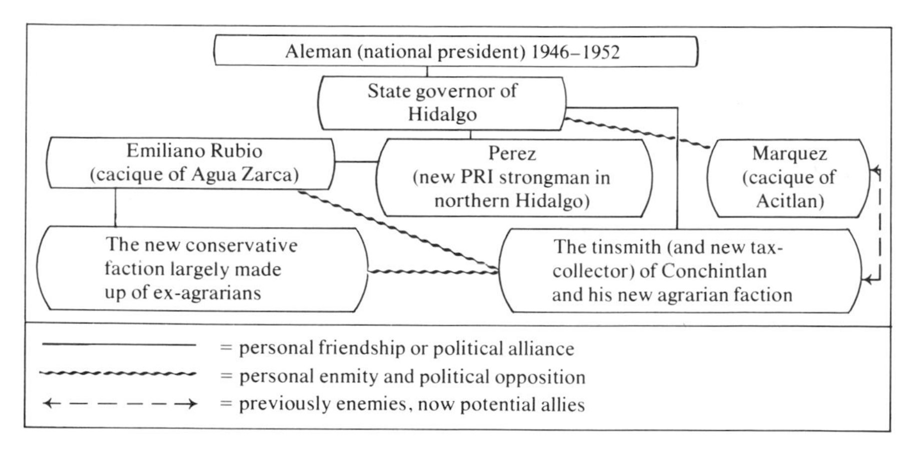

Chart III *The network of political links between local and regional politicians*

no other recourse but to go and see General Marquez in Acitlan. I spoke to him in the presence of his secretary and told him I no longer wanted to be his opponent. General Marquez advised me not to get mixed up with his group at that time because the state governor did not approve of him. He said that this might hurt me since I was already on good terms with the governor."

The network of personal contacts and political alliances in Conchintlan thus became so complicated that cross-cutting allegiances and competing loyalties emerged (see Chart III). Such conflicting loyalties and overlapping spheres of influence augmented the rapid change-over of local leaders and factional realignments.

The leader of the new agrarian faction and his closest associates, afraid for their lives, were forced to leave Conchintlan in 1948. However, because of their earlier support for Aleman, who became president in 1946, as well as their good connections with the new governor of the state of Hidalgo, the core members of this faction did not go unrewarded. The tinsmith was appointed to a public post in another part of the state by the governor, while his closest associate (a prosperous landowner with several properties in the mountainous zone of Conchintlan) became the president of a local chapter of the PRI in a nearby town. Both men have held minor positions on the regional level since then. Although neither became very wealthy the subsequent careers of these local politicians do illustrate the pay-offs (public posts, promotions in the bureaucracy, or even good business opportunities) available to entrepreneurial farmers and merchants who are able to successfully manipulate the patronage network of the PRI.

Politics Between 1950 and 1962

After 1950, the power of both the conservative Rubio and the various strongmen (including General Marquez and Perez) in northern Hidalgo declined. The network of personal links on the regional and state levels underwent changes and during this period a new and different type of political influence emerged in Conchintlan.

A native son, a local landowner and descendent of the founding family of Conchintlan, had made a political career for himself in the neighbouring state of Queretaro during the periods so far discussed. Beginning as secretary to Rubio, he later worked his way up to various administrative posts. In 1938, he sided with president Cardenas during the short-lived rebellion of Saturnino Cedillo,[11] although he had previously been more closely associated with the latter. A year later, he was appointed governor of the state of Queretaro while Cardenas was still in office. This politician played a very minor role in the local politics of Conchintlan during the 1930s and 1940s, but provided government jobs in the state capital to a number of friends and relatives from his home town. Most of these men also became agrarians in the state of Queretaro. Although very active in "defending the rights of the peasants" on the national level, the governor and his associates did not interfere in the internal politics of the community of their birth, probably because they did not want to antagonize Rubio.

After 1950, this man (now ex-governor) came to exert a great deal of influence in the social and political life of Conchintlan. In the early 1950s, he helped to promote the building of a feeder road to Conchintlan and is alleged to have nominated and helped to elect various authorities on the municipal level. Throughout this period he lived in the city of Celaya, Queretaro, or in Mexico City, where he held a number of important public posts. His influence over the political life of Conchintlan after 1950 represents a modified form of *caciquismo*. Although he owned land in the fertile valley of Conchintlan (which was rented out to several tenant farmers), he was not a local capitalist, but occupied a full-time administrative position on the national level. However, in order to legitimize his role as informal leader or patron of Conchintlan, he dispensed personal favours and sponsored public projects. In 1957, this new 'bureaucratic *cacique*' helped to re-establish agrarianism in Conchintlan by sending in a secret agent who arrived in town as a photographer during one of the festivals. The agent organized a small group of peasants who reactivated the long-forgotten struggle to obtain the land of the *hacienda* already discussed. Its absentee owners were the same two widows of the deputy who had bought this estate from the government in the 1920s.

In 1960, a part of the *hacienda* was invaded by a group of twelve peasants. They were small independent cultivators or wage labourers from the town of Conchintlan and from one of the nearby mountain hamlets. At first the local authorities were hostile and uncooperative but, with the public approval of the ex-governor, they too became supporters of the agrarians. At this point a member of the state congress of Hidalgo for the area, who was a personal friend of the ex-governor, took an active part in the internal affairs of the agrarian group. The new agrarian committee was soon dominated by rich peasants and small landowners. As in the '30s and '40s, this renewal of agrarianism in Conchintlan was obviously politically motivated. The ex-governor was at this time an active member of the agrarian league, a prestigious organization of veteran politicians. His active involvement in the implementation of land reform in his home town coincided with the coming to power of a reform-oriented regime (that of Lopez Mateos) on the national level, which would again step up the agrarian programme in a period of social and economic unrest (Anderson and Cockcroft, 1969). The establishment of an *ejido* would further enable him to use his connections with larger agrarian organizations to reward loyal followers.

Politics Between 1962 and 1973

Soon after the revival of agrarianism in 1960, a new burst of political turmoil and factional politics erupted. These conflicts were triggered by the arrival of a new parish priest to Conchintlan who undertook a number of public projects (a water line, finishing the new road, and the promotion of new agricultural techniques) and founded a peasant union connected with a larger Latin American Christian Federation (CLASC).[12] He also established Catholic schools throughout the *municipio* and began to preach against the "communist" tendencies of the Mexican government and the federal (public) school teachers. He received strong support from many landowners and most of the peasants in the mountain villages because of his close connections with several international organizations capable of providing financial help to local communities. The priest also dispensed medical aid and hand-outs to the local peasants. By introducing alternative sources of financial support and other forms of assistance, he thus eroded the legitimacy of the ex-governor and the local authorities who then lost a great deal of prestige and control over the local population.

The subsequent disputes took on a form similar to earlier factional conflicts. The authorities of Conchintlan tried in vain to have the priest transferred or removed and several threats were made on his life. The anti-government priest was then forced to utilize political resources within the PRI political structure which he had so ardently criticized. On the advice of one of his own local supporters, he established contacts with two PRI officials at a higher level, including a congressman and a regional *cacique* who wielded some influence in the area. These officials were personal enemies of the ex-governor of Queretaro and were not adverse to utilizing such an issue as a way of settling old scores.

The issues between the factions of the priest and his supporters, on the one hand, and the ex-governor and his local followers, on the other, concerned the status of local schools, the activities of the peasant union, and the functioning of community development projects.[13] These questions divided the inhabitants of many villages scattered throughout the *municipio* into supporters versus critics of the peasant union and the parish priest. A general pattern of cleavage emerged on the hamlet level: small peasant tenant farmers (middle peasants) became the leaders of the local peasant union, while their principal opponents were anti-clerical landowners who mobilized the poorest and most destitute elements of the hamlet population (the group most dependent on them). A few landowners who were favourably disposed to the priest actively supported the establishment of Catholic schools, although they were suspicious about such union projects as productive cooperatives and a credit union.

In order to boost their prestige and sagging influence, the ex-governor and his friends then pressured the Department of Agrarian Affairs to speed up the processing of the latest petition of the local agrarian committee (submitted in 1958) and to give one of the properties under dispute to the peasants of Conchintlan. An *ejido* was formally established in 1965 and many members of the Catholic peasant union also signed up even though their own organization had tried to buy or rent this land from the absentee owners only a half year earlier. Thus, after thirty years of endless petitions and feuding, about 800 hectares of very steep and badly eroded land (less than a tenth of the total surface area of the *municipio*) was granted to two villages in order to undermine the influence of a powerful local opponent – the Catholic priest.

However, the members of the Catholic union who had also become *ejidatarios* then clashed with the leaders of the *ejido* which was controlled by outside politicians and small landowning farmers. The local authorities, who were closely connected with the agrarians, did not want to recognize the Catholic union even though it was legally registered as a civil organization, and they tried to destroy it. Several union members were arrested and locked up overnight on charges of "drunken behaviour" or "being disrespectful of the authorities." Although one of the union leaders, a middle peasant from Conchintlan, was eventually elected vice-president (through the influence of the priest), he was not allowed to exercise any real power during his period of office. When, upon orders from his bishop, the "radical" priest left in 1966, the peasant union continued to operate in opposition to the local authorities and to a new priest who was appointed with orders to improve state-church relations in Conchintlan. The few landowners and rich tenant farmers who had been avid supporters of the priest abandoned the union, leaving it completely in the hands of small landless tenant producers (middle peasants) who tried to strengthen their organization scattered over seven hamlets. Over time, the peasant union disintegrated for a number of reasons: a lack of contact with the larger organization (CLASC) to which they were officially affiliated, internal disputes over cooperative stores, and the absence of a common enemy when political conflict with local authorities abated.

Neither the Almazan campaign in 1940, nor the intrusion of a radical priest opposed to the PRI and subsequent formation of a non-government peasant organization, upset the local balance of power. These failures in Conchintlan illustrate the difficulty of challenging the monopoly of power exercised by informal leaders supported by the PRI. This is all the more noteworthy since the dissatisfaction of the population at large made them receptive to the ideas propagated by the leaders of the peasant union and the criticism of the new parish priest. But, as we have seen, in order to operate effectively in Conchintlan, the priest was forced to seek support from a regional *cacique* and various PRI officials on the state level. Consequently he, like the peasant union, was forced to participate in factional disputes that also involved rival landowning families.

The last two municipal elections (held in 1969 and 1972) were again dominated completely by factions of landowners and merchants. Many people showed their disapproval of the official slate of candidates by defacing posters or refusing to vote. The majority of the peasants who had been active in the union and in agrarian committees in the past were only conspicuous by their complete non-involvement in, and feeling of alienation towards, these irrelevant manoeuvres.

SUMMARY AND CONCLUSION

This paper has focused on a peasant community characterized by a low level (but not the complete absence) of overt class conflict and the strong dependency of local politicians on external resources. Its predominantly factional pattern of political activity, commonly found in underdeveloped rural regions with a similar social and economic structure, took place in the context of a national system which forces all local opponents to compete for office and influence within the framework of a single party. The populist Mexican government is also officially committed to land reform and uses a leftist ideology which consistently fails to reflect the outcome of actual policy. It has been demonstrated that land reform in rural Mexico is not necessarily incompatible with the interests of members of the rural upper class. In fact, factional disputes fought over agrarian issues on the local level actually helped to preserve the *status quo*, regardless of who won. Such control over the local elite by a single party, combined with the policy of appeasing small groups of militant peasants (without basically altering the balance of power between employers and workers or the dominant position of the landed class), is most effective in backward rural areas.

I have also shown how the commercial and agricultural decline of one rural *municipio* over the past few decades made it that much more important for members of the local elite to gain access to resources available in the political system in order to protect their social and economic position. In my opinion, the popularity and the temporary success of the Almazan party in 1940 and of the 'radical' priest in the '60s, were directly related to the economic decline of the lower middle class in Conchintlan (the upper class of rich peasants and medium-sized landowners from the village perspective). Most of these downwardly mobile landowners, merchants, and artisans were eventually forced to compete for access to public posts and favourable connections with regional strongmen.

In order to understand this process of shifting competition from the economic to the political sphere, we must keep in mind the nature of the larger political system. Many political scientists who have studied the Mexican political system (see Hansen, 1971; Ugalde, 1970) have noted that the PRI offers many opportunities for promotion to aspiring politicians and that it has an amazing capacity for coopting local leaders.[14] The personal careers of many successful politicians from Conchintlan validate this thesis. Once its supporters are absorbed by the system, the PRI rewards them by granting consecutive posts in a bureaucracy and a party structure characterized by a high rate of rotation of such positions. For example, the ex-governor from Conchintlan (originally a landowning farmer) served as municipal president, member of state congress, state governor, director of an agricultural institute, and held numerous other minor posts. The use of an agrarian ideology and the support for token land reform by such a leader must be seen in this context of clientelist politics and economic decline.

The radical behaviour of the middle peasants on several occasions was related to the same economic pressures and downward mobility caused by wider economic changes which altered the relationship between various social classes. Several times the failure by factional leaders to distribute resources (particularly land) to this segment of the population caused sudden switches of allegiance or the transformation of intra-class disputes into class conflict. On the whole class conflict was quickly suppressed by local authorities or absorbed into the wider, factional structure. Thus, most of the transactions carried out on both the local and regional levels involved the realignment of a complex network of patron-client relationships typical of rural communities in underdeveloped regions.

My analysis also indicates that a detailed examination of class structure, as well as the interrelationship between factionalism and the opposition of class interest, can give greater insight into the dynamics of village political behaviour. The importance of factionalism as the predominant pattern of political activity in Conchintlan was directly related to the passivity of the poor, wage-earning peasants who represent the majority of the population.

Their lack of solidarity and political passivity can be explained by the characteristics of the productive process in which they are involved as both day-labourers (*jornaleros*) and part-time subsistence farmers.[15] Leading a precarious way of life, they lacked the economic security and the relatively greater personal independence enjoyed by the small tenant cultivators.[16]

Finally, I feel that the social situation described in this paper is representative of other areas in the marginal or underdeveloped rural sectors of Mexico. Conchintlan is today characterized by economic stagnation, general downward mobility, and declining standards of living among the majority of peasants. The resulting economic and social pressures are bound to give rise to even greater dissatisfaction and potential support for opposing political forces. However, we have seen that on two occasions, such political forces, openly hostile to the PRI, were met with resounding defeat in this area. The PRI was able to keep its monopoly on local political control despite popular dissatisfaction because of their strong position at the national level, their complete control over different resources available to local politicians, and their ability to co-opt or to repress politicians who threatened the *status quo* by introducing alternative sources of external support. Thus, factional disputes on the village level inevitably took the form of shifting alliances with regional strongmen or competing sectors of the official government party.

NOTES

1 All names of places and people (except for certain well-known national historical figures) are referred to by pseudonym in this paper. The fieldwork carried out in the community under investigation took place over a period of 6 years, totalling about 16 months.

2 The largest estate in the *municipio* of Conchintlan was just over 1000 hectares.

3 This process is the result of the growing unequal exchange between the local backward economy and the modern, external sector which provides much of the means of production and items of popular consumption. Although the prices of these commodities have increased, thereby increasing the local costs of production, declining productivity of the soil and technological stagnation have lowered the output of local agriculture.

4 The *trapiche* is a metal contraption consisting of two revolving wheels which crush the sugar cane when turned with the aid of animal power (mules or oxen).

5 Apparently Marquez got angry with Rubio when the latter refused to join him in a minor rebellion (that of de la Huerta) which occurred in 1923.

6 According to local oral accounts, Cardenas was met by an armed *entourage* headed by Rubio, who escorted him to the plaza of Conchintlan where an open air banquet awaited him. However, Cardenas refused to eat and instead took a chocolate bar from his pocket and walked over to a corner stand in the plaza to order a glass of water. They left almost immediately towards Agua Zarca.

7 This letter is on file in the archives of the Department of Agrarian Affairs in Mexico city.

8 The *ejido*, modeled after a form of communal land tenure found in colonial Mexico, is a form of landholding established by the revolution. The land is officially owned by the

community whose members enjoy the right of usufruct in perpetuity, but cannot sell or rent out the land they work.

9 Emiliano Rubio also founded a local chapter of a para-military organization known as the "veterans of the revolution" which was strongly anti-agrarian.

10 These men accused the local authorities of Conchintlan of bad administration and corruption. The state governor therefore replaced them with a "junta de administracion civil," an interim administration appointed directly by the state capital.

11 General Cedillo had been a close friend and associate of Cardenas but disagreed with Cardenas' pro-American stance just prior to WW II. Historical evidence suggests that Cedillo had also established close contacts with Nazi agents from Germany who encouraged him to start this rebellion (Kirk, 1942).

12 This international organization later joined together with two small independent peasant organizations in Mexico to form the "Authentic Labour Front" (FAT) which has since become Marxist.

13 In many cases such community development projects have greater political than economic significance and may even serve primarily as an expression of factional infighting without bringing any material benefit to the population at large.

14 At the same time one should not underestimate the element of physical coersion used in local-level politics. If you aren't co-opted, you are either killed, put in jail or forced to flee.

15 Another factor contributing to the dominance of factionalism and a low level of class conflct is the complexity of the rural class structure (see Tarrow, 1967:60) because of the many different forms of land tenure, the ambiguous position of many individuals in the class structure, and legal distinctions between different types of sharecroppers, smallholders, and wage-labourers.

16 Many middle peasant or small tenant farmers in Conchintlan have small reserves of corn, or more likely, coffee, that can be used to buy staples in times of scarcity. Although most of these peasants pay rents for the land they use, they are not dependent on landowners for employment or hand-outs. They are also likely to have dealings with many small landowners.

REFERENCES

AGUILAR, ALONSO and FERNANDO CARMONA
1967 *Mexico: Riqueza Y Miseria*. Editorial Nuestro Tiempo.

ANDERSON, B. and JAMES COCKCROFT
1969 "Control and Cooptation in Mexican Politics." *International Journal of Comparative Sociology*, 7(1):11–28.

HANSON, ROGER D.
1971 *The Politics of Mexican Development*. Baltimore, Maryland, John Hopkins Press.

KIRK, BETTY
1942 *Covering the Mexican Front*. Norman, University of Oklahoma Press.

MICHAELS, ALBERT L.
1971 "Las Electiones de 1940." *Historia Mexicana*, 11(1):80–134.

PARE, LOUISE
1972 "Diseno Teorico Para el Estudio del Caciquismo Actual en Mexico." *Revista Mexicana de Sociologia*, 34 (2):335–54.

SCHRYER, FRANS J.
1975 "Village Factionalism and Class Conflict in Peasant Communities." *Canadian Review of Sociology and Anthropology*, 12(3):290–302.

SIMPSON, EYLER N.
1937 *The Ejido: Mexico's Way Out*. Chapel Hill, University of North Carolina Press.

SINGER, MORRIS
1969 *Growth, Equality and the Mexican Experience*. Austin, University of Texas Press.
STAVENHAGEN, RODOLFO
1968 "Aspectos Sociales de la Estructura Agraria en Mexico." In R. Stavenhagen (ed.), *Neolatifundismo y Explotacion*. Nuestro Tiempo:11–15.
TARROW, SIDNEY
1967 *Peasant Communism in Southern Italy*. New Haven, Yale University Press.
UGALDE, ANTONIO
1970 *Power and Conflict in a Mexican Community (A Study of Political Integration)*. Albuquerque, University of New Mexico Press.

Furor Academicus[1] What There's to Learn from C. P. Snow

11

Robert Paine

"Our Court shall be a little Achademe."
Love's Labour Lost (I.i.13)
"Scholars are disputatious, almost by definition."
The Academic Marketplace (1965:165)
"... dons are not distinguished men. They are just men who confer distinctions upon one another."
The Affair (1962:62)

INTRODUCTION

My 'ethnography' for the following discussion is C. P. Snow's novel, *The Masters*.[2] Opening with the master of a Cambridge college dying in his lodge and with the first steps being made towards an inevitable election, the book is about the travail of the dons over this election. The setting is the 1930s when Snow, himself, was a don. Over and above its qualities of detail, consistency, and ring of authenticity as a narrative – all necessary prerequisites for the purpose to which I am putting the book – I am struck by its handling of interpersonal and small-group dynamics. Quite as much as using sociology to describe and analyse this novel, I propose to go to the novelist for insight for the places which friendship and hostility – in other words, *role of affect* – and ambiguity may have in the life histories of factional disputes.

I

Neither of the two factions is in power in *The Masters*, and it is this state of affairs which has to be resolved; nor is the issue around which the factions were formed – the election of a new master – fabricated in order to serve partisan designs or, as is often the case in party politics, to serve as a legitimator of the necessity for parties. The issue is forced upon the members of the college, throwing them into factions. At this point, however, individual members are held in the sway of their predispositions towards each other, as much as by 'rational' dispositions to the issue *per se*. However, the predispositions themselves change in the course of a crisis.

THE MAKING OF FACTIONS

Chrystal and Brown

Chrystal is Dean of the college and his close colleague, Brown is Second Tutor. In their middle-age, they "... were the solid core of the college ... but genuinely humble men ... neither thought that he was anything out of the ordinary. They knew that others round them were creative, as they were not; ... though they were the least conceited of men, they had complete confidence in their capacity to 'run things.' Between them, they knew all the craft of government ... . They never overplayed their hand ... [and] little of importance happened in the college which they did not support" (pp. 33–4).

But the two men sought different kinds of power. The kind Brown wanted "no one need know but himself. ... he wanted to handle, coax, guide, contrive, so that men found themselves in the places he had designed; he did not want an office or title to underline his power, it was good enough to sit amiably and see it work" (p. 61). Chrystal, too, "wanted to be no more than Dean," but "he wanted the Dean, in this little empire of the college, to be known as a man of power. ... he was not more ambitious than Brown – but irresistibly he needed to see and feel his power" (pp. 61–2). Together they became the 'campaign managers' for Jago, the Senior Tutor, in the election for the mastership. Chrystal is, true to his character, more obtrusively active in this project than Brown, but they work closely together as one team just as they had done on many previous occasions.

The election (it waits on the present master's death) has to be won by a simple majority of all the dons, whether or not all vote in the election. A majority is seven votes and when Jago's campaign opens, Chrystal and Brown have collected nearly seven pledged votes for him (excluding Jago's own). The other candidate is Crawford, slightly senior to Jago and a physiologist; Jago is in English Literature. Crawford started with four votes, excluding his own. As we shall see, the voting tally undergoes several vagaries during the ensuing months, and although the contest is a close one, Jago is the favourite for most of the course.

The Society

The dons of the college like to refer to themselves as a "society." Indeed, they share a number of corporate characteristics, including traits of xenophobia. However, their interpersonal relations are another matter: "I [Lewis Eliot] don't see ... why we should be so much divided." "We often are," said Jago ... "If fourteen[3] men are divided about most things, they're not specially likely to agree about choosing a new Master" (p. 15). "It was one of the odd features of a college, I sometimes thought, that one lives in social intimacy with men one disliked: and more than that, there were times when a fraction of one's future lay in their hands. For these societies were always making elections from their own members, they filled all their jobs from among themselves, and in those elections one's enemies took part ..." (pp. 45–6). In sum, then, the college is autonomous, an island unto itself, even to the point of deciding *that*. But the rider is that those who aspire to office in the college momentarily deliver power to their colleagues – and they may go "mad." "'You haven't seen a Master elected, have you Eliot? You'll find some people are mad enough for anything ...' said Chrystal" (p. 37).

Chrystal and Jago

Chrystal's relations with Crawford seem to have been distant and at this early stage, he supported Jago without having seriously weighed the two candidates. After all, during the years of the mastership now coming to an end, both men, Jago and Chrystal, worked successfully in the government of the college along with the master and Brown (p. 34). But as Figure 1 shows, Chrystal's support of Jago was given mainly on an indirect basis in that they shared the same feelings about two other men: Brown and Winslow. They both held Brown in high esteem (+) and both detested Winslow (–).

In the friendship between Brown and Chrystal, it was particularly Brown who was resolved on Jago:

> "Why was he so resolved? Partly through policy and calculation, partly through active dislike of Crawford, partly through a completely uncalculating surrender to affection; and, as in all personal politics, the motives mixed with one another.
>
> Most of all, Brown was moved by a regard for Jago, affectionate, indulgent, and admiring; and Brown's affections were warm and strong. He was a politician by nature; since he was set on supporting Jago he could not but do it with all the craft he knew – but there was nothing politic about his feeling for the man" (p. 53).

Still more senior than Jago, Winslow was in his middle-sixties and had been passed over in the previous election of a master. "He had a savage temper and rude tongue, and was on bad terms with most of his colleagues ... Between him and Jago there was absolute incompatibility. Chrystal disliked him unforgivingly ... Yet all the college felt that he was a man of stature, and responded despite themselves if he cared to notice them" (p. 24).

Eliot and Getliffe

However, there evolved an alternative pattern to the one just described, that of friends divided, and eventually several friendships were ruptured over the mastership. This happened early in the case of two close friends who were both in their early thirties; Getliffe, who was in Physics, and

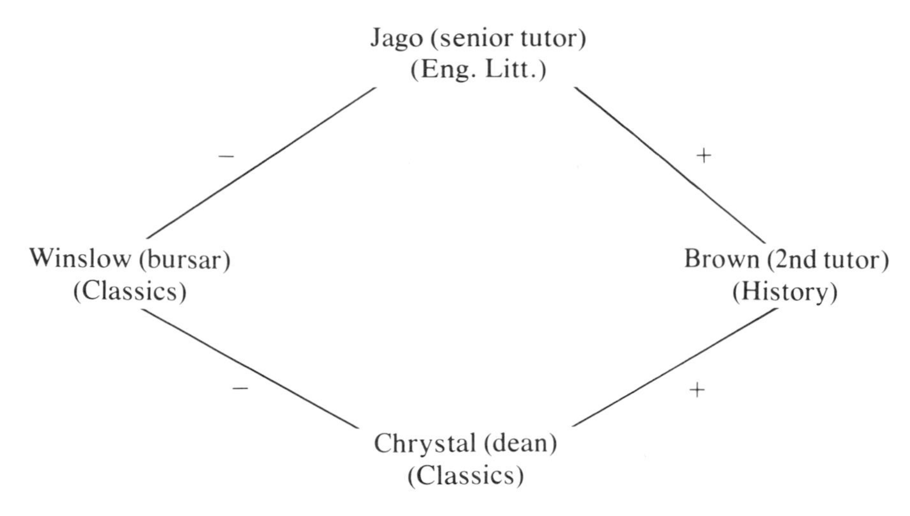

Figure 1 *Friends of a Friend, Enemies of an Enemy*

Eliot, who was in Law, each became an important supporter of their chosen candidate (Getliffe for Crawford, Eliot for Jago) even at the cost of their friendship. Witness this abrasive and bitter exchange which also tells us something about the issues:

"'The Master of the college must be a distinguished scholar,' said Francis [Getliffe].

'It's not so much what he's [Jago] done as what he is,' I [Eliot] said. 'As a human being there's a great deal in him.'

'I don't see it.'

'I can't begin to explain the colour red,' I said 'to a man who's colour blind. You'd better take my word for it – '" (p. 69).

Getliffe then tries another tack: political ideology. The two friends were both men of the left and Crawford was but Jago was not. However, one has already been told how "College politics often cut right across national ones," and we know that both Getliffe and Eliot had also worked with the "conservative" government of the earlier mastership (p. 34). Getliffe thrust this question at his friend:

"'Do you think this is a good time to elect conservative figureheads ... ?'

'For this particular job,' I said, 'I can't believe it's vitally important.'

Francis went on: 'He's got the right opinions. He isn't afraid to utter them ... There aren't many men of his standing with radical views ... Can't you see that it might be useful to have a Master of a college who is willing to speak out like that?'

'It might be very useful,' I said ... I added: 'He'd have no feeling. And no glow. And not a scrap of imagination.'

Francis flushed. ... 'It will be hard,' he said, 'for me to think you reliable again.'

'We'd better leave it,' I said. 'I've stood as much as I feel like standing – '" (pp. 70–2).

To summarize what is happening at this stage: on the one hand, the existing structure of relations among the senior members is predetermining their course of action, while on the other, the election is causing the younger members to choose between alternative principles, and not simply between rival sides; whether they want to or not, they are arranging disparate principles (scholarship, ideology, humanity) along a hierarchy. In addition, *each* member of the society is beginning to think more of the college in terms of the image he holds of himself.

From Common Room to Cabals

The public function of college meetings are held in the (senior) common room, also referred to as the ''combination room.'' It is also *the* clubroom of the ''society'' and, as such, is halfway between private and public (for absolute privacy, members retire to each others' rooms); members gather (around sherry or port) in the common room before and after meals, and guests from other colleges are often present then. Whatever is said by a member in the common room is said in '*his*' common room and so there is an uncertain degree of licence allowed in the direction of candour, especially for senior members – a situation which Winslow, for example, enjoys.

It is also in the common room that members sense the intimacies and hostilities in their society (which Eliot spoke of). It was there that Winslow opined about some members wishing to go ''outside'' for the mastership (p. 30). This idea was anathema to Chrystal and some days later there was this exchange:

> '' 'Good evening to you, Dean,' said Winslow. I said, in deliberate candour:
>
> 'We were just having an argument about Jago. Two for, and two against.'
>
> 'That's lamentable,' Chrystal said. 'We shall have to banish the Mastership as a topic in the combination room. Otherwise the place won't be worth living in.
>
> 'You know what the result of that would be, my dear Dean?' said Winslow. 'You would have two or three knots of people, energetically whispering in corners. Not but what,' he added, 'we shall certainly come to that before we're finished.'
>
> 'It's lamentable,' said Chrystal, 'that the college can't settle its business without getting into a state.'
>
> 'That's a remarkable thought,' said Winslow' '' (p. 64).

The ban went further, both unofficially and officially. At the college meeting shortly after, the motion that the mastership would not be discussed in a formal college meeting was carried (after contention) by seven votes to four. Winslow, Crawford, Getliffe and Nightingale (still to be introduced) were the four who opposed. Relations became strained, and even dinner in the hall was to become an ordeal: ''Men formed the habit of looking at the names of those down for dinner, and crossing off their own if there were too many opponents present. It became less a custom to stay for wine after hall'' (p. 146). In truth, the college split into two cabals that met

	Despard-Smith		
Gay		Pilbrow	('retired')
Winslow		CRAWFORD	
JAGO		Brown	('heavyweights')
Chrystal		Nightingale	
Getliffe		Eliot	
Calvert		Luke	('juniors')

Note: The society is markedly three-generational with the middle generation in control of the normal affairs of the college. I have labelled the generations: 'retired' (septuagenarians and octogenarians), 'heavyweights' (middle-aged) and 'juniors' (early thirties and under; the two most junior are without tenure).

Figure 2 *Seating Plan at Official Meetings.*

in members' private rooms for their business; pledges were renewed and speeches of support for the candidates (at least in the case of the Jago cabal which was Chrystal's doing) were requested and given (pp. 92 f). But there was still other college business to be conducted around the table in the common room.

Signals of Ambiguity

The seating at the college meetings was always to rule: "We took our places in order of seniority, one to the right, and one to the left of the chair" (p. 74). This produced the seating plan presented in Figure 2 with the deputy master in the chair.

Because it was not open to manipulation by the members, the seating plan was part of the arbitrary structure of this community. It is, of course, particularly in the arbitrary element (in the sense of customary) of a social structure that relations are furnished with symbolic or apparent final-cause explanations. The provision of this seating plan, then, is not itself an arbitrary act to be expected only of a novelist, but a prerequisite of an adequate ethnographic description of the college. And what symbolic explanations do we find? Snow offers this comment: "There was one feature of this curious system of seating: it happened at that time to bring side by side the bitterest antipathies in the college: Jago and Winslow, Crawford and Brown, Nightingale and myself [Eliot]" (pp. 74–5). But the seating arrangement produced yet another feature: it brought close friends facing each other across the opposite sides of the table: Brown and Jago, Brown and Chrystal, Eliot and Calvert.

Thus, one is dealing with the contrasting significance of 'full-face' and 'profile' relationships.[4] One can extrapolate from the text that both of these relationships have alternative meanings. Applied to Chrystal, for instance, we find full-face/friendship (Chrystal-Brown) and a distant but unambiguous relationship (Chrystal-Crawford); the profile relationship of strong antipathy is between Chrystal/Jago-Winslow and a relationship of no particular strength, but marked by ambiguity is that between Chrystal and Jago (as is eventually revealed). Here Snow seems to be telling us that this second pair of opposing affective relationships – distant but unambiguous *versus* ambiguous – is likely to spring into special importance in situations of crisis.

As the narrative unfolds, we see something of this process. Meanwhile one may note how, by the arrangement of this seating plan, the two candidates 'see' more support than they do opposition – for most of their supporters are seated across the table; conversely supporters 'see' their candidates surrounded by opposition.

Canons of Conduct

Even if Chrystal and most of the members of the college were unaware for a long time of this lurking danger of ambiguity in their personal relationships, both he and Brown showed early concern over the deleterious implications that factional divisions could have for college life. Such divisions were easier to divine, and their political experience told them what to do about that problem. Although they were protagonists over a position that would be judged as partisan by their opponents, adherence to canons of adversary conduct remained a matter of intrinsic importance to both Brown and Chrystal. This is not to say that there were no problems for them concerning both the interpretation and execution of such canons of conduct.

The matter of recruitment to the Jago party is a pertinent illustration. Clearly, the election was going to be extremely close; yet there were scruples to be observed when going after support: " 'I want to say where I stand on this [Chrystal said]. I won't be a party to over-persuading Luke. He's a young man, he's not a permanency here yet, he's got his way to make .... It stands to reason that Luke has to look to Crawford and Getliffe. They're the scientists, they're the people who can help him, they're the people who've got to make a case if the college is ever going to keep him. You can't blame him if he doesn't want to offend them' " (p. 89). Brown agrees: " 'The furthest I feel inclined to go,' said Brown, 'is to send him a note saying that some of us have now decided to support Jago. I'll tell him we're meeting on Sunday to discuss ways and means, but we're not inviting people who still want time to make up their minds' " (p. 90).

But before Brown had time to write, Luke heard of the meeting to which he was not going to be invited; Brown found himself facing an over-sensitive constituent:

" 'Brown, why haven't I been invited to this bloody caucus?'
'Why, to tell you the truth, Luke, we thought you might naturally want to vote for Crawford. And we didn't want to put any pressure on you.'
'I'm buggered if I vote for Crawford,' cried Luke. 'You might have given me credit for more sense. Jago would make one of the best Masters this college has ever had' " (p. 91).

The problem with another member of the college, Nightingale, of whom there will be more to say later, was quite different. " 'I want to find out,' he said, 'how the offices will go round, once Jago is Master' " (p. 104). Although they counted on Nightingale's support at that time, Chrystal and Brown resisted giving him the promise he sought; thwarted, Nightingale approached Jago directly. Jago, too, stopped short of a promise; nevertheless, he deprecatingly said of himself afterwards that he had been "despicably tactful" in his reply to Nightingale (p. 123). Actually, he had been instructed by Brown on this occasion: " 'You can be perfectly correct – without giving him the impression that the door is absolutely closed. Remember, indignation is a luxury which we can't afford just at present' " (p. 107).

These men, then, still remained within the bounds of their own moral rules, but "only just" (p. 90); and gradually tension developed between Chrystal and Brown over what we may call transactional tactics within the broad rules of the game. Whereas both judged Nightingale's approach as gross and inexcusable, they differed over the kind of relations that should be kept with their opponents. Impatient with what he perceived as a deadlocked situation, Chrystal wished to meet with the opposing side; Brown acquiesced most unwillingly in this course of action: " 'I like being as friendly with the other side as I can. But I don't like arrangements with them. You never know where they lead' " (p. 177).

It became clear that the moral burden of the whole election issue lay heaviest on Brown. Although the most intractable of all in his support of Jago, he was, at the same time, gravely concerned with the problem of how to rid the college of factionalism once the election was settled. Thus, although he distrusted the transactions in the meetings Chrystal convened (see below), Brown himself deliberately included some of "the other side" in his annual claret party that year (without Chrystal). What he had in mind is quite clear: " 'I'm inclined to think it would be rather statesmanlike. After all, we've got to live with the present society even if we slide Jago in. Mind you, I'm all against trying to make arrangements with the other side over the election. But I should regard it as reasonable to remind them that we're still capable of enjoying their company. It would be a descent gesture to invite some of them to the party' " (p. 154). Thus, the claret party consisted of Winslow, Crawford, Pilbrow, Clavert, Eliot and Brown himself.

Outsiders and Candidates

By the kind of paradox made familiar by Gluckman (1963), the college was, in some respects, never stronger than it was during the travail of the election. As was said earlier, those who aspired to office in the college momentarily delivered power to their colleagues. But this renewed strength also sprang desperately from xenophobic fears: "... [members] panicked at the idea of an outsider for master. It was as though our privacy were threatened: magic was being taken from us: this intimate world would not be so much in our power" (p. 184). Yet, if neither party obtained a majority, the "election" would be handed over to the college visitor, thereby becoming an 'outsider' matter on two counts: the visitor and not the college would choose, and (for various reasons) the choice would almost certainly fall on someone from outside. Such was the disdain and horror of the members for such a situation, that the Crawford party, after due deliberation, accepted a proposal from Chrystal at the first of the several bi-partisan meetings in his rooms. This could have meant handing the election to Jago. The circumstances were the following:

The predicted outcome, at that time, was a poll of six to five in Jago's favour (see Fig. 5): Nightingale had switched from Jago to Crawford (p. 135), and on Crawford's initiative, the two candidates themselves declared they would abstain from voting (p. 148). But as we said, a simple majority of all who were eligible to vote (thirteen members) was required; that is, seven votes. Hence, there seemed to be the bleak prospect of a statemate and its consequences. Chrystal saw the way out: the candidates, he told the meeting, must be instructed to cast their own votes for each other. This was done and a memorandum was sent to the candidates, signed by Winslow, Brown (with great misgiving), Chrystal, Getliffe and Eliot (p. 186).

When Jago objected to the "ultimatum," as he accurately but unwisely called the memorandum sent to himself and Crawford, he was unceremoniously put down:

> " 'When I find my party is negotiating behind my back –' "
> " 'This isn't a party matter, Jago,' Chrystal broke in. 'It's a college matter' " (p. 189).
> As Eliot commented: "... we enjoyed – there was no escaping the satisfaction – the chance of asserting ourselves against our candidate" (p. 184).

In truth, the college did not yet have a master.

WHY CHRYSTAL CHANGED OVER

Relations among the dons were ordinarily partly characterized by personal hostility and friendship; the college always had cliques. But it was also ruled by a cabal which cross-cut the affectively-based cliques and included friends and enemies (cf. Fig. 1). Conflict over the mastership, however,

for Jago	Crawford	
7	4	first line-up (shortly after Jago approached)
6	5	NIGHTINGALE switches
		on Crawford's initiative, the two CANDIDATES declare they will not vote; neither side has a majority any longer
7	6	the candidates forced to declare they will vote for each other (Chrystal's doing); by this device Jago has a majority, if there are no further switches; but these follow:
6	7	PILBROW returns from East Europe and withdraws support from Jago: he cannot support a "rightist" (even though he personally identifies with Jago rather than Crawford)
7	6	after a visit by Eliot and Calvert, the octogenarian, GAY, announces he is no longer committed to Crawford; it is believed (correctly) that he will vote for Jago
6	7	the evening before the election, CHRYSTAL crosses over and gives his vote to Crawford.
		(a simple majority of 7 is required for election)

Figure 3 *Summary of the Changing Poll*

tested each relationship in a special way. For ambiguities to be removed, they must first be revealed, and such is one likely implication of a crisis situation. Accordingly, there were not only changes of antagonists, but also changes in the antagonists themselves. Chrystal is used by C. P. Snow as the symbol of this process.

Chrystal switched his support the day before the election. The anticipated poll at this time was seven to six in Jago's favour, with Pilbrow now declaring his vote for Crawford, and Gay, the octogenarian, likely to vote for Jago (see Fig. 3); in other words, Chrystal expected his decision to give the mastership to Crawford. This is exactly what happened. What remains to be explained is Chrystal's desertion of Jago at the expense of his friendship with Brown.

Crisis and Ambiguity

Part of the tension associated with crises arises out of personal awareness that one is being forced to take a decision that really matters. Such was the dons' crisis. A question implicit in this situation is whether one is likely to be led to a self-realization of the ambiguities that underlie (and in a sense "falsify") particular personal relationships. I think this is the route by which C. P. Snow would have us approach the question of Chrystal's change of allegiance.

Yet account must first be taken of Brown's quite different reaction to the crisis. In his case it produced a *heightened commitment* to his existing network of personal relations and a zealous renewal of his faith in Jago. The pressure of ambiguity was, however, an assumption in both cases, and not in Chrystal's alone; the difference lies in the way the ambiguity was resolved. Brown repressed it, whereas Chrystal allowed it exposure: he re-examined his relationships.

The assumption that a crisis reveals ambiguities appears particularly reasonable when the issue around which a crisis emerges produces new role requirements. For example, whereas before there were but personal friends and enemies among the dons, the mastership issue added the roles of candidate, rival, supporter, opponent and waverer. In short, an issue such as this one carries its own symbolic organization through which all interpersonal relationships, for the time being, are likely to be refracted. Let us now go back to the C. P. Snow narrative.

The Flaw in Friendship

One source of ambiguity centres upon what Snow calls the "electric attraction of rivals."[5] It affected the two candidates: "They were drawn close in their rivalry. Even as they said [at a college meeting] they would not vote for the other, they felt an inexplicable intimacy. They found real elation in making a statement together; they enjoyed setting themselves apart from the rest of us" (p. 148). Earlier, note was taken of a similar elation which supporters found in asserting themselves against their candidate. Nor is a candidate's view of his supporters without ambiguity. People whom the candidate thought he knew well are seen in a new light – now that they are his rival's hope of his own defeat. He may be tempted to take his own supporters for granted; at the same time he may notice how they seem to play on his gratitude. It was left to the dying master to observe: " 'It's remarkable. People always believe that, if only they support the successful candidate, they've got his backing for ever. It's an illusion .... I assure you, one feels a certain faint irritation at the faces of one's loyal supporters. They catch one's eye and smirk .... Gratitude isn't an emotion .... But the expectation of gratitude is a very lively one' " (p. 170).

The attraction of one's adversaries may rival the attraction of friendship. "... rivals, whether competing for a job, opposing each other in politics, struggling for the same woman, are for mysterious moments closer than any friends" (p. 148). Indeed, a second and surely more important source of ambiguity is in what we may call the flaw in friendship. For it is the bond of friendship rather than the adversary relationship that can be intolerably constraining in periods of crisis: one's adversary is a target, but it may be painful to quarrel with a friend; in this sense adversaries are free where friends are bonded. "... soon I felt that Chrystal knew, right from the beginning, that he and Brown were bound to disagree. In his curiously soft-hearted way, Chrystal fought shy of a scene; he did not want to quarrel; he was afraid of the claims of friendship" (p. 176).

A crisis may place different claims on persons who, nevertheless, still try to claim each other's loyalty on the basis of a friendship antecedent to the crisis. A temporary resolution of the difficulty may be in one of the friends' deferring to the other (this may virtually amount to being drawn into a client role). But where this also involves the friend with people who are not his friends but his friend's friends, the strain may become too great and the friendship may suddenly snap.

This observation should be viewed in the light of its implications for Crawford's party. Only one person (Getliffe), among his original supporters, was involved in the four strong friendship dyads in the college: but three of the four friendships were eventually ruptured by the election;[6] then Crawford defeated Jago. Put another way, Crawford won the election even though the core of his supporters were the friendless persons in the college. The same difference is true of the candidates themselves: Crawford seemed to be without a close relationship, whereas Jago had warm relationships with at least three of the four junior members, in addition to his friendship with Brown (leaving aside his association with Chrystal).

Of the six men who were with Crawford at the end, three were constrained not by friendship but by its reciprocal, hostility; the other three (Chrystal, Getliffe and Pilbrow) were constrained by *the issue*, and for two of them this meant throwing over the constraint of friendship. The Crawford party won because, paradoxically, it was the 'freer' party of the two.

Chrystal

In the beginning, it was perhaps Chrystal more than any other of the principals whose judgement was pre-empted through the affective network in which he found himself placed; one also recalls how it was Chrystal who "irresistibly ... needed to see and feel his power." He came to realize that his chances in this respect were, after all, minimal with Jago. Eliot and his friend Calvert knew this, but they failed to draw the ineluctable conclusion (p. 51). On the other hand, Chrystal began to see how the Crawford party, because they were really little more than a stop-Jago group (see below), needed someone to run things; he began to see how Crawford too, if successful, would want a dean who would do just that. It is also true that the fascination of rivals was a particularly strong force with Chrystal: "As the months went on, Chrystal found he could endure the thought of Jago less and less. He felt free in the conferences with the other side: in the pacts with them ... he could assert himself. Everytime he was with the other side he felt that the whole election lay in his hands. In those meetings, in the hours at night with Jago's opponents, he came into his own again'' (p. 273).

Put more pragmatically, as the election dragged on over the months, Chrystal saw how it offered opportunities for new combinations; he began using the factional situation itself (especially the prospect of a stalemate) as a *political resource*. But for a time, he was hampered in this avocation as a Paretan ''fox'' not only by his friendship with Brown, but (and perhaps this was the more serious restriction) also by his aversion for Winslow. Then Winslow resigned as bursar in a pique at not having been consulted over a large endowment which Chrystal and Brown had secured for the college. Winslow's resignation meant that the aversion for the man burned with less intensity, and the success over the endowment renewed Chrystal's appetite for political management. At the same time, Jago's reaction to these linked events – the endowment and Winslow's resignation – placed more distance between Chrystal and himself.

> '''This is a wretched exchange.'
> 'I don't follow you ...'
> 'I mean,' cried Jago, 'that we're exchanging a fine Bursar for a rich man's charity. And I don't like it.'
> 'It's not our fault,' said Chrystal sharply'' (p. 210).

In his disenchantment with Jago and in his mood of self-realization, Chrystal attempted once again to impose his will on the college at a bi-partisan meeting in his rooms: '''Will any of you join me? I should like to find another man altogether''' (p. 252). The proposal was to drop both of the present two candidates and find someone else among their own number (Brown, most likely – who was angered when he heard of it). It seems that by this stratagem, Chrystal was hoping to separate himself from Jago without separating himself from Brown. When this endeavour proved still-born, there was no alternative combination left to him and so he went over to Crawford. With that decision made, the cloak of ambiguity fell from the Chrystal-Jago relationship: no longer was it held in place through Brown. Shortly before his decision, Chrystal confessed: '''There are times ... when I see the other side's case against Jago. He's too much up and down ... there are times when I have my doubts''' (p. 213). But now he tells Jago to his face: '''I don't mind Crawford being Master. I did once. It was my mistake. He'll make a good Master''' (p. 278).

In vain, Jago beseeches Chrystal to reconsider: '''We can make a working plan. I'm prepared to leave certain things in the college to you''' (p. 278). It is when all is lost that we are told what Jago really thought of Chrystal and of the chord of ambiguity running through Jago: ''He did not like Chrystal; they were as different as men could be; but that antipathy made Chrystal's support more precious. He resented Chrystal's management, he thought Chrystal was a coarse-minded party boss – but even when he wanted to quarrel, he thought with wonder and delight 'this man believes in me! ... If such a man believes in me, I can believe in myself!' " (p. 286).

Epilogue: The New Common Room

Glancing again at the old seating plan (Fig. 2), we can see the likelihood of Chrystal's switch in support signalled there: he was sitting alongside Jago. It was a profile relationship, and Chrystal became Jago's "Judas."[7] In the common room during the first evening after the election, Jago was beckoned to sit between the new master and Chrystal – Chrystal who, at the last moment, had put himself between Jago and the mastership. With Brown facing both Jago and Chrystal, ambiguity ran *across* the table as well. As Brown said in the privacy of his rooms: " 'It will be a few years before we stop being more divided than I should like' " (p. 282).

During the election, Eliot took Winslow's place in that tight network around Brown (cf. Figs. 1 and 4), but the defection of Chrystal ruptured all those relationships (except the one between Eliot and Brown). However, as a crisis, the election was an exceptional phase in the life of the college, for as far as one can judge from *The Affair*, a sequel to *The Masters*, college relations resumed their normal shape once there was a new master. Whereas changes in individual fortunes were remembered in personal friendships and particularly in personal hostilities, the governing clique or cabal – constituted, like its predecessor, independent of lines of friendship/hostility – kept to itself most of the government of the college. Its members were Crawford, Chrystal, Nightingale (as Bursar) and Brown. "... whoever had been Master, he [Brown] could not have avoided waiting there at his side. ... So when Crawford saw Brown settling himself to help ... he took him with open arms" (*The Affair*, pp. 131, 130). Jago, on the other hand, had withdrawn, as far as possible, from college life (*op. cit.*:111).

The Affair is set in the last year of Crawford's mastership; another cycle is nearly completed. Chrystal is dead; Brown is sixty-three and the Senior Tutor. It is widely assumed that Getliffe, who has both an international reputation and a knighthood in his possession, will follow Crawford. However, a group in the college, hostile to Getliffe, is gathering around Brown, urging him to declare himself a candidate. On a visit to the college, Eliot, now practising law in London, talks with Brown: " 'If I were to ask for your advice whether to let my candidature go forward or not, Lewis, I wonder what you'd say?' " (*op. cit.*:27).

II

While deliberative in his politics, Chrystal himself is an example of C. P. Snow's observation that "the more certain men are that they are chasing their own concrete and 'realistic' ends, the more nakedly do you see all the strands they could never give a reason for'' (p. 275). In other words, there is likely to be a 'structure' of motivation hidden from the view of the actors. It is especially the ''strands'' of affect that interest us and *The Masters* shows us how not only recruitment to factions but also the internal organization of individual factions can be directly related to the factor of affect. But before exploring this last point, more must be said about the strands of hostility – alongside those of friendship – in this small society of dons. It is here that among the *personae dramatis*, Nightingale moves to centre stage, and Coser's *The Functions of Social Conflict* (1956) is a useful, theoretically interpretative text.[8]

THE PROBLEM OF HOSTILITY

Coser on Conflict

Coser distinguishes between predispositions to engage in conflict, which he calls hostile sentiments, and conflict as transactions. Whereas hostility without conflict is prejudicial to the continuance of a group, ''a certain degree of conflict is an essential element in group formation and the persistence of group life'' (p. 31). But this general thesis of conflict as a form of socialization (an idea not new to anthropologists) is predicated on the distinction between *realistic* and *unrealistic* conflict (henceforth abbreviated as RC and URC). It is only RC that is transactional, in Coser's terms, for conflict is the chosen means – among other alternatives – for the correction of specific demands and services. But in URC, conflict is not an alternative means; rather, it is an end in itself – or it is used indiscriminately to attain release from tension (pp. 48–55). With URC, then, the only question is who is going to be made the object of conflict? ''Insofar as unrealistic conflict is an end in itself, insofar as it affords only tension release, the chosen antagonist can be substituted for by any other 'suitable' target'' (p. 156). URC is likely to imply ''a displacement of goal in the actor: he need no longer aim at reaching a solution of the unsatisfactory situation, but merely at releasing the tension which arose from it'' (*loc. cit.*).

Now, the chance of conflict within a small and homogeneous group correlates positively (in many, though not all circumstances) with the chance that the form of the conflict will include a good deal of URC. However, groups also need conflict. It is even dangerous for a group to suppress conflict; ''the fear of intense conflict may lead to suppression of hostile feelings; and in turn, the accumulation of such feelings is likely to further intensify the conflict once it breaks out'' (*op. cit.*:68). So the question becomes what kinds of circumstances allow for RC without promoting URC? We return to this after presenting more data from *The Masters*.

Nightingale and URC

Winslow, as already indicated, was affected by URC. Despard-Smith was too: " 'I've had a disappointing life .... It's a scandalous story. It would not be to the credit of this college .... And I lay it all to the blame of the people here' " (p. 263). But most of all, it was Nightingale who used URC through the long months of the election. As a young man, he showed great promise in his field of theoretical chemistry and awaited admission to the Royal Society. However, he was never admitted and the bitterness which overtook him made him a paradigm case of URC (p. 47). He had begun competitively (RC), but his failure left him suspecting all competition and everyone else's success: all that drove him now was the need to release the tension of the bitter conflict inside him.[9] His first 'target' in the election affair was, appropriately enough, Crawford, the successful scientist, the well-known Fellow of the Royal Society. Then Crawford was replaced by Jago. It was Nightingale (what irony in this name!) who "started a campaign against Jago." "It was a campaign of propaganda, concentrated with all his animosity and force .... The sneers did not aim at Jago himself, but at those around him. First his wife .... After Mrs. Jago, Nightingale's next point of attack was Jago's supporters and friends" (pp. 145–6). The effect was to implant the notion among Crawford's party that it was the others, the Jago party, who were departing from normative conduct, and among Jago's people, it drew a deepening distrust of the Crawford party. "We each found ourselves holding the other side *collectively* responsible for Nightingale's doings .... There were times when we all saw the other side through a film of enmity. We forgot who they were and what they were truly like" (p. 153).

In sum, the URC campaign fanned some characteristic factional (*ad hominem*) behaviour. Nevertheless, it did not do excessive damage to the college, and it is important to understand why.

Control over URC

Coser's treatment of our question regarding the circumstances that allow for RC without promoting URC, will be familiar enough to anthropologists: "Segmental participation in a multiplicity of conflicts constitutes a balancing mechanism within the [group] structure" and this reduces the affects of URC, if not its actual incidence. On the other hand, URC is most likely where adversaries "participate with their total personality," and this is most likely to happen where *one* issue cuts through a group (for then, the group is *not* "sewn together by its inner conflicts") (Coser, pp. 154, 58, 77). A mediator can "help to strip the conflict of its non-rational and aggressive overtones," but he can do so "only if each party believes the objective situation justifies reconciliation and makes peace advantageous" (p. 59). In other words, the success of his appeal against URC depends on his being able to reach the chords of RC in each of the adversaries. However, reduction of the URC element does not necessarily reduce the earnestness of adversary politics; on the contrary, protagonists may reject personal arguments and animosities precisely in order to improve the argument of their point of view. But the greater the RC element, the greater the likelihood of an ultimate "common goal" being retained among the adversaries, despite their arguments of "opposed aims" (pp. 111–19).

Now, in *The Masters* the balancing mechanisms were weak or absent because of the issue itself – the mastership. Although not all members entered into the fray with their total personality (Pilbrow did not, and Crawford managed to appear as though he had only a segmentary interest), such key persons as Jago, Brown and Chrystal did do so. However, Chrystal also mediated by means of RC arguments, whose appeal reached even Winslow. Nightingale was excluded from (or walked out of) the bi-partisan meetings convened by Chrystal. We noted how Chrystal seemed to use the factional situation itself as a political resource. Nightingale, in his own way, had tried to do something of the same. But whereas Chrystal succeeded, Nightingale failed and the explanation is to be found in the RC/URC difference. Chrystal, but not Nightingale, otherwise kept within the bounds of proper conduct (RC behaviour) which, itself, was another political resource. Towards the end, Crawford was scoring over Jago for the same reason: Jago's stand began at least to *look like* a URC one. Thus, despite the intensity of the conflict, or perhaps because of it, most of the adversaries kept in view a common goal at the same time as they pursued their separate interests; for example, they agreed that the election not be delayed and that it be made by the members themselves.

FACTIONS AS NETWORKS

The contending factions which centred upon Jago's and Crawford's candidacies formed distinctive networks: Jago's was a cluster and Crawford's formed a star.[10] From this distinction flowed a number of others which, in aggregate, suggested that as each faction coalesced it assumed a characteristic value structure. Affect had an important role in this process.

The Divided Cabal

The network evident in the early association of Jago, Brown, Chrystal and Winslow (Fig. 1) was maintained through status relations: these men were the four senior officers in the old master's government and they could not avoid being brought together. I call it a 'cabal' in view of its political nature; it was the network of the few who ruled. But that network was also remarkable as a constellation of affective relations: strong affinities and antipathies which were equally strong. Thus it was a 'divided' network.

Negative affect was centred upon Winslow who seemed to so charge most of his interpersonal relations; the positive centred on Brown. When the election of a new master became an issue, Winslow had to oppose Jago just as Brown had to support him, a state of affairs in which Chrystal found his own judgement curiously pre-empted. *The enemy of my enemy is my friend as is the friend of my friend*, and Jago was a 'friend' of Chrystal's on both accounts. Yet, there was little personal liking between the two men (p. 273).

Significantly, Crawford, Jago's actual rival, came into the picture only in a secondary way as the man whom Winslow (and others) chose to stop Jago from winning. Unlike each of the other four men, Crawford moved in a world that was not bounded by the college or even by his own university. For Winslow, this meant that his personal relations with Crawford were sufficiently distant and inconsequential as to be unambiguous and without (negative) affect. As viewed by Jago, Brown and Chrystal, however, supporting Crawford was an effort by Winslow to go "outside" – as far outside as he dared and was possible. Through Crawford, Winslow hoped to change the dynasty.

Cleavage: Cluster and Star Networks

These same forces of affect persisted in the emergence of the two college-wide factions. However, I am not suggesting anything quite as simplistic as a 1:1 relationship between positive affective relations and the formation of cluster networks, or negative affect and star networks. Closer examination of *The Masters* yields other factors that also contributed to this result.

One may wonder why a cluster network did not emerge around Crawford? What made a star network inevitable is that Crawford's people supported him separately, even to the extent of not sharing those reasons that they had in common. But why did the 'star' not generate relations of positive affect – or at least an *esprit de corps* that was so evident in the star network of the Norton Street gang made famous by William Foote Whyte (1955)? A large part of the answer lies in the domain of *personalia*. "Doc," the pivotal figure of the Norton gang, displayed aggressive 'stardom' in which his mastery over each gang member was matched only by his caring for each of them. It became his gang: the gang relationships not only converged on "Doc" but also radiated out from him. With Crawford, matters were very different: "'I'm afraid,' said Crawford, cordially, loudly, but without interest, 'that I'm very stupid when it comes to personalia'" (p. 146). Nor is this really unexpected: the Crawford followers had little in common except the separate URC motivations of some of them, and we now find, appropriately enough, that their 'leader' was a stranger, in this way too, to most of them. When Chrystal joined Crawford, he moved from a 'star' to a 'cluster' that needed him.

Turning to the other faction, why did Jago not emerge as another "Doc"? Why not a star network? It is not necessary to appeal to differences between street-corner youth and Oxbridge dons to explain this (and besides, street-corner gangs produce Jagos as well as "Docs"). As his party saw it, Jago was to be elected master because of the values he and his supporters all shared, and not because he, Jago, was different or even 'better.' That it was Jago and not Brown, for instance, who should assume the mastership was because Jago was the senior man. When master, he would be expected to assume leadership, so that a star network would be superimposed upon the cluster – though without destroying it. But as a candidate for the mastership, he was to leave matters largely in the hands (and the heads) of his party. His conduct during the pre-election months, as Brown and Chrystal instructed him, was to be "statesmanlike" (a favourite word for Brown) and, above all, discreet.

For network analysts, the diacriticum of a cluster is its high density of linkages (cf. Barnes, 1969:64), and it is exactly this that underwrites the distinction of the Jago party over Crawford's. Figure 4 attempts to portray how each party perceived themselves and each other. It was a case of mutual apprehension; for if Jago's people were aghast at the selfish, even spiteful alliances made around Crawford's candidacy, the Crawford people were as disturbed by the way the others 'held hands,' as it were, in a tight conspiratorial ring.

Incorporational and Transactional Values

The predominant value structures which I believe these affective inputs provided may be characterized as transactional in the case of Crawford's party and incorporational among Jago's (Barth, 1966).

It seems that the Crawford people discussed only how to secure the extra support needed for their majority. The Jago party was surely as interested in this matter, for it was to them that victory would likely fall; however, much of their talk with each other was about the reasons they were doing what they were doing: it was confessional and empathetic in character. The party placed a value on achieving a moral consensus. As noticed already, Brown (but not Chrystal) repressed ambiguity and this, too, is in accordance with the incorporational value structure.

The difference between the two parties is to be seen not simply in the inclusion of Nightingale and the URC factor in the Crawford party. More significant is that within its ranks there was room for both Nightingale and Getliffe. Getliffe was a person of as much moral purpose as his close friend Eliot and he was prepared to place that sense of purpose before his friendship. As we saw, Getliffe believed that the college should have as its master a distinguished scholar who, at the same time, was ideologically enlightened. Getliffe's anger and embarrassment over Nightingale's prop-

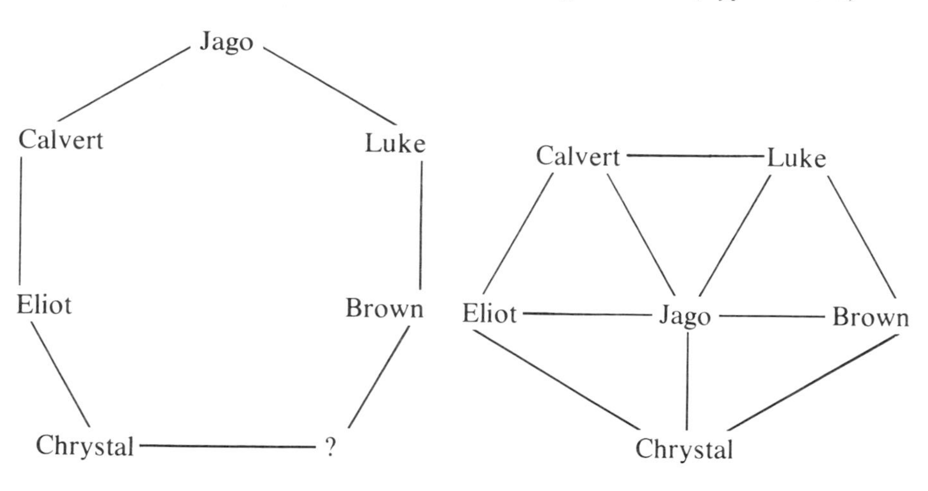

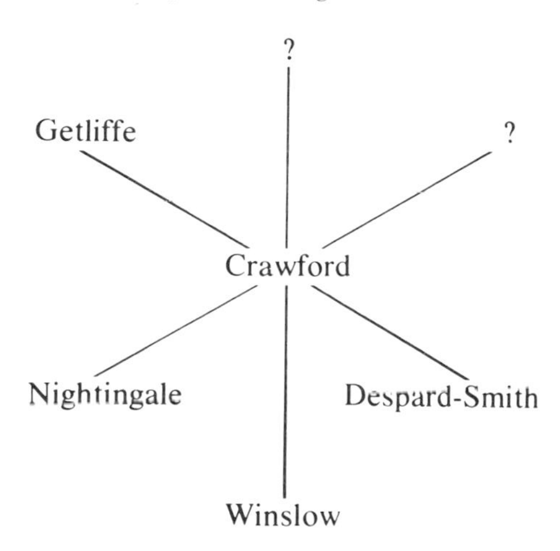

Note: "?" indicates the extra support each faction needed to obtain the necessary majority of 7.

Figure 4 *Jago and Crawford Networks (Simplified)*

aganda campaign[11] did not shake him in his resolve to support Crawford. His reasons for giving that support were his own. This was also true of the others, so that being a Crawford supporter carried minimal implications of membership for a Crawford party.

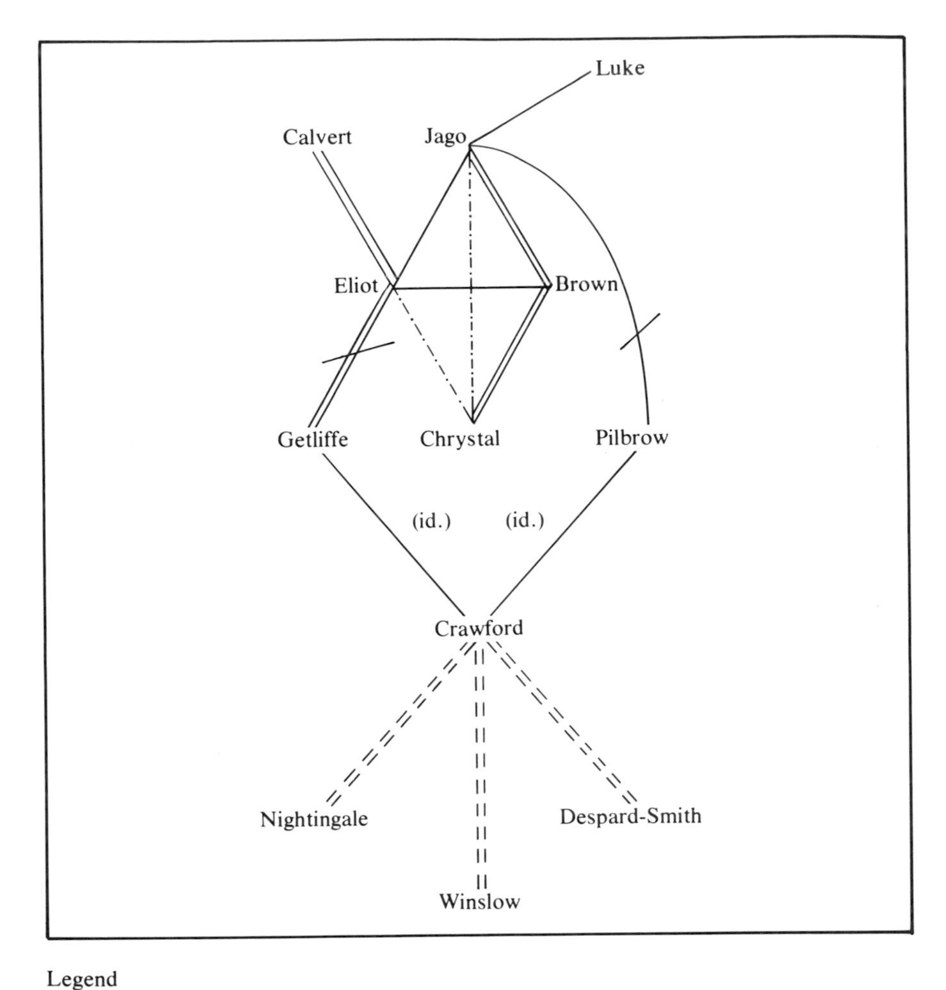

Legend

Direct links

positive: ═══ strong friendship

─── respect between equals, across generations (perhaps with growing friendship)

(id.) ideological identification with the candidate

negative: ⊁ broken relationship

Indirect links

positive: –· –·–·–· "friend of friend"

negative: = = = = = = support on basis of strong negative affect towards rival candidate and/or rival faction

(only those links that are discussed in text are shown; Gay, the eccentric octogenarian, not included here)

Figure 5 *Principal Motivational Links to the Candidates and Between Supporters*

Our discussion of the nature of the network links has been focused upon the candidate-supporter linkages. Over and above the general importance of affect in the formation of these links, two distinctions are significant. These are conveniently referred to as, (1) direct *versus* indirect links, and (2) positive *versus* negative motivations of links. Figure 5 attempts a summary presentation of the factions along these lines. It would be falling prey to a familiar piece of factional rhetoric to oppose 'transactional' and 'moral' – with the implication that transactional undertakings are without their own morality, or are amoral. Only if Crawford's party at all times reduced every issue to self-interested bargaining would this last characterization be justifiable. Such was not the case (witness their concern, shared with Jago's party, over a stalemate that would let in an outsider).

III

What have our labours with this novel achieved? Rather than bringing together the separate points that have been made, I think it would be more useful to conclude with a discussion around the sense of core problem in factionalism with which I came to *The Masters* and found well-demonstrated there.

THE CORE PROBLEM

Analytically, factionalism is, for me, the study of behaviour in structural situations of *internecine* discord. In particular, I associate factionalism with disputing in units that are without proper institutional arrangements for such an activity. For persons thus caught, the onset of factionalism may be expected to raise the spectre of social disintegration, however unfounded this fear may later prove to be. Of course, some units *are* constituted for disputing, and a parliament of political parties is an obvious example, but for other units – the political parties themselves, for instance – this is not so, and the danger of disputes degenerating into dysfunctional hostilities is particularly great. What of colleges and departments within academe?

Core Problem and Academe

It seems there is a myth throughout academe that it is quite proper for colleagues to dispute, and feasible for them to dispute properly. Caplow and McGee (1965:165) note that a favourite *self-definition* of professors is that of "men who think otherwise." Both the myth and the self-definition should deter us from supposing, *a priori*, that factionalism in academe is necessarily dysfunctional; where it is deemed (by those concerned) dysfunctional, it may, at the same time, be regarded as a necessary social cost of the need to dispute. This association of both academe and factionalism with disputing can also mean that individuals, far from feeling caught in the bind of factionalism, draw exhilaration from it. For that matter, even an assumption that the dysfunctional implications of factionalism are unintended and regretted may not always be true: contemporary academe certainly looks like a place where persons are able to challenge aspects of 'the system' that are assumed by others to be normative and, therefore, inviolate. Faction-fighting in academe sometimes tests (and perhaps revokes) such assumptions and where this is true, the disputes might be characterized as principled and selfless.

Caplow and McGee also report that "fights which began almost twenty years ago ... are still being carried on with great vigor, although all the original participants have departed from the scene" (p. 175) and that "many of the quarrels which disturb the peace of the ivory tower are nothing more than fights between two men of incompatible opinions" (p. 165). Some disputes, then, are remarkable for their longevity, intractability and their personal animosity as much as for their principle and selflessness. Furthermore, if academics are singularly factious, academe itself appears to be singularly unable to resolve the factions. This evidence (and more could be mustered) is good reason to query Lasswell's (1931:50) assertion that "factional strife subsides spontaneously," if by that he means factionalism *dies* easily. Or perhaps it is a particular hallmark of academe that factional strife once begun, is likely to be a long time dying?

Each of these points – the prevalence of factionalism, the recurrence of striking differences in normative character between one dispute or one faction and another and the longevity of many factional disputes in academe – may be usefully considered in the light of an apparent basic structural inconsistency or ambiguity, even contradiction, in academe. On the one hand, there is (what one may term) a general *lack of accountability* among academics of which a consequence is a high degree of job security. On the other hand, many academics experience circumstances of *arbitrary accountability* and hence, of job insecurity. Separately but especially in combination, these two factors open the way to URC behaviour.

Obviously, arbitrary accountability is particularly likely to be the perceived experience among non-tenured faculty, and C. P. Snow shows Brown and Chrystal to be sensitive to this matter. As Luke, the young scientist, does not yet have tenure, the two men hesitate to put a claim of loyalty on him that might prejudice his tenure case with the senior scientists all of whom happen to be in Crawford's party. By contrast, among tenured faculty, implications of non-accountability are seen, for example, in the behaviour of Nightingale, Winslow and others. It is this factor of non-accountability that I would single out as the salient one for our present discussion. If we ask to whom, or to what and when, or how the academic, established in his position, is accountable, the answer is surely that, compared with other walks of life, accountability is neither rigorously nor consequentially enforced. Arraigned against accountability is the shibboleth of academic freedom. A necessary shibbloeth, it can, nevertheless, mean that stands on principle are made by an individual without his having to make any realistic 'cost-accounting' of his actions – the cost either to himself, his institution or to others who belong to the institution. At worst, it means he can indulge his personal prejudices (and indulge a closed mind), protected by the ideal normative system of academe from effective sanction – even if his actions undermined that system.

Following Caplow and McGee (1965:177) again, we find a further dimension of structural ambiguity and/or contradiction in academe which also lends itself to factionalism. The issue is the location of esteem and, hence, the location of power in any academic institution. They have pointed to a "double system of ranking" and comment as follows:

> Academic rank is conferred by the university [or college], but disciplinary prestige is awarded by outsiders .... Every academic rank includes men of enormously different prestige. Power cannot, therefore, be tied to specific positions in the form of authority .... Yet power in some form must be exercised or the university of college cannot function. The solution to this dilemma which has evolved in the American university is to let power lodge pretty much where it may .... This is not the only possible solution; English universities have a different system and continental still another.

Although writing primarily about the American university, Caplow and McGee pinpointed two factors that were much on the minds of the dons in *The Masters*. First, on the assessment of the prestige of candidates for the mastership, there was a parting of ways among even close friends (namely, between Eliot and Getliffe). Secondly, on the protection of the autonomy of the college, even enemies sought a common front. The power of their college, it was realized, was more important to its members than the prestige of their Master; but because the two matters intertwine and both were, in the first place, in the hands of the dons themselves, there was factional fighting and intrigue. It cannot be supposed, however, that the opposite situation – where there is institutional pre-emption of responsibility by an outside authority – does not nurture factionalism. Gearing (1970:96) has written of "structural paralysis" on this account and noticed it to be a condition marked by mutual distrust and factional disputes. His finding was made on a Fox Indian reservation, but it is also one to bear in mind in the analysis of a number of situations within academe – perhaps especially at the departmental level but even at that of the university itself.

Four Questions

Our sense of core problem can be elucidated further by posing more questions about factionalism. Each question places in relief an aspect of the dilemma of internecine discord; each is likely to be in the minds of the persons involved, and where this is true their consideration is likely to generate constraints upon the behaviour of factional allies and adversaries. Brown and Chrystal constantly worried over such questions as those we are about to review and, at times, they found it difficult to agree on a common course of action that was at once reputable and politically effective. Eliot and Getliffe, although at odds with each other over the election, were both concerned with the import of these questions. Only Nightingale, almost entirely, and Winslow and Jago partially, ignored the dilemmas and spurned the constraints suggested by the questions.

Can a faction afford to win? This can be an agonizing question for members of the faction with the most power, for should their win imply defeat for the other faction(s), there is a real risk that the value structure of the unit to which they all belong will be destroyed. Nor is this dilemma encountered only in terms of an abstract value structure, but it can also have an equally strong pragmatic expression: faction A may be strong enough to defeat faction B and willing to do so, except for the consideration that it is not strong enough to sustain the unit competitively without B's resources. In this case, the question of loyalty (and of polarization of loyalties between, for instance, "our faction" and "the department") may be resolved through fine calculations about resources.

In sum, factional disputing is frequently conducted in the knowledge that "opposing aims" could, but must not be allowed to destroy the "common goal" (Coser, 1956:117–8). This sheds light on the reason factional relations are inclined to continue beyond the point at which a complete break would seem to an outsider (naive in his objectivity) to be indicated; in other words, why factions do not die easily. It is also an important part of the explanation of the persistent association, noted earlier, of factionalism with ambiguity.

How does one 'score' against a factional adversary without damaging the unit? Following upon what has just been said, the problem here is that although factions may perceive themselves to be in highly competitive and conflict-ridden situations, no formal declaration of war is possible (or desirable) because they are constituent groups of the same unit. This raises a number of matters.

What 'weapons' are available – which are permissible? Put another way, is the structural illegitimacy of factionalism (because it is internecine) likely to lead to the adoption of illegitimate tactics? When the Nuer fight the Dinka, it is war and they use spears, but when one section of the Nuer fight another section, that is something less than war and they use sticks (Evans-Pritchard, 1940). This shows that there are rules which the Nuer recognize and abide by for the less-than-war fighting. The piquant quality of factional fighting lies in the doubt about such rules. Indeed, it may be rules – those of the unit – that are in factional dispute. (The 1975 dispute inside the British Labour Party over the Common Market is illustrative of both questions: which weapons? which rules?)

Factions fighters are likely to be concerned (though perhaps along factional lines here too) about being observed by outside audiences and, in particular, about the intervention of outside authorities. In academe, these are likely to be faculty deans and academic vice-presidents or (as in *The Masters*) the college visitor. There are problems for the deans here as well, for any communication with one faction may be construed by the other(s) as a hostile act; it is precisely this factor which is likely to render ineffective, or even inoperative, any institutionalized locus of authority within the unit – a department chairman, for instance.

Once again, we find several considerations that tend to extend the life of factional activities: sanctions which the adversaries may place upon the prosecution of their own causes and sanctions against 'interference' by potential arbiters.

How is the expected dissonance of factionalism likely to be handled? The problem of 'scoring,' which was just under discussion, has a fascinating cognitive side to it. One may say of its logic that it is the reverse of the 'as if' genre of problem; for, x and y of opposing factions *are* enemies and yet they are not permitted, in some important ways, to act out that relationship. To compound the situation, x and y may also have been intimates and are likely still to draw upon (but as separately as possible) many things they hold in common. However, the attempted solution to the dilemma, insofar as cognition is concerned, may be of an 'as if' kind; each behaves as if the other does not belong to the unit. The salve applied to the wound of factionalism in cases known to me from the academic world has been joking and avoidance: joking within a faction about the other(s), and/or avoidance between factions. Besides being a coping mechanism, people also manage, by these means, to re-draw boundaries and re-design personalities (of group and individual) – acts they may not be allowed, or may not be strong enough to carry out, in the political realm.

That so much of the 'language' of factionalism is of this kind, serving evaluational rather than informational functions (cf. Bateson, 1951; Bernstein, 1973; Paine, 1976), is a further force towards the (self-validating) maintenance of factions and factional positions. Inasmuch as factional disputes attract *ad hominem* attacks, the latter can have a smoke-screen effect, for they are not the most effective way of drawing attention to issues of principle. While I do *not* suppose that is a reason for their use (certainly not in the case of Nightingale, for instance), the implication is still important: the outside audience will not learn much from the use of *ad hominem* abuse and the factional situation may well be prolonged through this process of closure. Germane to this point is a probable reaction, early in the factional process, of the person who finds that information is being withheld from him by others (an example is Nightingale while he was still courting the Jago party). Although he may acknowledge to himself that he no longer has easy social relations with these persons, he may be unable or unwilling to recognize that information, itself a social resource, is dependent on the persistence of social relations of other kinds; instead he 'blames' the conduct of others for his own situation, thereby setting in motion a cycle not only of *ad hominem* behaviour but also of self-fulfilling prediction – another characteristic, I believe, of factional relations, though, of course, not exclusive to them.

Are, then, factions a special case of conflict? Simmel believed that "the mere fact of engaging in conflict brings about, except in marginal cases, the common acceptance of rules governing the conduct of hostilities" (Coser, 1956:123). Factions may be the marginal cases. The principal reason for suggesting this may now be summarized as the 'They-in-the-We' perception of adversaries in factional situation. It is 'They' who either give offence to a 'good' structure or who selfishly support a 'corrupt' structure; in either instance their action is at the expense of 'We.' It is 'They' who are factional. In sum, factional relations are likely to be reciprocal in their practice but areciprocal in their perception.

NOTES

1 "Speaking as an academic man, I am sometimes inclined to believe in the existence of a special *furor academicus*": *The Affair* (1962:302).
2 Of course, I am not the first anthropologist to tap this source; Max Gluckman was there before me (Gluckman, 1962:44–5).
3 This figure includes the Master who is dying. The "I" (of the narrator) is Lewis Eliot.
4 For an art critic's discussion of "the general problems of 'frontal and profile' as symbolic forms," see Zerner's (1974) review of Schapiro's book *Word and Pictures: On the Literal and the Symbolic in the Illustration of a Text*.
5 The theme is found in *The Affair* too: "There was a curious accord between them. They stood at the two extremes, both utterly recalcitrant. As often with extremists, they felt linked. They had a kinship, much more than with their own sides, the safe and sensible people in the middle" (p. 181). It is a theme that should not surprise anthropologists too much: consider the Pathan chieftains. Yet we might ask ourselves whether we take enough account of it in our own analyses.
6 The surviving friendship was between Eliot and Calvert, the one farthest away from the power struggle.
7 Similarly coded information is provided by the seating plan regarding Nightingale: he was sitting between two firm Jago supporters even though he himself was counted as a Jago supporter; and it was only Nightingale who generated strong antipathies to either side.
8 Coser's book is, of course, an exegesis of Simmel (1955).

9 A distinguished war service, a peaceful marriage, and the bursarship of the college combined eventually to 'cure' Nightingale. (I would quarrel with C. P. Snow when, in *The Affair*, he builds up a case of guilt by circumstantial evidence against Nightingale: Skeffington rather than Nightingale seems to me the more likely source of URC in the circumstances.)
10 "Cluster" is a term from Epstein (1961) and is discussed by Barnes (1969:64). "Star" is a term developed by Barnes (1969:58). Though I do not burden the text with this extra term, it is quite clear that the factions in *The Masters* are of the "action-set" kind that "emerge in a specific context for a specific task" (Barnes, 1969:69).
11 Getliffe was deeply disturbed when told by Eliot of an attempt by Nightingale to coerce Luke into supporting Crawford. He undertook to stop it (p. 167).

REFERENCES

BARNES, J. A.
1969 "Networks and Political Process." In J. C. Mitchell (ed.), *Social Networks in Urban Situations*. Manchester, Manchester University Press.

BARTH, FREDRIK
1966 *Models of Social Organization*. Royal Anthropological Institute Occasional Paper, 23. London.

BATESON, G.
1951 "Information and Codification" (Chapter 7); "Conventions of Communication (Chapter 8). In J. Ruesch and G. Bateson (eds.), *Communication. The Social Matrix of Psychiatry*. New York, Norton & Co. Inc.

BERNSTEIN, BASIL
1973 *Class, Codes and Control, Vol. 1: Theoretical Studies Towards a Sociology of Language*. London, Paladin (Granada Publishing Ltd.).

CAPLOW, THEODORE and REECE J. MCGEE
1965 *The Academic Marketplace*. New York, Anchor Books (Doubleday & Co. Inc.).

COSER, LEWIS
1956 *The Functions of Social Conflict*. New York, Free Press.

EPSTEIN, A. L.
1961 "The Network and Urban Social Organization." *Rhodes-Livingstone Journal*, XXIX.

EVANS-PRITCHARD, E. E.
1940 *The Nuer*. Oxford, The Clarendon Press.

GEARING, F. O.
1970 *The Face of the Fox*. Chicago, Aldine.

GLUCKMAN, MAX
1962 "Les rites de passage." In M. Gluckman (ed.), *Essays in the Ritual of Social Relations*. Manchester, Manchester University Press.

GLUCKMAN, MAX
1963 *Custom and Conflict in Africa*. Oxford, Blackwells.

LASSWELL, H. W.
1931 "Faction." *Encyclopaedia of the Social Sciences*. New York, Macmillan & Co.

PAINE, ROBERT
1976 "Two Modes of Exchange and Mediation." In B. Kapferer (ed.), *Transaction and Meaning: Directions in the Anthropology of Exchange and Symbolic Behaviour*. Philadelphia, ISHI.

SIMMEL, GEORG
1955 *Conflict* (trans. Kurt H. Wolff). Glencoe, Ill., The Free Press.

SNOW, C. P.
1956 *The Masters*. Harmondsworth, Penguin Books.

SNOW, C. P.
1962 *The Affair*. Harmondsworth, Penguin Books.
WHYTE, W. F.
1955 *Street Corner Society*. Chicago, University of Chicago Press.
ZERNER, HENRI
1974 Review of *Words and Pictures: On the Literal and Symbolic in the Illustration of a Text* by Meyer Schapiro. *The New York Review of Books*, XXI:18.

ISER Publications

Studies

1 TOM PHILBROOK. *Fisherman, Logger, Merchant, Miner: Social Change and Industrialism in Three Newfoundland Communities.*

2 JOHN SZWED. *Private Cultures and Public Imagery: Interpersonal Relations in a Newfoundland Peasant Society.*

3 JAMES C. FARIS. *Cat Harbour: A Newfoundland Fishing Settlement.*

4 SHMUEL BEN-DOR. *Makkovik: Eskimos and Settlers in a Labrador Community.*

5 MELVIN M. FIRESTONE. *Brothers and Rivals: Patrilocality in Savage Cove.*

6 NOEL IVERSON and D. RALPH MATTHEWS. *Communities in Decline: An Examination of Household Resettlement in Newfoundland.*

7 CATO WADEL. *Marginal Adaptations and Modernization in Newfoundland: A Study of Strategies and Implications of Resettlement and Redevelopment of Outport Fishing Communities.*

8 ROBERT L. DEWITT. *Public Policy and Community Protest: The Fogo Case.*

9 OTTAR BROX. *Newfoundland Fishmen in the Age of Industry: A Sociology of Economic Dualism.*

10 LOUIS J. CHIARAMONTE. *Craftsman-Client Contracts: Interpersonal Relations in a Newfoundland Fishing Community.*

11 CATO WADEL. *Now, Whose Fault is That? The Struggle for Self-Esteem in the Face of Chronic Unemployment.*

12 GEORG HENRIKSEN. *Hunters in the Barrens: The Naskapi on the Edge of the White Man's World.*

13 ROBERT MCGHEE. *Beluga Hunters: An Archaeological Reconstruction of the History and Culture of the Mackenzie Delta Kittegaryumiut.*

14 A. P. COHEN. *The Management of Myths: The Politics of Legitimation in a Newfoundland Community.*

15 ELLIOTT LEYTON. *The One Blood: Kinship and Class in an Irish Village.*

16 DAVID W. ZIMMERLY. *Cain's Land Revisited: Culture Change in Central Labrador, 1775–1972.*

17 JAMES A. TUCK. *Ancient People of Port au Choix: The Excavations of an Archaic Indian Cemetery in Newfoundland.*

18 S. S. MENSINKAI and M. Q. DALVI. *Manpower and Educational Development in Newfoundland.*

19 DAVID ALEXANDER. *The Decay of Trade: An Economic History of the Newfoundland Saltfish Trade, 1935–1965.*

20 PAUL S. DINHAM. *You Never Know What They Might Do: Mental Illness in Outport Newfoundland.*

21 J. D. A. WIDDOWSON. *If You Don't Be Good: Verbal Social Control in Newfoundland.*

Papers

1 MICHAEL L. SKOLNIK (ed.). *Viewpoints on Communities in Crisis.*

2 ROBERT PAINE (ed.). *Patrons and Brokers in the East Arctic.*

3 ELLIOTT LEYTON (ed.). *The Compact: Selected Dimensions of Friendship.*

4 M. M. R. FREEMAN (ed.). *Intermediate Adaptation in Newfoundland and the Arctic: A Strategy of Social and Economic Development.*

5 RAOUL ANDERSEN and CATO WADEL (eds.). *North Atlantic Fishermen: Anthropological Essays on Modern Fishing.*

6 M. J. SCARLETT (ed.). *Consequences of Offshore Oil and Gas – Norway, Scotland, and Newfoundland.*

7 ROBERT PAINE (ed.). *The White Arctic: Anthropological Essays on Tutelage and Ethnicity.*

8 JOHN J. MANNION (ed.). *The Peopling of Newfoundland: Essays in Historical Geography.*

9 M. SILVERMAN and R. F. SALISBURY (eds.). *A House Divided? Anthropological Studies of Factionalism.*